miles
davis
and american culture

Malibu, 1989.
Photograph by
Jeff Sedlik

miles
davis
and american cultu

edited by
gerald early

Missouri Historical Society Press
Saint Louis

distributed by University of Missouri Press

Published in the United States of America by
Missouri Historical Society Press
P.O. Box 11940, St. Louis, Missouri 63112-0040

05 04 03 02   5 4 3 2

Library of Congress Cataloging-in-Publication Data

Miles Davis and American culture / edited by Gerald Early.
        p.   cm.
Includes bibliographical references.
ISBN 1–883982–37–5 (cloth : alk. paper). — ISBN 1–883982–38–3 (pbk. : alk. paper).
      1. Davis, Miles – Criticism and interpretation. 2. Davis, Miles – Influence. 3. Popular culture – United States – History
–20th century. I. Early, Gerald Lyn.

ML419.D39 M53 2001
788.9′2165′092 — dc21   2001030455
                                                                                                  CIP

Distributed by University of Missouri Press

Design by Robyn Morgan and Becki Hartke
Printed in Canada by Friesens Printing

∞ The paper used in this publication meets the minimum requirements of the ANSI/NISO, Z39.48–1992 (R 1997) (Permanence of Paper)

Cover: Miles Davis outside Café Bohemia, New York, 1956. Photograph by Marvin Koner. Courtesy of Sony Photographic Archive.

Contents

Boston, 1964.
Photograph by
Lee Tanner.

I remember Miles Davis as a friend, a beautiful person whom the rest of the world really didn't get to know. I remember him from the beginning, when we were both young trumpet players from St. Louis who shared a dedication to music and a passion for good clothes and for a good boxing match. We came from a place with a strong tradition in music, and that tradition helped both of us in our later lives in New York.

Over the years, St. Louis has been known as a trumpeter's town. Miles, Baby James, Bobby Danzig, Clark Stanley, George Hudson, Sleepy Tomlin, Lester Bowie, and even today, cats like Russell Gunn—all these cats were fine trumpet players. We all had a tradition to live up to. It got to the point where people would hear one of us and ask, "Are you from St. Louis?" The sound we all admired when I was coming up was crystal clear, not too much vibrato, a little like Shorty Baker.

It all started way back with Charlie Creath, who was The Man in the 1920s. He used to refer to himself as "Charlie Creath, the King of Cornet." He was a rather flamboyant, devil-may-care type cat, but he always had the great big sound and the dexterity. As Charlie went, the rest of the St. Louis trumpet players followed. As a result, most of the trumpet players interested in excelling rather than just getting some beer money for the weekend tended to play that way.

In the 1930s, I lived with my sister and her husband on Lawton Street in the Mill Creek area of St. Louis that later was destroyed by urban renewal. My brother-in-law used to play tuba in a band that played on the riverboats called Dewey Jackson's Musical Ambassadors. We used to call Dewey Jackson the loudest trumpet player that ever existed. People would know when to pick their kids up at the wharf by hearing Dewey singing out from two or three miles up the river.

I used to go to the band's rehearsals. The trumpet player, Louis Lattimore, would give me some candy from his candy store as payment for watching his trumpet during breaks. So I thought he was the greatest cat in the world, and I thought the trumpet was the greatest instrument in the world. On one occasion, he returned from a break to find me huffing and puffing away on the horn. He said, "Son, you're going to be a trumpet player." I was thirteen.

Foreword

by Clark Terry

Bands in St. Louis played the blues and standards. The big bands played a lot of the pop music of the day. We had a lot of big bands around town: Dewey Jackson's Salt and Pepper Shakers, the Crackerjacks, Jeter-Pillers Orchestra, the Fate Marable Band, Bunk Roberts. For the most part, when the small groups played, it was in a little joint or club, but a medium-sized to bigger-sized band played dance gigs whether on a boat or in a ballroom. As was always the case, half of the crowd was there to dance, and half was there to listen. I loved playing for dancers, and later when I played for Ellington and Basie, we played for the people who came right up front to the bandstand, just like we had back home.

I met Miles through his teacher, Elwood Buchanan. Buch used to always tell me, "Man, you've got to come over here to school; you've got hear this little dude. I've got a bad little dude over here." So finally one day, I went over to Lincoln High in East St. Louis and met this little skinny mother. He was so thin that if you had turned him sideways, they would have marked him absent. He was very shy. He couldn't look you in the eye; he would always look down and he spoke very softly. And I heard him play.

Well, he was a bad little dude then; he really could play, even as a kid. Buch used to keep a ruler with the tip wrapped in heavy tape on the end. He said, "The only problem with him is he likes to shake those damn notes," and when Miles shook the notes, Buch would hit him on the fingers and say, "Stop shaking those notes. You're going to shake enough when you get old." Miles was a big Harry James fan, but Buch made him start playing with a straight tone, without vibrato. Plus Buch's teacher, Joe Gustat, who played first trumpet with the St. Louis Symphony Orchestra, insisted that all his students play with Heim mouthpieces. Gustat taught Miles, too, and Miles got ahold of one and fell in love with it. So he always used to have me hunting for Heims for him. "Hey, man, you got any Heims?" he would say.

A few months later, I was working down in Carbondale, Illinois, with a bandleader named Benny Reed. We were playing for an interscholastic festival. Miles was with Buch's band when it came down. We played for the kids to dance. And this kid, Miles, comes up to me and says, "Hey, mister, can you show me some stuff?" I said, "Man, I don't want to talk about no trumpet. Don't you see all these pretty girls out here? Get the hell out of here."

Shortly after that, I went up to a favorite watering hole, the Elks, on Cardinal right off of Olive Street in St. Louis. A long flight of stairs led up into a loft where a lot of musicians, even visiting ones like Coleman Hawkins, used to hang out. So I ran up there to hear Eddie Randle's band, and I heard this trumpet solo, and I said, "Man, I've never heard that horn," because I didn't realize that Miles had become a member of Eddie's band. There he was, skinny as ever. So later I went up to him and said, "Aren't you the guy . . ." and he said, "Yeah, I'm the dude you fluffed off in Carbondale." We often laughed about it later. We became good friends after that and sometimes played at clubs together around St. Louis, like the Barrel on Olive Street.

Miles was instrumental in helping me decide I wanted to play the flügelhorn in about 1957. Miles played it with a trumpet mouthpiece. He used to let me take what he called his "fat girl" home to fix the valves, because I figured out a way to make the valves lighter, and I worked on a lot of his other trumpets, too. At about the same time, I was working with Selmer to develop their flügelhorn, and I used it on a Billy Taylor date the day I got it from the factory and played it with Duke's band that night. And of course, Miles played flügelhorn on the *Miles Ahead* album that year.

In the late forties and early fifties, Miles was addicted to narcotics, and needless to say, it set him back. He was fortunate enough to come through and managed to establish himself as one of the creators and innovators in the music world. I remember once he was in such bad shape. I was staying at the Hotel Americano, one of the fleabags on Forty-seventh Street. I happened to be walking up Broadway to get myself some bacon and eggs at a place on Fifty-third and Broadway, and I looked and saw this creature lying in the gutter in the street. I rolled him over and there was Miles. I couldn't believe it. So I picked him up, bought him some breakfast, then took him back to the hotel and put him into bed. I said, "Get some rest. I'll come back in a few hours and bring you some hot soup and tea or something." I was getting ready to go out of town on tour. I got back and my door was open. No Miles, no radio, no

clothes, no horn, no nothing. He had sold all my stuff. I saw Philly Joe Jones the next day walking down Broadway with my brand-new maroon long-collared shirt I had just bought.

He was still my friend. I knew he was sick. I knew he was a beautiful cat, too, and that once you got behind the "get the hell away from me" façade, he was a real pussycat. When I got sick the first time with my back in the 1980s, he called me from California: "Hey man, are you sick?" I said, "Yeah, man, I'm kind of laid up." He said, "M*****f*****, you die on me and I'll kill your ass." So a couple of days later, here comes a great big basket of fruit, nuts, crackers, meats, everything. A tub full of stuff.

We were in the hospital at the same time at the end of his life, on different coasts. I used to call him up at least a couple of times a week. At this point he couldn't talk. He would just have to respond with his eyes. I remember the last time I called him, I had them relay the message: "Tell Miles that it's me. Tell him to remember that we're two fighting trumpet players from St. Louis, and we're both in a battle royal, and we've got to kick everybody's ass to get out of here." They told me that when he heard the message, his eyes got real big. We had a beautiful friendship, and he was a sweetheart of a guy.

I remember Miles as Miles was. I remember him from the first time I heard

him at Lincoln High School, and I remember him at every stage along the way. In any setting, you could always hear the sound of Miles. He made so many records that even today I hear things that I didn't know he had made; but I can always tell it is Miles. People will continue to relate to him at those stages of his career, and will relate to the social changes that seemed to be part of the changing rhythms and styles in the music. But if you peel away everything that surrounds him, you will always find the essence of his sound: that beautiful tone that he first began to master in the classrooms and clubs back home in St. Louis.

Trumpeter and flügelhorn player Clark Terry was born in St. Louis on December 14, 1920. Terry played for both the Count Basie and Charlie Barnet Orchestras and enjoyed a particularly long stint with Duke Ellington throughout the 1950s. He was not adverse to playing in boppish settings. For instance, he recorded an album with Thelonious Monk, In Orbit, *in 1958. He made regular appearances on* The Tonight Show, *where his unusual style of scat singing earned him the nickname "Mumbles." Terry has been a remarkably active musician, playing in a variety of settings with some of the leading names of jazz into his eighties, and he has been an important teacher as well.*

miles davis

and american culture

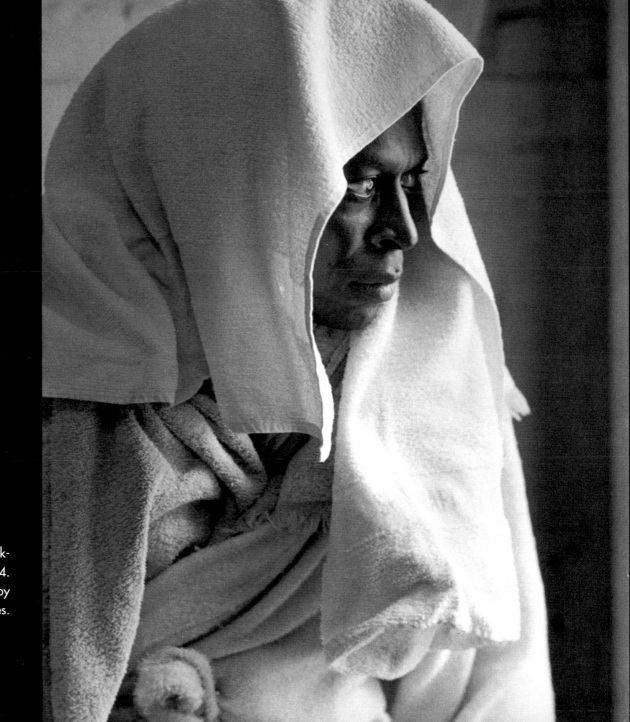

After a boxing work-
out, Boston, 1974.
Photograph by
Lou Jones.

When East St. Louis–born jazz trumpeter Miles Davis is remembered, it is usually recalled that he was a great innovator, that he had several distinct creative periods like Picasso, that he was a prickly, often unpleasant, personality. Davis is talked about often as a product of Cold War America and the "containment" culture it produced. (Was cool or Davis's reformulation of "free" jazz with his 1960s quintet versions of "containment" music?) He is contextualized within the civil rights movement of the 1960s and the height of jazz-rock fusion in the 1970s. He crossed several genres in his return to performing in the 1980s: hip hop, pop, smooth jazz, rock, world beat, probably none of them to the satisfaction of critics or even to hard-core fans of those genres themselves, although he was accorded an enormous respect and, of course, a sort of indulgence, by the last audiences he had before his death in 1991. He also made a great deal of money in the 1980s, more than he had ever made in his life. Curiously, his last project before his death was a new performance of some of his Gil Evans charts from the late 1950s under the leadership of longtime friend Quincy Jones. This might signal to some that he was ready to go back and revisit his past, and thus he had come full circle in some respect; but this is not likely. It was a project that he enjoyed but that he did with some reluctance, and it was not his idea to do it. For those who like to be especially antiquarian and source-oriented, Davis is contextualized as a St. Louisan, a man who emerged with a particular attitude and sound from a particular regional culture.

These various contexts and views of Davis are important—and, in explaining the man, of course, undeniably true. But the major, overarching context that, I think, explains him better than most is that he came of age when jazz music ceased to be a popular commercial music. Thus, he was faced with the dilemma of trying to make a living, of being something of a personality, in a music that had a dwindling audience and lacked the cultural and artistic presence it once had. He was enormously inventive, snappishly opportunistic, yet surprisingly principled In the simple act of making a living in a dying art, that is, dying as an art form with a large audience.

Jazz was searching for a role in the culture after World War II, and it tried several possibilities: as mood music (that combined pseudo, middle-brow intellectualism with its function as

The Art of the Muscle:
Miles Davis as American Knight and American Knave

by Gerald Early

background noise for mating—from Jackie Gleason to Don Shirley to Davis's *Kind of Blue*); as soundtrack for gritty, neorealistic crime cinema and television (from Ellington's *Anatomy of a Murder* to Davis's own soundtrack *Escalator to the Gallows*, from TV's *Peter Gunn* to *77 Sunset Strip* to *Ironside*); as experimental neoclassical music (from Stan Kenton's neophonic orchestras to John Lewis's Modern Jazz Quartet to Keith Jarrett's solo concerts); as politics in the form agitprop-aesthetics (the black revolutionary "new thing" to the regressive New Age-ism of the holistic Paul Winter). There might be other roles we can think of as well, and jazz certainly fulfilled these functions, more or less well, though to some degree with increasing frustration for the men and women who wanted to play this music. But no music can be played, realistically, in the United States and expect to withstand the pressures of the marketplace. No music can eschew its own commercial dimension, and if it does, as jazz sometimes has during this era of lacking commercial viability, it only winds up, paradoxically, trying to sell itself on the basis that it is non-commercial and somehow purer and less tainted than other music being sold. This is elitism, not necessarily or a priori a bad thing, but jazz certainly succumbed to this during the era that Davis was a star. What is interesting about Davis was that he clearly and cleverly made use of this elitism while always eyeing how he could maintain himself in the popular realm, walking a fine line between art and commerce. So the secret of Davis's success, his importance to us today as we remember, is not that he was a questing musician. He was hardly unique in that regard in the field of jazz after 1945: was he any more searching than Stan Kenton or Ornette Coleman or John Coltrane or Charles Mingus or Eric Dolphy or Lee Morgan or Jackie McLean or Bud Powell or Herbie Hancock or a dozen others? How Davis succeeded was being able to "sell," as an image, the iconoclastic romance of the searching jazz musician as a representation of the "committed" artist that a sizable portion of the American public wanted to buy, enough to make it possible to support himself in style as a jazz musician. He was able to do this, in part, because of his race, because of the instrument he played, because of his looks (he was thin and smolderingly handsome), and because he had considerable talent. Timing helped immensely and, of course, he was lucky. Young audiences were very open to highly experimental pop music in the late 1960s and to a kind of jazz-rock sound or a sound that expanded the idea of the typical popular song, in part because of groups like Cream; Traffic; Blood, Sweat, and Tears; and, of course, the Beatles.

I think it also helped him that he had an analogue and antithesis of sorts in pianist Thelonious Monk, a fellow bopper, who never really played bop (or he played the slowest bop in the world), who was never the technical wonderman that Parker and Gillespie were. (Neither was Davis.) Monk, who recorded for Columbia in the 1960s, as did Davis, and who was on the cover of *Time* magazine in 1964, essentially never changed his style of music from the 1940s (it was so terrifically unusual at the time that it took the public a number of years to catch on to it), although he continued to write new compositions and reconfigure his music by playing it in different settings (from solo to trio to quartet to septet to big band). But Monk was able to remain the conservative revolutionary for his breakthrough in the 1950s to the end of the 1960s, when Columbia allegedly fired him for refusing to do an album of

Beatles covers. Davis, in his own way, mirrored this kind of conservative revolutionary stance until the end of the 1960s—both Davis and Monk shared important sideman John Coltrane, a story in itself—when he went in an entirely different direction than Monk, doing albums like *In a Silent Way* and *Bitches Brew*. Both men, part of a revolutionary movement in bebop, expressed contempt for the avant-garde of the 1960s. Monk continued in the path that he always had and Davis decided to embrace the avant-garde, on his terms, through rock, Indian ragas, and the like in a surprisingly daring way. Despite the criticism he endured, this change in direction did not destroy him or marginalize him, as Monk was marginalized at the end of his life. It put him at the center of everything, and remarkably, he absorbed it and remained identifiably himself, the questing, restless artist forever, like the American pioneer, seeking new frontiers. In a sense, what Davis wanted to do was transcend jazz and simply embody modern musical innovation. More than any other jazz musician, he virtually succeeded at this, and that story, of the complexity of that success, is one worth knowing and telling. Miles Davis, the American bad boy of jazz, our Huckleberry Finn, the adventurous capitalist artist, our great American picaro, who "lit out for the territories" and survived. It is one of the great tales of "manhood" and morality in modern American culture.

Part One: The Fighter

Only the strong survive in jazz.

—Miles Davis

Feels like love when it looks like this.

—jazz singer Patricia Barber

In 1953, at the age of twenty-seven, Miles Davis was a drug addict and his musical career was uncertain. It had seemed a long time ago when he was the rising star on the jazz scene with *The Birth of the Cool* sessions that he had done, with a racially integrated set of musicians, in 1949 and 1950. Most of his records since were not good. His stage performances were poor. He looked shot. His appearance was sloppy.

His clothes were dirty and unkempt. He was nodding out. He smelled bad. He had kicked his habit once by going back to East St. Louis and living on his father's farm in Millstadt, Illinois. But he went back to narcotics as soon as he left his father's house and went to Detroit, where he also became a pimp. While in Detroit, though, he threw off the habit again. As Davis tells the story in his 1989 autobiography:

Anyway, I really kicked my habit because of the example of Sugar Ray Robinson; I figured if he could be as disciplined as he was, then I could do it, too. I always loved boxing, but I really loved and respected Sugar Ray, because he was a great fighter with a lot of class and cleaner than a motherfucker. He was handsome and a ladies' man; he had a lot going for him. In fact, Sugar Ray was one of the few idols that I ever had. Sugar Ray looked like a socialite when you would see him in the papers getting out of limousines with fine women on his arms, sharp as a tack. But when he was training for a fight, he didn't have no women around that anybody knew of, and when he got into the ring with someone to fight, he never smiled like he did in those pictures everybody saw of him. When he was in the ring, he was serious, all business.

I decided that that was the way I was going to be, serious about taking care of my business and disciplined. I decided that it was time for me to go back to New York to start all over again. Sugar Ray was the hero-image that I carried in my mind. It was him that made me think that I was strong enough to deal with New York City again. And it was his example that pulled me through some real tough days.[1]

There are several observations to make about what I call the mythology of black masculinity that Davis constructs here. First, Detroit is a significant location because Sugar Ray Robinson was born there, as Walker Smith. He became Ray Robinson when he embarked on his amateur boxing career in Harlem. Detroit was also where Joe Louis, the great black boxing champion of Davis's boyhood, grew up and started his career. (Louis was born in Alabama.) Detroit, therefore, is the symbol of an assertive, disciplined, stylized black manhood as it is connected with the two most accomplished black boxers and,

indeed, two of the most publicized black male public figures of the first half of the twentieth century. The Midwest, the center of the United States, its "heartland," takes on a complex set of mythologized meanings in Davis's book and holds a particular relationship with New York City, the center of jazz life. I shall speak more about Davis's views of his midwestern origins later.

Second, Robinson was six years older than Davis. They were close enough in age to have much in common in taste and style and to be considered of the same generation. They were far enough apart in age so that the younger man could admire the older one. They were also close in size. Robinson fought professionally as a welterweight

(maximum weight: 147 pounds) and a middleweight (maximum weight: 160 pounds). He was a bigger man than Davis, but on the whole, as a fighter, he was smaller than the average man. He was clearly smaller and younger than heavyweight Joe Louis, and this almost certainly made Robinson a more accessible hero-figure for Davis than Louis would have been. The fact that Robinson was a very dark-skinned man, like Davis himself, and that Louis was light-skinned, also may have intensified Davis's identification with Robinson.

Robinson would have appealed to Davis not simply because of his age and his size but also because of the way he fought. As Davis writes in his autobiography, "Boxing's got style like music's got style. . . . But you've got to have style in whatever you do—writing, music, painting, fashion, boxing, anything. Some styles are slick and creative and imaginative and innovative and others aren't. Sugar Ray Robinson's style was all of that, and he was the most precise fighter that I ever saw."[2] Robinson was, without question, the most stylish, beautiful-looking fighter ever to enter the ring (with the possible exception Muhammad Ali, who admitted that he modeled himself after Robinson, who was his hero, too, when the future heavyweight champ was a teenager growing up in Louisville in the 1950s). With his mop of processed hair (the sign of ultimate cool for black men before the 1960s) flopping across his head, Robinson used his lightning-quick hands and dancing feet to pound and dazzle opponents into submission. Nearly every official boxing body has voted Robinson, not Ali, the best pound-for-pound boxer in the history of the sport. The disciplined beauty of Robinson's art was something Davis wanted to emulate in his own life and in his art. In a sense, there was something Oscar Wildean about Davis's obsession with Robinson, as if the major lesson he derived from Robinson was learning to make all life a form of aesthetics or, more precisely, a series of aesthetic postures, poses, and propositions.

Third, boxers and jazz musicians historically have occupied the same world, at least black boxers and black musicians have. It was a world referred to by the turn-of-the-century phrase, "the Sporting Life." (One of the most noted characters in Dubose Heyward's 1925 novel, *Porgy,* is called Sportin' Life, and he represents exactly all the virtues and vices of this underground class: urbanity and city life, stylish dress and figure, and drug addiction.[3]) This is the netherworld of nightclubs, gambling, prostitutes, pimps, hustlers, the world of black entertainers, including athletes, musicians, actors, and the like. It was a world of interracial sex, drug addiction and alcoholism, atheism and agnosticism. But it was also a world of wit and spontaneity, of hatred of hypocrisy and pretence, and a kind of expressive fluidity that many found comforting and some even found inspiring. It was a subversive setting, undermining all the assumptions of respectable society, including self-repression, false morality, and racism (though, unfortunately, not sexism), but it was a vicious, often criminal, almost Darwinian world as well that had little pity for losers. The denizens of this world were outcasts from the bourgeois black world of striving middle-class respectability and the work-a-day world of ordinary black Christians, such as those depicted in James Baldwin's 1953 novel, *Go Tell It On the Mountain.* So, Davis and Robinson shared a milieu, an ethos, a way of life, and more profoundly, a history that went back well into the nineteenth century and the beginnings of modern popular culture. Since he came from a black bourgeois background, Davis would have been drawn, as many bourgeois people are, particularly to this type of world. He became a jazz musician, to be sure, for many reasons, and this, the type of world the jazz musician inhabited and the type of people he associated with, was probably one of the rebelliously striking attractions. Robinson was an athlete who had to maintain a Spartan regimen, and thus possessed a kind of physical virtue, but he was also a sybarite who enjoyed the sensual experience, was indeed a connoisseur of it. Embodying this type of contradiction as a style, a measure of trying to be true to both aspects of being a man— monkish abstinence and satyr-like but highly aesthetic indulgence—became an important aspect of Davis's immensely appealing form of 1950s and 1960s cool, a kind of black male existentialism that forged a moral code from the imperatives of the male body as it alternately functioned as a symbol of engagement and detachment, of punishing discipline and plush pleasure that operated cooperatively, not in conflict, if rightly understood. Beyond that, there was no reality. Nothing transcended the senses. What was right was what was instinctively felt to be right. The body was the cosmos, the root of all self-consciousness that mattered, and if it could not explain itself, the body could, on some levels, realize and actualize itself. The Hemingway code meets the priapic poetics of Henry Miller. Davis is describing this change in his life, his defeat of his drug habit, this great admiration of Robinson, in 1954, the year Hugh Hefner starts *Playboy* magazine, which espoused a similar code of masculine cool for the white corporate bourgeoisie. Three years later, Norman Mailer offered a further elaboration of this idea in his famous (or infamous) essay "The White Negro," and Jack Kerouac offered a view of life rather like this in his famous novel, *On the Road* (1957). The striking irony is that Davis, who believed so much in the discipline of the body, suffered so much from ill-health nearly all of his life— calcium deposits, an auto accident from which he never fully recovered, which spurred bouts of drug-addiction particularly from the 1960s on. And he so mistreated his body with jags of dissipation. Perhaps that was also in keeping with his admiration of boxers: theirs is not a healthy sport, and ultimately they suffered severe physical, and in many cases mental, deterioration. But Davis went further than merely admiring the great boxer and wishing to apply, in a figurative way, the athlete's discipline to his art. He became a boxer:

I had convinced Bobby McQuillen that I was clean enough for him to take me on as a boxing student. I was going to the gym every chance I could, and Bobby was teaching me about boxing. He trained me hard. We got to be friends, but he was mostly my trainer because I wanted to learn how to box like him.

Bobby and I would go to the fights together and train at Gleason's Gym in midtown or at Silverman's Gym, which was up in Harlem on 116th Street and Eighth Avenue . . . on the fourth or fifth floor in this corner building. Sugar Ray used to train there, and when he came in to train, everybody would stop what they were doing and check him out. . . .

A lot of people tell me I have the mind of a boxer, that I think like a boxer, and I probably do. I guess that I am an aggressive person about things that are important to me, like when it comes to playing music or doing what I want to do. I'll fight, physically, at the drop of a hat if I think someone has wronged me. I have always been like that.[4]

There are several important aspects to Miles Davis's mind here, his mythmaking, if you will. It was risky, even foolish, for a trumpeter to become a fighter, even as an avocation. One punch in the mouth and Davis would be out of work for months. Severe punishment could have ended his career. I suspect, therefore, that neither McQuillen nor anyone else ever pushed Davis seriously in the ring or even took this boxing venture as much more than a lark, a way for Davis to keep physically fit. For Davis, considering the risks, boxing had to be a form of brinkmanship, living on the edge. And that is important in understanding Davis's approach to his art. As others did with Davis, so Davis did with Robinson and fighters generally: he shamelessly romanticized their profession and their craft to find a black masculine analogue for his own life. Jazz musicians were like fighters in the sense that they were an itinerant breed; they worked in an arena that spotlighted their individualism and that was a merciless meritocracy; and they were largely an enclosed cult that outsiders found difficult to penetrate. It was the closest thing—being a boxer or a jazz musician—to being a knight, an urban paladin. Added to this was Davis's own needs to be an assertive black man at a time when a few assertive black men were becoming major figures in American culture: Jackie Robinson, in 1954, was not the non-violent martyr he was in 1947 when he broke the color line in Major League Baseball. He was argumentative, outspoken, overly sensitive to slights, intensely competitive, and aggressive. He had gone from being beloved by the white press to being disliked, even hated in some quarters. There was Paul Robeson, who refused to back down from being a Stalinist in a repressive Cold War America, virtually daring his country to silence him. James Baldwin had published *Go Tell It On the Mountain* and was to become a new assertive voice for black America in the 1950s and arguably, along with Amiri Baraka, among the most politically engaged writers of his generation, although he was never an avowed leftist. (Baldwin modeled his writing not only after other writers, but also jazz musicians, principally Miles Davis. Other black writers of the post–World War II period were deeply affected by jazz as well, especially poets like Ted Joans, Michael Harper, Yusef Komunyakaa, Sonia Sanchez, Carolyn Rodgers, and prose writer Nathaniel Mackey. John A. Williams, Toni Morrison, and William Melvin Kelley are among several black writers who have written fiction about jazz. Baldwin's "Sonny's Blues" is considered the best jazz short story ever written and, without question, the most anthologized. Indeed, Davis's impact, as well as that of post–World War II jazz in general, can be felt among white writers

as well, from the Beats to Delillo and Pynchon.)

Black men generally had become more assertive as a result of two war experiences that occurred within a span of ten years: World War II and the Korean War, the last being particularly important as it was the first military conflict where American troops were racially integrated. So Davis fashioned himself the fighter as well and made a literal identification with this psychological mode by actually becoming one. Fashioning himself as a fighting black man made Davis an outsider. But he was more than that. Davis, for most of his career, as James Lincoln Collier once noted, was also an insider. After all, Sugar Ray Robinson, by the way he handled himself and the way he appeared, "like a socialite," according to Davis, was something of an insider, and so was Jackie Robinson by virtue of being a success in America's pastime. He also had testified reluctantly before the House Un-American Activities Committee, countering statements that Robeson had made just a few years earlier about African American

unwillingness to fight in a war against the Soviet Union. Robinson would not have been called to do so if he had not been considered "loyal." Both Jackie and Sugar Ray Robinson asserted themselves but neither challenged the validity of the systems under which they worked. Davis came along at the right historical moment when he could use his outsider status as a way to be attractive to the bourgeoisie, both white and black. Davis may have abhorred the "Uncle Tom" image of smiling and shuffling, but so did a good portion of the hip, nonconformist black and white audience of the 1950s and 1960s to whom he wished to appeal, especially the young. Moreover, despite being black, Davis's rude, surly image of uncompromising artistic involvement satisfied the romantic yearnings of his white audience, which had come to accept this sort of thing from a black, partly as a refreshing novelty, to be sure, just as they had accepted it from white artists for more than one hundred years. Whites were quite willing, even thrilled, to let Davis be as Byronic as he wished. Columbia Records, for whom Davis recorded for most of his career, from the mid-1950s to the 1980s, found that the image could be marketed, and thus, the Prince of Darkness was born: the black American knave as American Heroic.

Davis used his boxing connection in a vivid and complicated way some years later when in 1970 he recorded the soundtrack to a documentary about the boxer Jack Johnson. Johnson, born in Galveston, Texas, or thereabouts in 1878, right after Reconstruction, and thus, something of a New Negro, that is, according to Southern mores, a black who did not know slavery, was the first black to become heavyweight champion when he beat Tommy Burns for the title in 1908. Before this, from the reign of John L. Sullivan to that of Jim Jeffries, no white heavyweight champion would consent to fight a black. (Blacks, during the late-nineteenth and early twentieth centuries, held boxing titles in lighter weight divisions—Joe Gans, Joe Walcott, George Dixon—but the heavyweight title was considered one of the grand titles in all of sports. It was felt to be symbolically troublesome for an inferior black—and blacks at this time were considered to

be, by scientific evidence, not only intellectually inferior to whites but physically inferior to them as well—to compete and win this honor.) But Johnson came of age as a boxer ironically during the era of Jim Crow segregation that culminated in the *Plessy v. Ferguson* decision of 1896 and during the age of social reformism called Progressivism. It was this reformist urge that got him a shot at the title in 1908. And Johnson was undone by the very reformism that led him to the title. He had a penchant for white women, most, but not all of whom, were prostitutes. He tried in no way to conceal this and was eventually convicted under the 1910 Mann Act, which prohibited taking women across state lines for "immoral purposes," a federal measure meant to stem the rising tide of prostitution among working-class women. (The famous Leo Frank case of 1913, in which a Jewish factory owner was convicted, and eventually lynched, for killing a fourteen-year-old girl who worked for him, dramatically demonstrates, whether Frank actually committed the crime, the sexually exploitative atmosphere that most working-class women and girls had to endure. For many, it was easier to become a prostitute.)

Howard Sackler wrote a play about Johnson in 1969 entitled *The Great White Hope* that became a Broadway hit and a successful film. What inspired Sackler was the saga of Muhammad Ali, the young boxer who won the championship in 1964, converted to the

Nation of Islam immediately after, a group little understood by whites at the time (or many blacks, either), known mostly for its fiery minister, Malcolm X. A few years later, an outspoken Ali refused to be drafted into the armed services during the unpopular Vietnam War, making him a hero to many non-conformist liberals, although a villain to many others, especially those, including many athletes, who had served in World War II and the Korean War. Ali was convicted of violating the Selective Service Act and sentenced to five years in prison, which he never served. Ali was banned from boxing for more than three years while he appealed his case, an act that generated a great deal of debate and made Ali a martyr for his beliefs, something that endeared him to a certain section of the public as a man of principle. Sackler wrote his play during Ali's exile years, 1967 to 1970. He saw a parallel between Ali and Johnson, and so did many during this period, including Ali himself. There was not nearly as much similarity between the two boxers as many at the time thought, but what was there was important.

Davis himself, by 1970, had radically changed directions in his music. This had started with such late 1960s albums as *Filles de Killimanjaro* and *In a Silent Way*, which made use of electric pianos, electric bass, electric guitar, and the like and used rock rhythms. The big breakthrough album for Davis was *Bitches Brew*, made from several August 1969 sessions. As drummer Tony Williams put it, "[Miles Davis]'s trying to get further out (more abstract) and yet more basic (funkier) at the same time." *Bitches Brew* was Davis's most commercially successful record and, along with the 1959 *Kind of Blue*, his most legendary. In 1970, he recorded *Jack Johnson*, possibly his most successful fusion of jazz with hard rock. In his autobiography, he writes:

> When I wrote these tunes [for "Jack Johnson"] I was going up to Gleason's Gym to train with Bobby McQuillen, who was now calling himself Robert Allah (he had become a Muslim). Anyway, I had that boxer's movement in mind, that shuffling movement boxers use.

They're almost like dance steps, or like the sound of a train. . . .

> Then the question in my mind after I got to this was, well, is the music black enough, does it have a black rhythm, can you make the rhythm of the train a black thing, would Jack Johnson dance to that? Because Jack Johnson liked to party, liked to have a good time and dance . . . .[5]

Davis thought of a record, of music, about a black boxer as being connected with his own boxing, and the record had a certain political resonance not only because it was about Johnson, a black rebel figure, but also because Johnson, in the cultural view of those living in the 1960s, adumbrated Muhammad Ali. Davis, who abhorred liner notes, wrote the notes, succinct but telling, for this album. He opened with: "The rise of Jack Johnson to world heavyweight supremacy in 1908 was a signal for white envy to erupt. Can you get to that? And of course being born Black in America . . . we all know how that goes." But this fear and loathing of black masculinity that Davis saw in the America of Jack Johnson was part of a larger, ongoing drama that, in many ways, Davis saw as explaining himself and his music in mythical terms of assertion and resistance to "white envy." So *Jack Johnson* was a record about black male heroism that spanned and collapsed two distinct historical eras. The fact that the music was so contemporary-sounding intensified Davis's own claims as a rebel through his rebel-sounding jazz—a music that tried to be both abstract and funky, both black and white—which, in turn, intensified his identification with the rebel boxers— Johnson and, indirectly, Ali. In a most profound sense, Davis saw himself as operating within a black male heroic tradition, and black male heroes were men like Jack Johnson, not typical black leaders like W. E. B. Du Bois or Martin Luther King and certainly not someone like Booker T. Washington, whom even Johnson himself disliked.

Davis thought *Jack Johnson* his most danceable record and he thought Columbia did a terrible job promoting it. However, I remember the record well when it was released, as I was a college student then. It was a popular record but hardly considered by anyone a dance record or a party record in the sense that music by James Brown or Sly Stone was. One can sense overwhelmingly the influence of guitarist Jimi Hendrix (Buddy Miles, a drummer who had worked with Hendrix's last band, Band of Gypsies, was supposed to be the drummer for the session), but Hendrix, however much his music might be considered "black" (and it certainly had little appeal to black people at the time), did not make dance music in any conventional understanding of the term. *Jack Johnson* was toe-tapping but still fairly abstract for many people. The record was, nonetheless, commercially successful and probably Davis's most "liked" record of his early 1970s period because it was less cluttered and more simplified than *Bitches Brew* or *Big Fun* or *Get Up With It* or *On the Corner* and more coherent and structured than his live albums. The documentary itself has the virtue of showing extensive good footage of Johnson, reminding the world that he clearly was the most photographed black man of the early 1900s and that boxing was essential to the rise of the film industry, but little else. (Brock Peters's speeches throughout are simply the wrong characterizations of Johnson; one has only to read Johnson's 1927 un-ghosted autobiography to realize that Johnson did not express himself in the way the filmmakers have Peters speaking.[6]) Oddly, in watching the documentary today, one is struck by how jarring and out of place the music seems, how much better the documentary would have been had it used period music. In looking back, the Davis music seems rather quaint and dated, reflecting more its own time than anything about Johnson. It is just this time-bound quality of the music that Davis made during these years, its broad reach that seems both so

courageous and so quixotic, that makes it difficult to access, to tease the art from the conceited, youth-obsessed artifice. The music of *Jack Johnson* has the virtues of being well-played and even brilliantly conceived, without being very good soundtrack music or very good "popular" music. But jazz, in its modernist conceit, was supposed to express the modernist, urban energy of Johnson's age. The more modern the jazz, the more powerfully wrought would be Johnson's own modernism, his own startling revolt as a "New Negro," so the filmmakers probably thought. The greatest irony of all perhaps is that Johnson, by the time he wrote his autobiography, was not a fan of jazz: "I am not a jazz enthusiast, but I will admit that this age, which has come to be known as the jazz age is better than the preceding. . . ."

The radio and the player pianos, to say nothing of phonographs, are grinding out with ceaseless energy the latest jazz, which, while it amuses and is quite in keeping with the rapid movement of life and the lure of dance halls, nevertheless, is not of lasting substance, and its inspiration is only for

the moment. For my own part, I find my delight, as far as music is concerned, in the splendid compositions of the old masters, who not only wrote music in its highest forms, but who made it live with the reality of life, transferring into it such depth of feeling and such height of expression that it arouses the best qualities of human nature.[7]

But in 1954, when Miles Davis was inspired by the heroism of Sugar Ray Robinson to change his life and re-dedicate himself to his craft, it was the moment that truly began the public life of Davis, the moment that made the man. Of course, Davis had been a professional musician for more than a decade, had played with Eddie Randle, Billy Eckstine, and Charlie Parker. But if he had died in 1954, Davis almost certainly would have been, at best, a minor footnote in jazz and possibly forgotten altogether, just as Freddie Webster, Gil Coggins, and Dodo Mamarosa are. That summer of 1954, when the Supreme Court, in *Brown v. Board of Education*, declared Jim Crow unconstitutional and integrated America's public schools, Davis recorded *Walkin'*, one of his classic works that signaled his return not only as serious musician, but as one of the best jazzmen of his generation. Despite the ups and downs of his later life, no one ever considered him, from that moment on, to be anything less than a major presence and a major myth in twentieth-century American music. And he knew it, too.

Part Two: Miles Davis and American Music

Now, I had learned from the jazz musicians I had known as a boy in Oklahoma City something of the discipline and devotion to his art required of the artist. . . . These jazzmen, many of them now world-famous, lived for and with music intensely. Their driving motivation was neither money nor fame, but the will to achieve the most eloquent expression of idea-emotions through the technical mastery of their instruments (which, incidentally, some of them wore as a priest wears the cross) and the give and take, the subtle rhythmical shaping and blending of idea, tone and imagination demanded of group improvisation. The delicate balance struck between strong individual personality and the group during those early jam sessions was a marvel of social organization. I had learned too that the end of all this discipline and technical mastery was the desire to express an affirmative way of life through its musical tradition and that this tradition insisted that each artist achieve his creativity within its frame. He must learn the best of the past, and add to it his personal vision. Life could be harsh, loud and wrong if it wished, but they lived it fully, and when they expressed their attitude toward the world it was with a fluid style that reduced the chaos of living to form.

—Ralph Ellison,
"Living With Music"

Arguably, the three jazz musicians who were young men, virtually teenagers, when the bebop revolution of the 1940s took shape, and who had the biggest influence on or exerted the greatest presence in American popular music after 1945 were Miles Davis, Quincy Jones, and John Coltrane. Each man, so different in personality and geographical origin—Coltrane was from the South; Jones, by way of Chicago, grew up in Seattle; and Davis was from East St. Louis—exercised his force in distinctly different ways.

Jones became a noted arranger, record and film producer, film scorer, and popular music mogul, astute in the ways of the business practices of the industry, and open to a number of musical styles from bebop jazz to hip hop, from avant-garde film score to teen-aged pop. He produced Sinatra and Basie, Dinah Washington and Ray Charles, and the biggest-selling album in the history of American popular music—Michael Jackson's *Thriller* (1982). His music is ubiquitous, although many people may not recognize it immediately as his, and he has had more commercial success than any jazz musician of his generation, perhaps of any jazz musician in history. But he did not become a major instrumentalist, nor did he develop an identifiable sound as a bandleader, although he fronted very good bands during his heyday as an active, touring musician. He was charming, handsome, talented, dependable, and willing to work extraordinarily hard. But unlike the other two men we are considering here, he did not develop a personality cult or a stylized personality or public persona that attracted people to him for reasons other than his music.

Coltrane became perhaps the greatest technical master of the saxophone in the history of modern music. He recorded a number of albums in the early 1960s that enjoyed some considerable commercial success, despite the fact that they were undiluted, uncompromising modern jazz, in other words, highly stylized art music. Records such as *My Favorite Things, Giant Steps, John Coltrane and Johnny Hartman*, and, notably, *A Love Supreme*, did well in the marketplace,

attracting, particularly, young people and those possessing a genuine or pseudointellectual interest in music. The civil rights generation of young people, iconoclastic, nonconformist, and romantically inclined about both politics and art, were particular fans of this music. Coltrane's later, more radical records of the period—*Ascension, Meditation, Kulu Se Mama*, and the like—did not sell as well but nonetheless had a worshipful audience. (So worshipful, in fact, that a church has spawned in San Francisco dedicated to John Coltrane.) Indeed, listening to and owning these records became a sign of being a member of the jazz and cultural cognoscenti, in a decade when spontaneity and emancipation became

virtual political and psychological obsessions. Coltrane, in important ways, signified the inchoate yearnings for change and self-improvement of his age: for blacks, his highly spiritualized racial consciousness seemed almost an aesthetic and a political aspiration; for whites, this same spiritualized racial consciousness seemed the romanticized ideal of a counterculture impulse that rebelled against a hypocritical, racist, materialist America. Coltrane, previously a sloppy drunk and drug addict, cleaned himself up and found redemption in the purity of art or the quest for pure artistic expression. He became essentially the anti–Charlie Parker, not a man who was a slave to his appetites but a man who seemingly had mastered them or, in effect, transcended them for a higher consciousness. The 1960s might be seen as the age of two gentle black male radicals who ironically were responsible for a great deal of gut-wrenching disruption: Coltrane and Martin Luther King. After his death, no one had a greater influence on aspects of 1970s popular music than Trane. No jazz musician was ever so honored by tribute songs as Coltrane was in both jazz and pop circles, and no jazz musician ever so overtly influenced how musicians wanted to live since the drug-days of Charlie Parker. Doug and Jean Carn, Carlos Santana, John McLaughlin, Billy Gault, Joe Lee Wilson, Chick Corea, McCoy Tyner, Elvin Jones, Terry Callier, the Rascals, the Last Poets,

Archie Shepp, and Gil-Scott Heron were some of the many jazz and pop artists who reverently honored Coltrane, either before he died or after or both. And tributes continued to flow later from such musicians as Vanessa Daou, Sonny Fortune, Kenny Garrett, Benny Golson, Dave Liebman, and Suzanne Pittson. Coltrane is mentioned more in socially conscious rap music than any other jazz musician. Coltrane single-handedly made the soprano saxophone, a technically difficult and often unruly instrument, which Sidney Bechet once played with vibrato and abandon back in the 1920s and 1930s, one of the most popular reed instruments of the last quarter of the twentieth century in popular music and jazz. But he was not a mogul, like Jones; not a noted composer or arranger of music; not someone very open to anything other than a certain sort of jazz that emerged after 1945. He was a genius player, period, and this intensified his myth and etherealized his achievements. He also died at the relatively young age of thirty-nine, when his work as an artist hardly had come to its full maturity.

Perhaps of the three men, Miles Davis is the most complex figure. Like Coltrane, Davis was a genius player, but not the same type of genius. Coltrane was one of the most technically accomplished saxophonists ever; but no one would say that Davis was one of the most technically accomplished trumpeters ever to emerge in jazz. Almost certainly Louis Armstrong, Roy Eldridge, Fats Navarro, Clifford Brown, and Dizzy Gillespie were better players technically. Many, I am sure, feel that Clark Terry, the late Lee Morgan, and possibly Wynton Marsalis are better players in their ability to get around the horn. But few players in jazz or in modern music ever matched Davis's ability to convey deep emotion, a poetic lyricism with an instrument. And very few jazzmen ever have been able to construct better solos, use space and silence so well, and make a few notes sound so telling. Kenneth Tynan called Davis "a musical lonely hearts club."[8] Davis was more than *that*, but the fact that the public could understand him as being *that* was important to his success: he was a high-level musician whose playing was accessible, romantic. His haunted, touching sound, so moving, particularly on ballads, that seemed so much like an abstraction, distillation, and improvement of Freddie Webster, an early influence, and his uncanny ability to swing at any tempo, like Armstrong, made him a formidable musician. (Davis was capable of playing fiery enough when he wanted, and one can hear him to good effect in this vein on some live albums he made in the 1950s and 1960s, particularly some live sets he made with Coltrane: *Live at the Blackhawk* and *"Four" and More*. He could produce this effect in the studio as well, on tunes like "Gingerbread Boy," "Salt Peanuts," and "Freedom Jazz Dance." Although he purposefully limited his range on the instrument—to take advantage of his strengths—technically he was more accomplished than some were willing to give him credit for.) Davis was probably not only one of the half-dozen or so greatest soloists in jazz in the last half of the twentieth century, but he was probably one of the finest conceptualists of music in American history; arguably, only Ellington, Armstrong, Thelonious Monk, Charles Mingus, Billie Holiday, and Parker matched or exceeded him in this realm.

If anything, Davis was able to generate a greater mystique about his playing than Coltrane did with his; and Davis, never in his life, affected any sort of religious or spiritual persona that would tend to romanticize himself or his music as something transcendent. He was a die-hard sensualist and secularist his entire life. Davis became one of modern American music's extraordinary personas, much to his benefit and sometimes to his detriment. Davis could be inspiringly prideful, incisive, determined, principled, and wondrously knowledgeable about music and people. He also could be remarkably crude and cruel, vain and foolish, and unnecessarily, childishly obscene in speech. Great flaws and great contradictions are often the marks of great people.

Like Jones, Davis was able to maintain himself in music, as an important voice in popular culture, far beyond the years of his youth. Indeed, at middle age, Davis reached an entirely new audience of young people in the 1970s with a kind of swaggering hipness and unbridled audacity virtually unmatched anywhere in American popular music, just as Jones, during those years, reached college-aged audiences with albums like *Smackwater Jack, Body Heat,* and *Gula Matari.* Davis changed his sound radically over the years, but unlike Jones, he unmistakably stamped the sound he became associated with. No matter what he was playing, whether tightly stated cool or wild-angled fusion, everyone instantly recognized a Miles Davis record, even if everyone did not like it instantly or eventually. Davis was not a mogul or a producer like Jones; nor was he an arranger or a composer of note. (Davis has been accused of taking credit for tunes he did not write, although the few tunes he is credited for having composed have become standards in jazz: "Milestones," "Nardis," "All Blues," "So What," "Blue in Green.") Yet on the strength of his ability and reputation as a player and particularly the image and reputation he cultivated as an innovator, an explorer, he kept himself more current and he managed to keep himself vital longer than most jazz musicians ever do.

Miles Davis, the musician and the man, is largely the result of certain cultural cross-currents that emerged after World War II. If there was a New Negro that philosophy professor and Harlem Renaissance broker Alain Locke could describe in his seminal 1925 essay, "The New Negro," which appeared in his famous anthology of the same name, it is very possible to talk about an even Newer Negro after World War II, more militant, more worldly, more urban, more alive to a changing world that was overthrowing European colonialism. Miles Davis's biggest years were between 1954 and 1975, the age of "colored" self-determination around the world. Both his music and his attitude reflected this. Davis also emerged during the age of the drug revolution, where people experimented with consciousness-alteration, with looking at what had been forbidden before (only people like jazz musicians took drugs) and to find out for themselves what these things were like. ("Better living through chemistry," as one wag of the 1960s put it.) Davis came into his own during the age of the sexual revolution. From the Kinsey Report

and *Playboy* magazine to the birth-control pill, legalized abortion, the gay rights movement, and the rise of the hard-core porn industry, Davis saw not only changes in the public attitude about and cultural depiction of sex, but he saw a change in the role of women in society. His own attitudes may not have changed much, and he still may have had, until the very end of his life, the old hustler's view of women as "bitches" who occasionally needed a man "to put his foot up their asses," but the attitude of the women in the world around him changed. And this has affected very deeply how he has been interpreted since the 1980s and particularly since his death in 1991. In the jazz world, of course, as in the sporting life itself, since the nineteenth century, a great deal of casual sex and interracial sex occurred. What Davis saw happen over the years of his prominence was that the sex of the jazz world became the sex of the mainstream world. What had once been considered criminal or bohemian became rather standard by the 1960s and 1970s, particularly. Davis was at his height during the years of protest and dissent in America about Vietnam and civil rights. And in some subtle ways, there was much protest in his music, and in some blatant ways, much protest in his attitude and self-presentation. Davis chose very much to be a jazz musician on his own terms, defining this music as he felt it necessary. But Davis clearly benefited by coming of age as an artist in an age of personal experimentation that touched the core of mind and body and challenged established authority, the state, the school, the church, the family. This gave Davis's own restless quest for experimentation not only a cultural and social context but an incredibly sympathetic ambience.

Davis's most ardent admirers claim that he changed the direction of modern music four times or more in his career. First, he single-handedly created cool—when bebop grew stale and clichéd—when he did the sessions that became *The Birth of the Cool* in 1949 and 1950 and set the jazz world on its ear. He invented hard bop with *Walkin'* and his sessions for Prestige in the mid-1950s. Then, he was credited with reinvigorating orchestral jazz with the Gil Evans sessions of the late 1950s; he invented modal jazz with the seminal *Kind of Blue* album in 1959, the single most influential jazz album since World War II; he walked a line between freedom and tradition with his 1960s quintet that has become the basis of virtually all small-group jazz being played now; and he invented jazz-rock or fusion in 1970 with *Bitches Brew*.

There is truth in this, but these claims rather miss the truly complex nature of Davis's genius; it is certainly always the case that admirers suspect the genius to be auteur of all he or she ever touched. This is far from accurate.

Davis had a knack for being around very talented young musicians—he saw jazz as a young musician's art—who not only understood and appreciated him but whom he understood, and in some sense, liberated. In other words, musicians who played with Davis were able to develop their own ideas and many went on to fruitful careers. When Chick Corea, Dave Holland, and Jack DeJohnette played as Davis's rhythm section in the early 1970s, they often would drop out of the music and play material that sounded very much like Corea's avant-garde group of the time, Circle. Davis permitted this, just as he did Coltrane's long solos when the latter was in his 1950s band. When Herbie Hancock was in Davis's band in the 1960s, he sounded very much like Hancock with his own band. And Keith Jarrett's solos with Davis in the 1970s sounded very much like the sort of thing

Jarrett would play in his own band on an acoustic piano. In short, Davis provided his musicians with a context where they played something clearly identifiable as his music or his sound, but in that context they not only remained themselves, they very often found themselves. This is why nearly all the musicians who played with Davis during his career speak so highly of the experience.

The character of Davis's music changed significantly, depending on who was in his band. Davis became interested in modal music when pianist Bill Evans was in the band, and much of the music on *Kind of Blue* sounds like the sort of thing Evans would write (and some say, indeed, that Evans did write it, particularly "Blue in Green," "All Blues," and "Flamenco Sketches"). Yet, and this is the sign of Davis's genius, no one would ever mistake *Kind of Blue* for an Evans album. Gil Evans was the architect for Davis's orchestral sound and had much to do with the success of *The Birth of the Cool* sessions (along with saxophonist Gerry Mulligan). Wayne Shorter was the main composer for the sound of Davis's 1960s band. Davis was far from being the inventor of jazz-rock. Drummer Chico Hamilton's band, which had members like guitarists Gabor Szabo and Larry Coryell, bassist Al Stinson, and saxophonist Charles Lloyd, did far more innovative things in that direction in the mid-1960s than Davis during the same time. So did vibes player Gary Burton, saxophonist Eddie Harris, and Lloyd himself. Davis caught the wave at a certain height with the right musicians to move fusion ahead in a way that no one had quite envisioned. Timing was a significant factor in his success; for instance, the *Sketches of Spain* album had much to do with a craze for Spanish—not Latin American—culture in the United States in the late 1950s. Garcia Lorca's poetry was hot; flamenco music was big; Henry King made his film version of *The Sun Also Rises* in 1957, and bullfighting was the rage with the American intelligentsia. (*The Brave Bulls* and *The Bullfighter and the Lady*, two other bullfighting pictures made in 1951, had been successful as well and reflected the strong interest in this subject expressed throughout the

decade.) Disney's *Zorro*, set in Spanish California—with constant references to the mother country, Spain—was a popular television program. It was a good time to make a Spanish—not an Afro-Cuban—record, and part of *Sketches of Spain*'s appeal is that it makes use of what Jelly Roll Morton called "the Spanish tinge" in a remarkably fresh way. The timing for *In a Silent Way* and *Bitches Brew* could not have been better. Jazz was losing its audience; there were few venues left to play it. If one were going to make a living as a jazz musician, it was necessary to find a way for this music to be played in rock venues. Davis discovered a way to do that. Some thought of it as selling out, but Davis's music remained incredibly abstract and strikingly noncommercial despite being gussied up and marketed as youth music. (Sometimes I think critics of Davis's music during this period mistake the marketing of the music for the music itself.)

In short, there was much about what Davis did in his career that was sui generis. The Gil Evans sessions were remarkable, but Ellington and Basie were still the best big jazz bands of the period and Stan Kenton was far more experimental. The Prestige small group sessions with Coltrane, Red Garland, Paul Chambers, and Philly Joe Jones—a more unpromising group of mismatched musicians could hardly be imagined, yet Davis made it work brilliantly and those men never sounded better—were influential hard bop records, among the

best ever. But the hard bop records from the period that are considered quintessential are Art Blakey's, Horace Silver's, Hank Mobley's, and organist Jimmy Smith's. Davis operated in a separate sphere, in part, because the quality of his music was so high, yet he never seemed imprisoned by any of the periods or styles he recorded in. Davis had the three instincts necessary for genius: he was an opportunist; he was not afraid of talented people, even if, in some particular area, they were more talented than he; and he had supreme confidence in his ability to make anything he'd try work. Moreover, Davis understood his limitations: he wrote music, but he was not a composer in the way that Ellington or Mingus or Monk were. He was not an arranger in the way that Gil Evans was or Billy Strayhorn or Quincy Jones or Gerald Wilson were. He was not a producer like Quincy Jones or Teo Macero. Indeed, he had a rather careless attitude about his music and needed a producer in the way that a writer like Thomas Wolfe needed an editor. He had no real sense of business, although he fronted bands for many years. He discovered talent, but he was not a cultivator of it in the way Stan Kenton was. If he had had a greater entrepreneurial impulse, he probably would have made a great deal more money than he did. (As it was, he was enormously successful financially for a musician who made, for the most part, music with meager commercial appeal.) Yet it all came together for him and worked amazingly well for a number of years. His biggest gift was that he was neither afraid of his audience nor of himself.

This lack of fear is apparent in Davis's autobiography, for the book generated much controversy, not only for what was in it but how it was expressed. Stanley Crouch and Jack Chambers have said the book is largely plagiarized. Others are displeased with the crude language and the mistakes. Still others are annoyed with Davis's treatment of women. Yet, despite its shortcomings, it is one of the most fascinating jazz autobiographies ever written. Davis talks insightfully and incisively about music and music-making, about his bands and the life of a working musician. What drives a musician to make music is not at all the same as what drives an audience to listen to it. What a musician gets from making music is entirely different from what an audience gets from listening to it. This is true despite the fact that a musician understands precisely what sort of effect his or her music likely will have on an audience, because the emotional response to certain tones and keys is

well established and almost never varies. Davis conveys very well the sense of music to a musician but does so in a way that a reader who is not a musician can fully understand. It is important that Davis was able to explain his craft on his own terms. After all, jazz is the most persistently explained music ever invented in America and may be the most explicated popular music in the world, despite that most of its major artists dislike critics. With his autobiography, Davis, who hated critics while in some sense he artfully courted them, became his own critic.

To appreciate better Davis's book, one might do well to compare it with *Hamp*, Lionel Hampton's autobiography published the same year. *Miles* and *Hamp* give us two distinct views of black musical innovators: drummer and vibes player Hampton, who sees himself transparently as an entertainer willing to give the people what they want; and Davis, who sees himself egotistically as the rebel who is almost opaque, impenetrable, misunderstood, and mistreated because he is black. Hampton smiles incessantly when he performs;

Davis never smiled, and, indeed, for a good portion of his career, he never even spoke to or acknowledged his audience. Both attitudes symbolize the intense, inescapable racial consciousness of the two men and the unrelenting anxiety of playing for the white establishment, which, frankly, as both books make clear, made them possible by creating and sustaining their fame. There is a sense with both men, Hampton's accommodation and Davis's resentment largely becoming reflections of the same sensibility, that jazz has only a white audience and that the poses, after all, are the only possible ones available to them. Of course, any historian of this music is well aware that Davis and Hampton, for most of their careers, had sizable black followings. Because there were so few black movie and television stars before the 1960s, black musicians and black athletes were the pop-culture aristocracy of the national black community. Yet both Hampton and Davis always must have felt that the real powers in jazz—from the concert promoters to the nightclub owners to the record company executives, from the large portion of the record-buying public to the critical and reviewing establishment—were exclusively white. How they responded to this says much about their careers and the kind of books they wrote about themselves.

Nothing demonstrates this aura of whiteness and the difference in how both men handled it more compellingly than their view of the white political establishment. Hampton writes with pride of his long friendship with Richard Nixon and his association with conservative Republican politics, of the number of Republican presidential balls he played: "I walk within the Republican party and do what I have to do, as long as Republicans are in it. . . . I believe in a lot of principles of Republicanism, like not being wasteful."[9] Later, in discussing the 1988 campaign of George Bush, Hampton says:

I had high hopes for a Republican victory in November. I believe that the country was better off after eight years of Reagan. The country had gone more conservative, and in my opinion there was no other way for

it to go. Things were really getting out of hand. They talk about getting our teenagers tuned to a better way of life and good citizenship, and then they let all this filth in. There was a time when divorce was a damnable sin. Now a couple of movie stars can shack up and have a kid out of wedlock, and they're heroes.[10]

One, of course, cannot be sure who "they" are. Perhaps Hampton means Democrats or liberals generally. It is noteworthy that his condemnation of liberalism, on the ground of corrupting the innocent, is precisely the ground upon which jazz as an art form was condemned in the 1920s and even, to a lesser extent, the 1930s, the era when Hampton emerged first as an apprentice, a major musical presence. Jazz, at one time in this country, when Hampton was a young man playing it in Los Angeles and later with Benny Goodman, represented a kind of liberalism and artistic dissent. It was an attack on the status quo until the late 1940s, when a certain kind of jazz had become the status quo. Later, Hampton became associated with rock and roll, another rebel music for the young that threatened the status quo. His post–World War II band was largely a rhythm and blues, jump band. He was, for instance, featured prominently in Alan Freed's 1957 film, *Mr. Rock and Roll.* (Indeed, if the film is read right, Hampton *is* Mr. Rock and Roll.) It is not strange, in the

end, that Hampton defends the establishment and the status quo; he sees it as the culmination of his career, arriving at a level of respectability and recognition, not from critics, not from fellow musicians, not even from the general public, but from an elitist group of conservative social climbers. Finally, when he writes about how the Republican White House paid homage to him, his exchange of honorifics with President Reagan seem hollow:

The following September the Reagans paid me just about the greatest honor I've ever had when they gave me a special reception at the White House. George Bush had a lot to do with that. It was his way of thanking me [for campaigning for the Reagan-Bush ticket in 1984]. About eight hundred people gathered on the south lawn of the White House, and President and Mrs. Reagan greeted everyone. Then we did a concert. . . . After the concert, the president called me a great American, and I called him the greatest star in the world. I was deeply honored.[11]

Miles Davis, on the other hand, never talked about politics, never indicated that he had ever voted in an election, saying only that he has "never liked that kind of political shit." (This attitude explains why he steered clear of the civil rights movement and comes very close to the view of Ralph Ellison: the artist must focus on his art, not politics, although Davis's feeling borders on utter cynicism and contempt, not simply detachment and indifference. He does not find politics distracting but outrageously immoral.) Davis writes of attending a 1987 presidential reception and ceremony for Ray Charles, who was getting a Lifetime Achievement Award:

When I met the President I wished him good luck in trying to do what he was doing, and he said, "Thanks, Miles, because I'm going to need it." He's a nice enough guy when you meet him in person. I guess he was doing the best he could. He's a politician, man, who happens to lean to the right. Others lean to the left. Most of them politicians are stealing the country blind. It don't matter whether they are Republicans or Democrats; they are all in it for what they can take. The politicians don't care anymore about the American people. All they think about is how they're going to get rich just like everybody else who is greedy.[12]

The affair was painful for Davis, as he was insulted several times by whites who were ignorant of his art: "That was some of the sorriest shit I've ever been around. That was a hell of a feeling I had down there in Washington, feeling embarrassed because those white people down there who are running the country don't understand nothing about black people and don't want to know!"[13]

What explains the difference beyond merely pointing out that both men are of different generations? Both were midwesterners, but Hampton came up from the Deep South, whereas Davis was born in Illinois. Davis makes a considerable point of his background on at least three occasions in his autobiography. First, in assessing why he, Coleman Hawkins, and Charlie Parker got along as artists, he explains, "We—Bird, me, and Bean—were all from the Midwest. I think that had a lot to do with us hitting it off musically, and sometimes—at least with Bird—socially; we kind of thought and saw things alike."[14] Second, Davis uses his background to explain the difference between himself and the two "clown"

princes of jazz trumpet, Dizzy Gillespie and Louis Armstrong: "I come from a different social and class background than both of them, and I'm from the Midwest, while both of them are from the South. So we look at white people a little differently."[15] Finally, he speaks of region in explaining why he and his second wife, Frances, were attracted to each other: "Frances was from Chicago and I was also from the Midwest, so that might have had something to do with us hitting it off so quick, because we never did have to explain a lot of shit."[16]

Unlike Hampton, who from his youth when his family ran a bootlegging operation to his early days as a musician when he played in clubs owned by the likes of Al Capone, tended to see strong white men in authority—whether gangsters or Republican politicians—as protectors, Davis was unimpressed by white men in authority. Indeed, Davis saw himself as something of an outlaw: a dope addict, a pimp, a jazzman, a boxer. He had adopted many of the fearful guises of the black man who rebels against white male authority in the United States. In this way, we must understand everything about Davis as artifice and masculine stylization. It is also a book about being at war with white masculinity and the white male presumption of power. This is perhaps in the end why Davis's book, where the language is itself so stylized after the masculine rituals of context insulting—a performance feature of both boxing and the street-corner hustler—and the authoritative, sexist denigrations of the pimp, is, by far, one of the most morally obsessed jazz autobiographies ever written. For Davis, jazz history is the allegorical battle for the black man's body and his ethical and aesthetic principles, which explains why Davis's book has richer assessments of the musicians he played with, the creative processes that constitute the making of jazz, and the artistic workings of a jazz band than any extant jazz autobiography. What Davis condemns consistently throughout the book is greed, selfishness, and people's unwillingness to pay the price for what they do. He calls not only white politicians greedy, but also the greatest musician he ever played with and possibly one of the finest musicians

America ever produced, Charlie Parker. Davis suggests that not even great art can save one morally, and that it is presumptuous, as in the case of Parker, to believe that it should or that it confers a kind of preemptive grace. This is a profoundly remarkable and moving idea, because there is no self-pity in it, nor sentimentality, nor any attempt to escape the immediateness of this life and its necessity that we answer for who we are with what we are by appealing to something transcendent, not even art itself, no matter how impressive that art is.

This collection of essays—by blacks and whites, men and women, jazz and nonjazz scholars—looks at various facets of Davis's career, from his influences in East St. Louis and St. Louis when he was growing up to an examination of what he means to black women. There are pieces that look at Davis in the political context of the civil rights movement, within the context of the avant-garde movement of the 1960s, and during the Watergate and Reagan periods in the early 1970s and 1980s. Interspersed between the essays are interviews with people who knew Davis, record producers and musicians. The appendices include a detailed chronology of African American and jazz history during Davis's lifetime, as well as the famous interview Davis did with Alex Haley for *Playboy* magazine in 1962. A certain amount of dispute has arisen about the latter. First, it is said that Davis beat up Haley in the ring before consenting to the interview, displaying,

for his detractors, Davis's cruelty and inclination to have people kiss his ass. (Davis mentions in his autobiography that Haley did enter the ring with him.) Recently, Jack Chambers has suggested that the interview was plagiarized. Nonetheless, it remains the most noted interview Davis ever did. It is hoped that this collection will provide a full view of the life and music of Davis, why the man was discussed and thought about while he was alive and continues to be discussed—and deserves to be—since his death. No jazz musician in history, with the exception of Duke Ellington and probably Count Basie, made as much good music for as long as Davis. And no jazz musician other than Ellington made as much different music, that was good, as Davis. It is difficult to understand modern American music without thinking about the role of Miles Davis. It is impossible to know modern American culture since 1950 without knowing what he did and why. Here is a beginning.

1   Miles Davis with Quincy Troupe, *Miles: The Autobiography* (New York: Simon and Schuster, 1989), 174.

2   *Miles: The Autobiography*, 181.

3   The novel became a successful play that Heyward coauthored with his wife, Dorothy. In 1935, in collaboration with the Gershwin brothers, the play became the folk opera, "Porgy and Bess."

4   *Miles: The Autobiography*, 180–81.

5   *Miles: The Autobiography*, 314–15.

6   This description of Johnson, from James Weldon Johnson's autobiography, *Along This Way* (1933), is pertinent in this regard: I think the most interesting person I met was Jack Johnson, who was to be, three years later, the champion prize fighter of the world. I saw him first at the theater, where he had come to see Bob [Cole, one of Johnson's songwriting partners] and Rosamond [Johnson, James's brother and another songwriting partner]. He came frequently to our apartment, and his visits were generally as long as our time permitted, for he was not training. These visits put the idea in my head of improving myself in 'the manly art of self-defense'—the manner in which gentlemen used to speak about taking boxing lessons. Jack often boxed with me playfully, like a good-natured big dog warding off the earnest attacks of a small one, but I could never get him to give me any serious instruction. Occasionally, he would bare his stomach to me as a mark and urge me to hit him with all my might. I found it an impossible thing to do; I always involuntarily pulled my punch. It was easy to like Jack Johnson; he is so likable a man, and I liked him particularly well. I was, of course, impressed by his huge but perfect form, his terrible strength, and the supreme ease and grace of his every muscular movement; however, watching his face, sad until he smiled, listening to his soft Southern speech and laughter, and hearing him talk so wistfully about his big chance, yet to come, I found it difficult to think of him as a prize fighter. I had not yet seen a prize fight, but I conceived of the game as a brutal, bloody one, demanding of its exponents courage, stamina, and brute force, as well as skill and quick intelligence, and I could hardly figure gentle Jack Johnson in the role. . . .
—James Weldon Johnson, *Along This Way:*

The Autobiography of James Weldon Johnson (New York: Viking Press, 1938), 208. Johnson's books, *The Autobiography of an Ex-Colored Man* (1912), *Black Manhattan* (1930), and *Along This Way* provide excellent accounts of the black sporting life of which Johnson, as a popular songwriter in the 1890s, was a part. For more on Jack Johnson and how he challenged the reformist era with his prizefighting and his ownership of a nightclub (where his first white wife committed suicide), see Kevin J. Mumford, *Interzones: Black/White Sex Districts in Chicago and New York in the Early Twentieth Century* (New York: Columbia University Press, 1997), 3–18, especially. Also see, Gerald Early, "Jack Johnson: A Man Out of Time," in Michael MacCambridge, ed., *ESPN SportsCentury* (New York: Hyperion Books, 1999), 34–49.

7   Jack Johnson, *Jack Johnson—In the Ring—and Out* (Chicago: National Sports Publishing Company, 1927), 217, 221.

8   Quoted in Dan Wakefield, *New York in the Fifties* (New York: Houghton Mifflin, 1992), 300.

9   Lionel Hampton, with James Haskins, *Hamp: An Autobiography* (New York: Warner Books, 1989), 167.

10 Ibid.,174.

11 Ibid.,168.

12 *Miles: The Autobiography*, 378.

13 Ibid., 381.

14 Ibid., *77.*

15 Ibid., 83.

16 Ibid., 227.

Davis (back row, right) in
Eddie Randle's Rhumboogie
Orchestra,
St. Louis, ca. 1943.

Miles Davis's readiness to innovate and his defiant personal style have allowed some to imagine him outside the main currents of history. To imprison him within historians' lumbering generalizations may seem to deny the creative capacity that he brought to bear on music. But even a free and creative spirit like Davis had a childhood and a youth shaped by the dreams and delusions of his time. He was as caught up in the sticky web of history as everyone else, and his fiery attitudes toward racism gave ample evidence that he knew it. A closer look at the period from his birth in Alton, Illinois, in 1926 to his departure for New York City in 1944 reveals that the East St. Louis–St. Louis area provided him with personal and musical experiences that contributed in important ways to his subsequent career. Influences in the Mississippi valley made it likely that he would play jazz on the trumpet and that he would associate his music with a search for identity, opportunity, and freedom.

Davis spent most of his first eighteen years in East St. Louis, Illinois, his hometown. He made clear in his autobiography that that swiftly growing city had left its mark: his father, mother, and hometown teachers like Elwood Buchanan had done a good job, encouraging him to dig under the surfaces, to lay a solid professional foundation, and to be proud of himself. Davis remembered many influential individuals and formative events from his youth. When he decided to get involved in jazz, he entered a particularly rich, complex stream of African American musical life that surged through the Mississippi valley around St. Louis and East St. Louis.

For example, one of his early decisions, an important one, was, despite his mother's disapproval, to play his music on the trumpet. That step, according to *Miles: The Autobiography*, emerged from his negotiations with his high school music teacher, Elwood Buchanan, and with his father, but the ideas of those two men were in turn influenced by the St. Louis "school" of the trumpet. The black St. Louis school of jazz trumpeters included Robert Shoffner, Leonard "Ham" Davis, Irving "Mouse" Randolph, Eddie Randle, Harold "Shorty" Baker, Charles Creath, Dewey Jackson, Ed Allen, Clark Terry, and George Hudson, to mention only those who gained a measure of fame in jazz. Many others, like Levi Madison and Bruzz Woods, were known only within the region.[1]

Just before Miles:

Jazz in St. Louis, 1926–1944

by William Howland Kenney

The trumpet played an important role in European concert hall music, of course, but that was not where young black musicians encountered it. Early in the twentieth century, grass-roots musical training for boys in black St. Louis emphasized the cornet and trumpet. The Mound City Company "C" of the Knights of Pythias and the Fourteenth Regiment Odd Fellows Band both championed military-influenced wind ensembles heavy on brass instruments—cornets, trumpets, trombones, French horns, and alto horns. The pioneer jazz musician Dewey Jackson, who became president of the black musicians' union Local #44, for example, started playing trumpet at age thirteen in the Odd Fellows Band under the instruction of P. B. Langford.[2] Saxophonist Sammy Long took lessons for fifty cents a week in the Pythian Lodge Childrens' Band, learning "the fundamentals of music."[3] The community's newspaper, the *St. Louis Argus*, underscored the importance it attached to the involvement of young men in musical education. The paper reminded its readers that young boys in these bands learned "discipline," "deportment," and "self confidence" in addition to music itself. Such qualities, the paper editorialized, were particularly important to young black males who, "unlike whites, had little prestige and race development behind them."[4] Robert Lee "Bob" Shoffner and Edward C. "Ed" Allen, two St. Louis trumpeters who performed in a number of different jazz groups during the 1920s, appear in

newspaper photos as proud, young Odd Fellows musicians.[5] The two organizations' music programs for youth disappeared from the newspaper's pages after 1916, so those grass roots of the St. Louis school of trumpet may have disappeared as well. Pythian Hall, however, remained the black community's major dance hall throughout the jazz age.

The developing lines of commercial music in St. Louis and East St. Louis also shaped the field of possibilities from which Miles Davis made his choices. Not long before making his famous move to New York City, Davis began his jazz performance career by working with a variety of musicians in a network of black jazz and "hot-dance" bands in Missouri and Illinois. Hot-dance, as dubbed by the region's black musicians, was the music performed and promoted by blacks for blacks on riverboats. The self-consciously African American jazz form arose in the early 1920s and remained a recurrent force, weakened, but by no means destroyed, by the Great Depression. Some of the region's hot-dance groups and musicians came from or through East

St. Louis, but during the second and third decades of this century most of them found most of their jobs across the river in St. Louis. East St. Louis and Brooklyn, Illinois, developed more active nightclub scenes during the 1930s and 1940s. These cities held a central position within an active network of musicians and bands entwined by the river, the railroads, and the highways that paralleled them. This "hot-dance" tradition—as Miles labeled it in his autobiography[6]—that flourished in and around black St. Louis helped Davis begin to find his way as a working professional and also brought him advance news from jazz's wider worlds. As he put it:

And I think when I was growing up it was because of the people—especially black musicians—moving back and forth from New Orleans. St. Louis is close to Chicago and Kansas City, as well. So people would bring the different kinds of styles of those places back to East St. Louis.[7]

The railroads and highways played an important role in shaping the economy and society of East St. Louis while influencing land use as well. As recently as 1970, East St. Louis ranked second only to Chicago in the amount of land devoted to railroad use. The trains and highways brought musicians through East St. Louis, while the riverboats brought them through St. Louis. The particularly important role of transportation in the area enriched the musical sounds that reached the ears of the region's young musicians,[8] but, inevitably, also took musicians away from the area, making it difficult to establish long-term St. Louis traditions.

In his autobiography, Miles emphasized that "playing with Eddie Randle and His Blue Devils for one year starting in 1943 when he was 17 years old had to be one of the most important steps in my career. It was with Eddie Randle's band that I really started opening up with my playing, really got into writing and arranging music."[9] We tend to look back at that period knowing what an accomplished musician Miles Davis became, but a photo of him playing with Randle's Rhumboogie Orchestra at the Rhumboogie Club,[10] located in the Elks' Club in downtown St. Louis, reminds us that he was a very youthful teenager. Eddie Randle placed his own recollections of the neophyte jazzman in the perspective of 1943. Actually, he had taken a chance in hiring Davis:

In fact, all the guys in the band wanted to quit when I hired Miles. . . . But I could see the possibilities, I said, "boy, the sky is the limit for this kid." And the rest of them said, "well, you got a chance to get this other fellow with all this experience." And I says, "well, he's got the experience and he's not going any further. He's like me. He just going to play good and that's it." And I said, "sky is the limit for this young fellow." And so by being the boss . . . I didn't let them out talk me. And I was proud that I gave Miles the chance. And Miles has given me a lot of credit for giving him his chance.[11]

For his part, Davis reserved his favorite tough-guy accolade ("a motherfucker") for Eddie Randle's band; they were "hot," "could play their asses off," and "everybody used to come to hear us play, no matter what kind of music they themselves played."

Bandleader and trumpeter Eddie Randle possessed several of the same capabilities that would mark Miles Davis's career: he preferred the more abstract, theoretical elements of music, the managerial and promotional challenges of band leading, and the process of judicious recruitment of sidemen. In the early 1940s, when Miles Davis began his career in jazz performance, Eddie Randle had the best, most popular hot-dance band in St. Louis. Many musicians who went on to national fame in jazz came to listen to his Rhumboogie Orchestra—Clark Terry, Sonny Stitt, Benny Carter, Roy Eldridge, and Kenny Dorham.

Randle epitomized the struggles and achievements of black musicians in the river valley. He had been born into a musical family in Pulaski County, Illinois, near Cairo, and came to live at 3112 Lucas Street in St. Louis at age seventeen.[12] Taught the trumpet by an uncle, Randle discovered his "own groove" on the instrument, but always lamented his lack of formal schooling both on the trumpet and in music generally. He revealed that he always had loved knowing about music's formal elements. In fact, "I just loved music more than I wanted to play." He avidly pursued musical knowledge, commenting: "My grandfather who raised me was a great musician, in fact all of my people played and I listened . . . [since] training for us was limited." Randle learned how to read and write music in his family and became proficient enough to lead and write compositions and arrangements for a ten-piece orchestra. When the New Orleans jazz trumpet soloist Henry "Red" Allen replaced Louis Armstrong in Fate Marable's Orchestra on the Streckfus Line riverboats in 1924, he came to Randle to learn how to read the Marable band's charts.[13]

Randle built his band's reputation the hard way, beating the bushes in small towns in Missouri, Illinois, Indiana, and Kentucky,[14] performing on radio stations WEW and KMOX, and playing from time to time on the riverboats. He braved the prejudice of country club and radio station managers to book his band. He persisted and soon found jobs as much as one year in advance, the 1930s passing in a constant round of one-nighters. The turning point in his career occurred in the fall of 1932 when he managed to get Eddie Randle and His Blue Devils on the air regularly at WEW. His knowledge of the fundamentals of music helped him get this important job. Upon applying, he had suspected that racial prejudice was hidden beneath the station manager's initial refusal to hire his band. That person had claimed that the band played too many tunes registered with the American Society of Composers, Authors, and Performers

(ASCAP), and since radio stations had to pay performance fees to ASCAP for airing such material, this would make Randle's airtime too expensive. The bandleader surprised the station manager by assuring him that his band would perform nothing but original works on the air, thus sparing the radio station all of the usual ASCAP performance fees. The group landed the job, which became one of their rare regular gigs, one that attracted many young listeners like Miles Davis from the St. Louis, East St. Louis, and Missouri area.

In 1943, when the seventeen-year-old Miles finally got the courage to call about a job opening on trumpet, Randle's was the best in a crowded, changing field of hot-dance bands

working the region. The Mississippi River valley around St. Louis enjoyed a surprising number of ten- to twelve-piece hot-dance bands that read arrangements enriched with solo improvisations and enlivened with plenty of rhythmic intensity. In addition to Randle, Eddie Johnson, Chick Finney, Elijah Shaw, Dewey Jackson, James Jeter, Hayes Pillars, and Charles Creath all led bands in the area from the time of Davis's birth to the time of his departure for New York City. They influenced the rising generation of the 1930s and early 1940s with their emphasis on the fundamentals of music: sight reading, composing, and arranging, as well as the other qualities commonly associated with jazz, like rhythmic swing and improvisation. Davis's jazz mentors from the region believed in stylistic versatility so that they could perform for both white and black audiences, dances, balls, riverboats, radio stations, and vaudeville and cabaret acts. The "jazz" label, so easily bestowed by the media on all African American musicians, falsely implied a narrower musical focus. Miles took this probing musical versatility, if not the idea of the hot-dance band itself, with him to New York, where he vastly expanded the musical parameters of jazz.

The Mississippi River played a central role in the growth of the regional hot-dance band culture that surrounded the young Miles Davis in the 1930s and early 1940s. During the one year that Davis played professionally in the area, before moving on to New York City, he never played on the riverboats; the riverfront of East St. Louis had not been developed commercially and was owned throughout Davis's lifetime by the railroads and the Wiggins Ferry Company. Despite persistent efforts to secure control, the city could not develop the waterfront to its benefit in the way that St. Louis had.[15] Moreover, World War II had shut down the excursion-boat tourist business. In 1943–44, when Davis was seventeen to eighteen years old, no one played on the riverboats. Barges carrying supplies for the war effort overwhelmed the Mississippi and its major ports. The United States Coast Guard[16] even commandeered some of the paddle wheelers, and the region's versatile, hot-dance bands were forced out of business by the induction of their sidemen into military service. Miles Davis left East St. Louis in 1944, not only to work with Charlie Parker and Dizzy Gillespie in New York City, but also because World War II had sunk the hot-dance band business, especially for blacks.

For the musicians of Elwood Buchanan's generation, jazz, both on and off the river, was a matter of racial, musical, professional, and social pride. Miles Davis absorbed this orientation. All-black hot-dance bands had grown up with the racially segregated riverboats during the 1920s, and this kind of band managed to survive the depression of the 1930s under increasingly difficult circumstances. The relatively inexpensive steamboat excursions remained a major, popular activity during those difficult years. Regular employment on the riverboats during the spring and summer months, therefore, furnished an economic base in St. Louis for ten- to twelve-piece black bands. These bands were by no means the only foundation for jazz in St. Louis, nor was "the old saying that St. Louis is a dead town for musicians" true.[17] But pianists Fate Marable, Eddie Johnson, and Chick Finney, and trumpeters Charles Creath, Dewey Jackson and Ed Allen, Eddie Randle, and Hayes Pillars all led bands on the river during this period. Their orchestras all worked on land as well as in downtown East St. Louis clubs, those of St. Louis, in the white country clubs that dotted the entire region, and at the varied venues controlled by the black Local #44 of the American Federation of Musicians. But the established riverboat business, working the lucrative popular white market six nights a week and the smaller African American market one and sometimes more times a week, provided a solid economic foundation for black orchestras in the region. The boats did not pay lucrative wages, but they offered St. Louis/East St. Louis musicians regular nightly work from May 1 to the end of September.

Most of the writers who have shown an interest in riverboat music have been smitten by the graceful white wooden paddle wheelers, beautiful swan-like craft that stirred the white imagination with images of the antebellum South. But the romance of those racially segregated vessels appealed mostly to whites.[18] The riverboat companies had promoted segregated Monday evening cruises for African Americans from at least the turn of the century, and the Streckfus Line carried that Jim Crow tradition into the 1920s, 1930s, 1940s, 1950s, and 1960s. Racial segregation on the riverboats came to an end only in 1969.[19]

African Americans in St. Louis during Miles Davis's youth chafed under this as under all other forms of segregation, but still devised ways to enjoy cruises when someone "from our group," as their newspaper phrased it, organized them. The steamboat excursion companies filled the decks with passengers by sending out representatives well in advance of the cruises themselves.

During the late winter months, salesmen usually succeeded in convincing civic and fraternal organizations to sponsor one or more summer cruises. As the segregated African American market was proportionally smaller than the "white" one, the steamers usually convinced two or more business, religious, civic, or social groups to "sponsor" a summer cruise together. Here are the names of just some of the social groups in black St. Louis that enjoyed cruises:

Prudence Crandall Club, Owl Boys, White Rose, Flor de Melba Girls, Clinging Rose Social Club, Red Rose Social, Silver Bell Social, Finney Avenue Circle, Yellow Jackets, Arrow Boys, Arabian Boys, Stanwix Boys, the Melrose, Liberty Boys, Monarch Boys, Yale Boys, Belvedere Club, and Lajovial Girls.[20]

So too, such black St. Louis professional, religious, and union groups as the Knights of Pythias, Original Ostend Club, Scullin Steel Company, the Colored Waiter's Alliance, People's Hospital, Medinah Temple Mystic Shrine, the Wheatley Branch of the YMCA, Union Memorial Church, St. Paul AME Church, Lane Tabernacle Church, and the St. Louis Negro Business League sponsored cruises.

Despite their Jim Crow policies, a few specific excursion steamers offered regular employment for black musicians. Streckfus Steamers, Inc. based its operations in St. Louis, and its musical director, Fate C. Marable, hired orchestras, thereby creating musical opportunity in that city for ten-piece hot-dance bands. During Miles Davis's youth, this company dominated the Mississippi and the Ohio River tourist trade with six large steamboats, two of which, the three-hundred-foot *St. Paul* and the somewhat smaller *J.S. Deluxe*, steamed out of St. Louis with all-black orchestras. Fate Marable, who regularly performed in St. Louis clubs during the winters, recruited the best musicians he found there to make "water music" during the warmer months. Riverboat employment played an important role, therefore, in holding musicians in the St. Louis area. When World War II, federal regulations, air conditioning, the interstate highway system, and old age led to the dismantling of the old wooden excursion boats, a crucial economic foundation for the region's hot-dance band tradition disappeared. But until that unfortunate time, hot-dance bands featured such St. Louis trumpeters as Clark Terry and Harold "Shorty" Baker, as well as the saxophonist Talmadge "Tab" Smith and double-bassist James "Jimmy" Blanton, who all worked in one or another of the maritime bands.[21] Many exceptionally talented musicians who did not earn fame also played in these bands, including drummer and vocalist Floyd Campbell, the saxophone and trumpet virtuoso Lee Hilliard, pianist Burroughs Lovingood, and flautist Lloyd Smith.

The racially segregated riverboats remained contested public space despite Jim Crow law. Miles Davis would become more outspoken than the musicians of his father's generation, but he was by no means the first to associate jazz with racial pride. The popularity and pervasiveness of hot-dance music illustrates this fact. The Streckfus Line ruled the waters but was not without competitors. Black riverboat jazz, moreover, possessed a resourceful champion in the band booker, recording company scout, music store proprietor, taxicab entrepreneur, and excursion cruise promoter Jesse J. Johnson of St. Louis. For the jazz musicians of Miles Davis's father's generation, jazz on and off the river was frequently a matter of racial, musical, professional, and social pride. The young trumpeter certainly took this tradition with him to New York.

The long performance career of East St. Louis trumpeter Charles Creath, born in Ironton, Missouri, in 1890, illustrates the intermixture of race relations with jazz in the generation that immediately preceded that of Miles Davis. Just after World War I, Creath, who lived in East St. Louis and became the most famous jazz trumpeter in the region during the 1920s, started leading his own bands for dates in the most publicized black St. Louis venues, like the Keystone Club at Compton and Lawton and Tom Turpin's Jazzland. In Late 1919, he sallied forth to the St. Louis Country Club, where his Keystone Jazzers bested Chicago's all-white Gene Rodemich Orchestra in a battle of the bands. By as early as 1920, he was sending out a variety of bands from his "Sensational Jazz-O-Maniacs" office at 2234 Market Street.[22] His newspaper advertisements read: "Give a Thought to Music. For Real Time, Rhythm, Jazz Dance Music call C. Creath, 4257A Kennerly Ave.," and "The Water's On! There'll be a Hot Time in the Old Town."[23]

During the winter months, Charles Creath's Jazz-O-Maniacs performed in all of St. Louis's major dance halls—the Paradise Dance Palace at 930 Sarah Street, Pythian Hall at 3137 Pine Street, Bohemia Dance Hall at 2246 Market Street, and Argus Hall at 2312–2316 Market Street, owned and rented by the *St. Louis Argus*. His bands varied in size from three to as many as twelve musicians and usually included drummer and vocalist Floyd Campbell and string bassist George "Pops" Foster.

Creath, the founding father of St. Louis jazz trumpet playing and of the city's jazz in general, recorded with his Jazz-O-Maniacs for the Okeh label in 1924, 1925, and 1927.[24] The leader himself excelled in the hot, cup-muted style related to that of Joe Oliver, but the St. Louisan played with his own ringing purity of tone. His range seems narrow, especially on the earliest of his recordings, but that tone is burnished, centered, and sure. He urgently punches out his leads, his lines paraphrasing the melody. His nine-piece band of two trumpets, a trombone, three saxes, piano, banjo, and drums blends jazz

band polyphony with the harmonized saxophone choir, defining the early hot-dance band style. The trombone, clarinet, and cornet improvise polyphonically, while the saxophones chant the melody in heavy vibrato. Creath gambled, according to the New Orleans string bassist George "Pops" Foster, and lost his first band to drummer Floyd Campbell. He rebuilt another one and recorded his slickest sides in 1927, his solos as hot as before but more adventuresome, his sax choir tighter, the arrangements showing the influence of Fletcher Henderson.[25]

Miles Davis remarked that musicians from St Louis knew how to play the blues, and Creath's Jazz-O-Maniacs proved that point. The band recorded popular songs, novelty songs, but mostly blues. Their recordings of "Market Street Blues" (a reference to the black entertainment blocks in downtown St. Louis) and "Every Man That Wears Bell Bottom Britches Ain't No Monkey Man" feature the full, rich vocals of drummer Floyd Campbell, who either must have inspired Jimmy Rushing or learned from him. Campbell insisted that he was the first male vocalist to record the blues.

Creath's enterprising jazz activities extended well into the late 1930s, when he still could be heard playing on the Streckfus Line. When, from time to time, work disappeared in St. Louis, he moved to New Orleans and played on the *Capitol* with Fate Marable. He was a hard-working star trumpet player for nearly twenty years and set an example followed by Dewey Jackson, Eddie Jefferson, Chick Finney, and Eddie Randle. All of them also received the invaluable support of Jesse Johnson, the "Kingpin"[26] of jazz bookers in the region. Johnson began his influential career promoting riverboat cruises for the St. Louis African American community. His first efforts predated jazz, when, in 1916, he organized riverboat excursions every spring on the *Grey Eagle* so that civic-minded citizens could enjoy an outing down to the orphanage at Montesano Springs. He sometimes combined this trip with one honoring the year's high school and trade school graduates. Johnson negotiated with the steamboat captain, hired a St. Louis band, usually invented a new dance step to introduce along the way, and acted as master of ceremonies. In June 1916, while most of the adults went ashore to picnic with the orphans, the younger set remained on board to make some music of their own. Not long thereafter, jazz became Johnson's music of choice for river cruises.

In 1919, when the first of his promotions of Charles Creath was announced in the *St. Louis Argus*, Streckfus Steamers, Inc., despite a long-standing tradition of racially segregated Monday night river cruises in the St. Louis area, had yet to advertise any cruises for blacks. Their first efforts to attract customers to segregated cruises did not occur until September 10, 1920. Johnson had gotten the white company's attention by negotiating with the *Liberty*, *Grey Eagle*, *Pilgrim*, and the *Majestic*, all rivals to the Streckfus Line that tramped the upper Mississippi.[28] Following a tradition of dance music on the river, Creath's band played "sweet strains of music" for that occasion. He and Johnson broke all attendance records and goaded the Streckfus Line into belatedly offering a few racially segregated cruises after Labor Day 1920.[29]

Jesse Johnson promoted cruises for black people on the *Grey Eagle* from 1916 to 1918, at which time that steamer was crushed by river ice. He then teamed with Charles Creath aboard the *Majestic* during the summer of 1921, after the Streckfus Line finally had entered their market. That summer, Creath went one-on-one against the Streckfus Line's biggest and most famous boat, the *St. Paul*, and its acclaimed trumpeter—Louis Armstrong—whom then was backed by Fate Marable's Metropolitan Jazz-E-Saz Orchestra ("the other bands are trying to imitate them"). The Streckfus Line subsequently beat its St. Louis competition by default when, in

May 1922, the *Majestic* unexpectedly burned in winter quarters on the Illinois River.

The following summer found Johnson and Creath in charge of the music on all but one of the *St. Paul*'s Monday evening "colored boats." Johnson and Creath, however, refused to give in completely to the segregated Streckfus Line and promoted cruises for African Americans on the smaller steamer *Pilgrim* four nights a week. They advertised this boat as "The Only Steamer on the Mississippi Operated by Colored People. Concessions are also Operated By Our People. Steam Calliope, Four Spacious Decks, 1500 Chairs, 500 Rockers, 3000 Jazz Lights!"[30] Jesse Johnson even promoted Fate Marable's bands, known to history as the house bands on the Streckfus Line's "colored boats," in competition with that dominant company. He did so, moreover, explicitly to fight the established pattern of segregation on the river. On May 14, 1926, Johnson promoted an inaugural cruise on the "City of Cairo." Taking out a full-page advertisement in the *Argus*, Johnson, always involved in dance as well as music promotions, featured "Prof. Jesse Johnson and his Paradise Boys and Girls," demonstrating to the music of Fate Marable and His Jazz Syncopators in a Big Saturday Nite Midnight Ramble for "the Exclusive Use of Our People." The "officers on our steamer are members of our group":

Churches, Social Clubs, Fraternal Organizations and Labor Organizations will not have to group together to secure a date on the "City of Cairo," due to the fact that our steamer is not confined to Monday Night only but EVERY NIGHT. We feel sure that each and every one will appreciate this step forward and will co-operate individually and collectively to make this mamouth undertaking a grand success.[31]

Somehow these efforts to unite music and dance in the name of racial freedom on the river repeatedly foundered in tragic accidents: just as the *Grey Eagle* sank in 1918, the *Majestic* burned in 1922, and the *City of Cairo* suddenly sank during the winter of 1923. The *Pilgrim*'s draft proved too deep for the river, and she was towed away to Tampa, Florida, where she rotted away.[32]

Despite these maddening reversals, St. Louis riverboat pianist Chick Finney insisted that Jesse Johnson be remembered as a great benefactor of his race. "He was a great contribution to St. Louis and to our race, I have to say that. He worked in civic, religious, and he had a dream like Mr. Randle said, to give St. Louis something to put them on the map for entertainment." Bandleader Eddie Johnson called Jesse Johnson, "the black Streckfus. If you wanted to play the boat then, you came to Jesse Johnson. He made a lot of contributions to the black community."

Jesse Johnson epitomized the spirit in which Miles Davis learned the roots of jazz. He also promoted the jazz careers of orchestra leaders who followed Creath: trumpeter Dewey Jackson, drummer/vocalist Floyd Campbell, Eddie Johnson, and pianist Chick Finney. Born in St. Louis in 1900, one of eleven children of Augustus and Nettie Jackson, Dewey Jackson took his first lessons with the Odd Fellows Band in 1912 and 1913.[33] He organized his first band in 1920 with Harry Dial on drums, Boyd Atkins, violin and sax, Sammy Long, tenor sax, Andrew Luper, trombone, and Jane Hemingway at the piano. He led his St. Louis Peacock Charleston Orchestra on a Vocalion recording date in 1926, performing both of the riverboats and at Jesse Johnson's Regal Nite Club and Paradise Dance Hall.

Jackson led his own bands right through the worst of the depression, appearing with them in a variety of black clubs and dance halls, on radio stations, and, of course, on the Streckfus Line's steamer *St. Paul*. He broke race barriers by playing at St. Louis's Castle Ballroom and Sauter's Park. On February 24, 1933, Jackson's orchestra starred in an unusual integrated dance sponsored by the Catholic magazine *Interracial Review* in the Saint Louis University gymnasium. This Catholic thrust for greater racial understanding also produced the program "Interracial Hour" over radio station WEW. On June 10, 1933, the Dewey Jackson Orchestra performed for a "Depression Dance" at the People's Finance Building, 11 N. Jefferson, the proceeds going to the Scottsboro Boys Defense Fund. Whenever times got too tough, he landed back in the Fate Marable Cotton Pickers Orchestra, playing for long periods on the *Capitol* in New Orleans. World War II drove Dewey Jackson, like most of the other jazz musicians of his generation, out of the business.

Eddie Johnson's own career in Monday night cruises on the *St. Paul* began in 1929 and was as deeply intertwined with Jesse Johnson's promotions as Creath's earlier work had been. Born in East St. Louis in 1912, Eddie Johnson had played piano in the Oliver Cobb Band and took over that group upon Cobb's death, renaming them Eddie Johnson & His Crackerjacks. Under his direction, this band played in such St. Louis clubs as the Dance Box, the Chauffers' Club in the Finance Building, the Palladium at Delmar and Franklin, the Paradise Ballroom at Sarah and Hodiamont, the Casa Loma Ballroom, Riviera, the Carioca Ballroom at Sarah and Finney, and the Showboat at Delmar and Taylor. Johnson, moreover, secured a regular broadcast on KMOX Radio. St. Louis youngsters used to gather in a candy store near Vashon High School to listen to Johnson's programs.

Jesse Johnson promoted Eddie Johnson's Crackerjacks on several successful tours to various sections of the country. Trombonist Winfield Baker reorganized some of the band's members into the St. Louis Crackerjacks

with his brother Harold "Shorty" Baker on trumpet. In 1935, Chick Finney joined them on piano; he and William "Bede" Baskerville wrote arrangements for the band. It remained popular until 1938. Under Finney's leadership, the band tramped on the steamer *Idlewild*, owned by Henry Meyers, from Alton, Illinois, up and down the Ohio River to and from Louisville and Cincinnati, before the Streckfus family invaded that territory in the early 1940s.[34] The Crackerjacks played on the *Idlewild* for five months each year, earning an enviably solid economic foundation. As Martin MacKay put it: ". . . the money was practically clear. You could leave you money up and collect at the end of the season and no expenses and whatnot. And you had the opportunity to travel quite a bit."

Chick Finney led the band on a productive Decca recording session in 1936.[35] The group plays with cohesion, attack, intonation, and more sophisticated arrangements, moving well beyond the 1920s world of Charles Creath and Dewey Jackson. A strong inclination toward the blues and gospel gives the Crackerjacks continuity with the past, but this St. Louis aggregation has jettisoned hot polyphony for the seduction of silky smooth section work and a big-league rhythm section. The Original St. Louis Crackerjacks reached for and seized the major concepts, if not the glamour and ballyhoo, of the Big Band Era.

The band may have taken its inspiration from records by the Duke

Ellington, Fletcher Henderson, and Cab Calloway bands, but they also had the opportunity to hear these bands in person. During Miles Davis's early years, Jesse Johnson promoted important, musically educational concerts of the best jazz musicians in the country, bringing to St. Louis such national stars as Louis Armstrong, Duke Ellington, Fletcher Henderson, Thomas "Fats" Waller, Claude Hopkins, Jimmie Lunceford, Cab Calloway, and the International Sweethearts of Rhythm, presenting them on the *St. Paul*, at the Coliseum, and in the various ballrooms. Jesse Johnson showed younger musicians of Miles Davis's generation the possibilities for careers in jazz. He first brought Henderson's Orchestra to the Coliseum in 1926. In two marathon appearances that would have tested the strongest embouchure, Armstrong performed on Sunday afternoon February 5, 1928, from 2:00 to 7:00 P.M. at the Paradise Dance Palace, 930 North Sarah St., and again from 9:00 P.M. "'til Late" at the Capitol Palace at Twenty-Third.[36] Alphonzo Trent's Orchestra backed Armstrong.[37] Many eager fans had to be turned away from this concert. Listeners were struck not only by Armstrong's playing but also that of Trent's saxophonist Lee Hilliard and violinist Stuff Smith. Hayes Pillars played in Trent's band for that concert and made some contacts that eventually led to a triumphal ten-year gig in St. Louis. Johnson also promoted the Cab Calloway and Duke Ellington bands in

1933, in both cases hiring an airplane to drop thousands of advertising flyers over East St. Louis and St. Louis.

Jesse Johnson always found ways to promote simultaneously the best local bands as well as the national stars by staging "Battles of the Bands" against the visiting groups or simply promoting a musical bill with at least two bands, one of which came from the St. Louis area. For example, he put the Creath, Jackson, and Marable bands on the bill with Fletcher Henderson, while the Crackerjacks went on tour with Fats Waller from Cincinnati throughout the East Coast. Johnson used national stars to promote concerts in such venues as St. Louis's Forest Park Highland that normally contracted exclusively with the white American Federation of Musicians (AFM) Local #2. The whites controlled music in the best hotels, opera, and other theatrical productions, but as Eddie Randle put it:

> . . . the Negroes had just a better dance band in those days. This is the way that came about. Because this was the only thing that we could play and it was a matter of making it. We applied ourselves. We practiced. We had arrangers that would sit up all night writing to put us in this position where if our kind of work came along, we could do it . . . and we did a good job of it.

Because of racial segregation and Jim Crow law, jazz and hot-dance music in the Mississippi River valley became an expression of racial antagonism and pride. Miles Davis noted several instances where he knew that race discrimination had cheated him. He remained an outspoken "race man" throughout his career. He could well have mentioned, but did not, the history of St. Louis Local #44 of the AFM. That story pulled together the struggles of the entire generation of black jazz musicians who prepared the way for Miles Davis.

According to drummer Elijah Shaw, who had been born in Jackson, Tennessee, on September 9, 1900, and who arrived in East St. Louis just after the infamous race riot of 1917, African American musicians in St. Louis organized before a national musicians' union existed. In 1896, when the American Federation of Musicians was born, black St. Louis musicians sent pianist John L. Fields to the first national convention. The AFM formed forty-four unions at that meeting. As Fields was the only black representative, his local got the last number. After thirty-five years of uninterrupted activity in St. Louis, a combination of racism and economic hardship stemming from the depression combined to kill what was then referred to as "the colored union."[38]

African American hot-dance bands, known for their jazz, had sought jobs in dance halls, nightclubs, and riverboats because organized white musicians dominated the vaudeville and silent movie theaters, the legitimate theaters, the opera houses, and concert halls. When sound came to motion pictures in 1927, white musicians lost those jobs, and in 1929, the Crash drove most of them out of many of the remaining jobs controlled by the "white" Local #2. Shaw remembered the 1920s, "while the bulk of musicians in St. Louis, being white musicians, played in all the theaters. They played little or no dance work."

In 1931, black musicians in St. Louis learned that their union charter had been revoked one year earlier. According to Shaw, the Streckfus Line had requested a low "concession price" from both black and white locals, one that would have reflected the hard times. Local #2 rejected the price. Captain Joseph Streckfus therefore decided that "instead of using three white groups on the two boats they ran out of here at that time, they were going to use four colored bands" from Local #44. Local #2 formed a special committee, headed by Harry Lang, bandleader at the Castle Ballroom and the Forest Park Highlands, "to wait on Capt. Joe about this crisis." Inevitably, the whites decided that without a union charter, black musicians could not possibly negotiate with the Streckfus Line at all. Therefore, the river captains installed three white bands and one all-star black band that included Marable, Dewey Jackson, Floyd Campbell, and Charles Creath. None of the white bands that now found themselves on board had any prior experience in riverboat work.

For two years, the *St. Louis Argus* made practically no comment on this terrible blow to the economic, political, and racial foundations of black music performance. In 1932, the paper reported "much confusion in Local #44," as "hostile forces" worked to get #44 "out of all white jobs."[39] Several months later the organization was referred to as the Musicians' Protective Association.[40] Finally, in September of that year, the *Argus* revealed that the American Federation of Musicians also had revoked the charters of the black locals in Kansas City and Denver and reported that the Kansas City musicians had refused to accept the decree. So too, the paper reported that the black San Francisco Local #648 had gone to court to prevent the white local from barring black musicians from all venues.[41] The *Argus* darkly suggested that the compliance of #44 in St. Louis had led to its becoming "a subsidiary local, paying dues to the white local but not receiving equal benefits in return."[42]

Why did Local #44 in St. Louis acquiesce? Certainly the importance of Streckfus steamers to black union membership and the payment of membership dues had something to do with it. Once a series of reversals had sunk Jesse J. Johnson's efforts to establish independent black riverboats, black musicians relied exclusively on the white company that, to its credit, consistently had hired at least some black bands. Floyd Campbell, Charles Creath, and Dewey Jackson abandoned their bands and joined an all-star black unit under Creath and Marable's direction. Had Local #44 fought the AFM, the white St. Louis Local #2, and the complicity of "Captain Joe," those precious jobs would have been lost.

During the 1930s, nonunion dance bands dominated the black St. Louis and East St. Louis halls, regularly playing under scale. Racism within the American Federation of Musicians had seriously undermined the union movement among black musicians in St. Louis. Elijah Shaw remained a steadfast champion of unionism in St. Louis, going so far as to compose a song entitled "Close the Halls to Non-Union Bands." His bands sang it wherever they performed. For the most part, however, black dance-band musicians had to work where they could.[43]

Black bands did not disappear entirely from the riverboats. St. Louis musicians played for the smaller excursion companies that worked the Ohio River. The Streckfus Line hired bands like the Jeter-Pillars Orchestra that had recently arrived in St. Louis after touring extensively across the nation. New Orleans musicians, who had never been unionized, also worked for them, as well. Pianist Walter "Fats" Pichon ("Fats Waller's Double") and, of course, Fate Marable made water music throughout the 1930s. In the meantime, Elijah Shaw took time off each year to attend the AFM national conventions, where he "harassed the officers" about getting back an AFM charter for the once robust St. Louis Local #44. Finally, in 1944, the national organization chartered St. Louis Local #197. That remained the black musicians' union in the Mound City until 1971, when the white and the black locals finally integrated for the first time.

As the economic depression wore on through the 1930s, an increasing number of black musicians adjusted to the decline in the number of jobs on the river by taking jobs outside the city for at least part of the year. Charles Creath, Dewey Jackson, and Fate Marable played out of New Orleans. Many of the other St. Louis musicians worked with a variety of bands that toured the country, returning to St. Louis when a lucrative job beckoned from the dance halls. Floyd Campbell moved first to Cincinnati and then Chicago; Ed Allen, Leonard Davis, and Irving Randolph to New York City. Many of these musicians brought the St. Louis tradition of hot-dance music to the orchestras of Fletcher Henderson, Benny Carter, Cab Calloway, Andy Kirk, and Teddy Wilson.

At the same time, St. Louis musicians tried to merge their local bands with national trends by recruiting a number of recognized musicians from around the country into their orchestras, using the connections these men brought to promoters in other cities. During the early 1930s, Eddie Johnson replaced many of the local musicians who had played in his Crackerjacks orchestra with out-of-town musicians like saxophonist Tab Smith. Excellent local groups always faced this temptation to "go national," sacrificing their river city identity for inclusion in national media circuits.

The blending of St. Louis–based jazz styles with influences from around the United States became more pronounced with the arrival of the Jeter-Pillars Orchestra in 1934. Led by saxophonists James Jeter and Hayes Pillars, this band settled in for a ten-year run at the Plantation Club, a segregated club catering only to whites. After many years of arduous touring from Arkansas to Maine and Oklahoma, Jeter and Pillars were content to bring rising young instrumental stars to St. Louis. Among these rising stars were trumpeters Harry "Sweets" Edison and George Hudson, trombonist Lawrence "Snub" Mosley, string bassists Walter Page and Jimmy Blanton, and drummers Joe Jones and Sidney Catlett. Like St. Louis's other hot-dance bands, the Jeter-Pillars Orchestra prided itself on musical versatility, playing floorshows with such visiting stars as the Mills Brothers, Ink Spots, and Nicholas Brothers. In 1944, the band moved to Club Riviera, a racially integrated establishment run by Jordan Chambers, a prominent African American undertaker.[44]

Miles Davis drew upon these regional experiences with jazz and race. His father, Dr. Miles Davis, and his high school trumpet teacher, Elwood Buchanan, turn up repeatedly in the "East St. Louis News" column of the *St. Louis Argus*. The two men, who were major influences on the young Miles Davis, Jr., appeared at Jesse Johnson's concert promotions and in the clubs where St. Louis's best hot-dance bands performed, listening and dancing to Duke Ellington, the Crackerjacks, Cab Calloway, and Don Redmond, Eddie Randle at the Coliseum, the Harlem Nite Club in Lovejoy, the Palladium, Huff's Summer Garden, and other venues where the black upper middle class gathered to see and be seen.[45]

Hot-dance music, as played by the best black East St. Louis and St. Louis musicians in the best clubs, was the preferred music of the area's black elite. The society column usually carried reports on local musicians who performed for the elite, describing the bands, music, the tunes, and the ambiance. Some musicians, like Horace Eubanks, were related to members of the upper crust. That someone of Miles Davis's privileged background, with the encouragement of his father and his music teacher, became a jazz musician, by way of the hot-dance bands, should come as no surprise. He had been born and raised to it.

The young Miles certainly did move swiftly and permanently away from hot-dance music, but his career, it must be recalled, began just as that style crumbled under the pressures of the depression and World War II. Bebop's leaders were trying to create a new niche for themselves in a music business decimated by the war. Recording studios and smaller, more intimate clubs meant for listeners, not dancers, became the new focus of bebop, and Miles Davis followed these trends in the late 1940s.[46]

Davis, moreover, carried into the jazz world of the 1940s and 1950s Eddie Randle's desire to bring formal musical knowledge to bear upon jazz. Bebop and Davis's subsequent stylistic innovations had to do with a greater sophistication in the applications to jazz of harmonic theory, particularly of the higher chordal intervals and modal scales. Miles Davis was able to "think outside the box" placed before him. Eddie Randle and many other hungry musicians in the territory bands had had to search on their own for such knowledge. When Eddie Randle, Jr., a symphonic musician, took courses with a Mr. Lambiasi in St. Louis, the elder Randle sometimes took the lesson for his son just "to see how wrong I was when I was playing for a living." While the younger Randle played with the St. Louis Philharmonia, Eddie Randle, Sr., took only a few lessons before going back to independent searching. Similarly, Miles Davis lasted only one year at New York City's Juilliard School, preferring to work out bebop's approaches to the higher knowledge outside of the conservatories.

Through all these matters ran the hideous history of race relations in the Mississippi valley. Miles became known for his refusal to adopt the on-stage mannerisms associated with Louis Armstrong's generation of jazzmen. He wouldn't play for dancing. He wouldn't grin and shuffle. He often refused even to look at or speak to his audiences. And he managed to use the recording studios to place his sound over that of whites "so that the black thing would be on top."[47] He surely served as a young prince to the older generation of musicians from the St. Louis/East St. Louis area, making jazz more of an artistic activity and less a social dance music. Miles Davis created new styles that whites could not as readily imitate, garnering in the process fame and wealth of which the older generation had only dreamed. It had all begun back in East St. Louis, when Elwood Buchanan had warned Davis away from the flashy swing-band vibrato of Harry James, urging him to develop his own cooler sound. Miles took that approach, combined it with the ambitions of the St. Louis school of trumpet, and, leaving the excursion boats to the white Dixieland combos, succeeded beyond all expectations in making himself heard throughout the nation and the world.

1. *St. Louis Post-Dispatch,* May 25, 1975.
2. John Cotter, "The Negro in Music in St. Louis," ts., 326–27 (National Ragtime & Jazz Archive), Southern Illinois University, Edwardsville, Illinois.
3. Irene Cortinovis interview with Sammy Long, April 18, 1973, ts., University of Missouri–St. Louis.
4. *St. Louis Argus,* March 19, 1915, 4.
5. *St. Louis Argus,* April 21, 1916, 3.
6. Miles Davis with Quincy Troupe, *Miles: The Autobiography* (New York: Simon & Schuster, 1989), 38.
7. *Miles: The Autobiography,* 38.
8. Robert E. Mendelson, *East St. Louis: The Riverfront Charade* (Edwardsville: Southern Illinois University, 1970), 1.
9. *Miles: The Autobiography,* 42–43.
10. For the photo, see Richard Williams, *Miles Davis, the Man in the Green Shirt* (New York: Henry Holt & Co., 1993), 13.
11. Irene Cortinovis, interview with four jazz Musicians: Eddie Johnson, Elijah Shaw, Chick Finney, Eddie Randle, August 20, 1971, ts., University of Missouri–St Louis.
12. Randle gives his age upon moving to St. Louis as seventeen in Doris Wesley, Wiley Price and Ann Morris, eds., *Lift Every Voice and Sing: St. Louis African Americans in the Twentieth-Century* (Columbia: University of Missouri Press, 1999), 67.
13. Ibid.
14. Smithsonian Institution Interview of Hayes Pillars, St. Louis, Mo., March 2, 1977, ts., Institute of Jazz Studies. Thanks to Dan Morgenstern for sending me a copy of this marvelous document.
15. *East St. Louis Daily Journal,* January 15, 1918, 1.
16. Kenney interview with Captain William Francis Carroll, St. Louis, Mo., January 20, 2000.
17. Frank Mitchell, "Musicians' Chatter Box," *St. Louis Argus,* September 7, 1928, 5.
18. Interview with Danny Barker, William Ransom Hogan Jazz Archive, Tulane University, New Orleans.
19. David Chevan, "Riverboat Music from St. Louis and the Streckfus Steamboat Line," *Black Music Research Journal* 9, no. 2 (1989): 158.
20. *St. Louis Argus,* January 4, 1924.
21. Cotter, "The Negro in Music in St. Louis." This is an invaluable compendium of bands and their personnel during the 1930s. "Singleton Palmer Memoirs" and Leon King Memoir, ts., NRJA.
22. *St. Louis Argus,* August 15, 1919, 1; December 5, 1919, 4; July 2, 1920, 5.
23. *St. Louis Argus,* October 13, 1922, 3; February 23, 1923, 3.
24. The 12 sides cut by the Jazz-O-Maniacs have been reissued on the CD "Jazz in Saint Louis, 1924–1927," Timeless Records CBC 1-036 Jazz. They also can be heard on the World Wide Web at www.redhotjazz.com/maniacs.html.
25. George "Pops" Foster with Tom Stoddard, *The Autobiography of a New Orleans Jazzman* (Berkeley: University of California Press, 1971), 127.
26. Eddie Johnson in Cortinovis interview with Johnson, Shaw, Finney, and Randle.
27. *St. Louis Argus,* June 23, July 7, July 21, 1916.
28. *St. Louis Argus,* June 4, 1920, 5.
29. *St. Louis Argus,* June 18, 1920, 2.
30. *St. Louis Argus,* July 23, 1922, 3, 12 includes a photo of the boat.
31. *St. Louis Argus,* June 4, 1926, six includes a photo of the boat.
32. Frederick Way, Jr., *Way's Packet Directory, 1848–1994* (Athens: Ohio University Press, 1983), 90, 304.
33. John W. Randolph, "Dewey Jackson: King of the Riverboat Trumpets," *Jazz Report* 6, no. 4 (May 1958): 7–8, 10.
34. Irene Cortinovis Interview with Martin Luther MacKay, May 21, 1971, ts., University of Missouri–St. Louis.
35. Cotter, "TheNegro in Music in St. Louis," 334–38.
36. *St. Louis Argus,* January 27, 1928, 3.
37. "The Floyd Campbell Story," as told to Bertrand Demeusy, ts., NRJA, Southern Illinois University–Edwardsville.
38. Cortinovis Interview with Shaw.
39. *St. Louis Argus,* February 26, 1932, 5.
40. *St. Louis Argus,* May 13, 1932, 5.
41. *St. Louis Argus,* September 21, 1934, 1.
42. *St. Louis Argus,* September 9, 1932, 5. According to James Neal Primm, *Lion of the Valley: St. Louis, Missouri, 1764–1980* (St. Louis: Missouri Historical Society Press, 1998), 442, "black members were allowed to form a subsidiary totally dominated by the white organization."
43. Ben Thomas, "Musicians' Local and Non-Union Bands Air Their 3 Years Conflict," *St. Louis Argus,* October 29, 1937, 5.
44. Cotter, "The Negro in Music in St. Louis," 341.
45. *St. Louis Argus,* March 16, 1935, 12; June 14, 1935, 9; July 12, 1935, 12; August 30, 1935, 3; July 24, 1936, 6B; November 20, 1936, 6B; February 5, 1937, 6B.
46. Scott Deveaux, *Bebop: A Social & Musical History* (Berkeley: University of California Press, 1997), 236–69.
47. *Miles: The Autobiography,* 184.

With Howard McGhee,
New York, ca. 1948.
Photograph by
William Gottlieb.

Quincy Delight Jones, Jr., has achieved greater fame and commercial success than virtually any other jazz musician of his generation. Born in Chicago in 1933, he grew up in Bremerton and Seattle during World War II. He learned to play the trumpet as a schoolboy and eventually played around Seattle with the likes of Ray Charles, taking lessons from Count Basie trumpeter Clark Terry. Eventually, he wound up doing arrangements for bassist Oscar Pettiford and became a member of Lionel Hampton's band. He became a successful freelance arranger, working with a number of artists including Dinah Washington, Cannonball Adderley, Art Farmer, Clifford Brown, James Moody, Sarah Vaughn, Billy Eckstine, and Count Basie, as well as a variety of nonjazz acts. In 1956, Jones was the musical director for Dizzy Gillespie's band when it toured Africa, Asia, and the Middle East under the auspices of the State Department. He studied composition in France under the tutelage of Nadia Boulanger. He became an A-and-R man for Mercury Records, rising to the vice presidency of the company. It was during his years at Mercury that he began to produce pop music and a great deal more rhythm and blues, including some classic Ray Charles sides.

In 1963, he left Mercury to try his hand at film scoring in Hollywood. Sidney Lumet's *The Pawnbroker* was his first film. Jones encountered some resistance at first in trying to break into an industry so thoroughly dominated by whites. But after a slow start he succeeded in scoring many films, including *Walk, Don't Run, In Cold Blood, In the Heat of the Night*, and *The New Centurions*. He also scored a number of television shows, including *Ironside, Sanford and Son,* and *The Bill Cosby Show*.

Jones went on to produce films—*The Color Purple*—and to co-produce some of the most successful records in the history of popular music—Michael Jackson's *Off The Wall, Thriller*, and *Bad*, as well as the single "We Are the World," all in the 1980s. His production company developed such television shows as Roots and *The Fresh Prince of Bel Air*, which made a megastar of Will Smith. Jones is the founder of the hip-hop publication *Vibe*. He has won more Grammys than any other musician.

Yet despite his enormous success in many areas of popular culture, he remains, at heart, a jazzman and a great lover of the music that inspired him to become a musician and arranger many years ago. He was particularly eager to talk about his peer, Miles Davis.

"I Just Adored That Man": Quincy Jones

interview by Gerald Early

"I first met Miles in 1950 in New York at the Downbeat Club, run by Monte Kay and Pete Cameron," he said.

Oscar Pettiford had brought me to New York. I wrote some arrangements for him in Boston, and he liked them and said, 'I'd like for you to come to New York.' It was the first time I had ever been in New York in my life. I had been dreaming about it my whole musical career.

I came down to New York, and I was like Liberace in Boys Town, Dracula at the blood bank. Bird, Miles Davis, Dizzy, Bud Powell, Mingus. It was just ridiculous.

Bird and Miles were off and on at Minton's. They were also playing at Big Nick's on 110th Street. Stuff was all going on. Fifty-second Street was smoking then. Oscar Pettiford was at Snookie's. That's where somebody sat on Dizzy's horn and bent it, and it became a style. We had so much fun. I was a kid then. I was only eighteen years old.

Jones describes his first encounter with Davis, then about twenty-four years old:

When I first saw Miles, he was playing. The first time I met him he didn't have as much of a rasp. I heard a voice behind me—and I'll be very gross but that's the way Miles was—and he said, 'I was hanging out with some freak and heard some motherfucker trying to play like me.' He had heard me with Lionel Hampton on a tune called 'Kingfish.' I was terrified. I knew it was him. He was strung out then, too, and it was just amazing. Everybody was. But I was just flabbergasted because he was my idol and everything.

I just adored him, just adored him. I tried so much to play like him. I don't consider myself a trumpet player. I was always into writing. I was with Hamp [Lionel Hampton] then, and I was always into writing.

One thing led to another and we got closer and closer. He had such a gruff exterior, but somehow I could feel it was more bark than bite. But everybody did that. All the beboppers. The beboppers invented what the rappers are trying to do now. You know, be cool, the underworld, subculture language, the body language, the lifestyle. You had to be cool.

Jones went on to discuss the impact Davis and the beboppers had on him as a teenager:

Hip and cool. I always loved that because it gave me a target to aim for, to hold on to. It was a way to be dignified and proud and individualistic. And just to be a real man. There weren't many models then.

[The jazz players] were very sophisticated. That's the one thing I loved about that whole circle I started in. They dressed better than everybody else. And they were global because the Europeans understood that this was an art form real early. Jazz is the Esperanto of the world. Always has been.

Jones talked about the influence of the work of arranger Gil Evans and how he worked with Davis in 1991 to re-create the famous Evans orchestral charts, the only time Jones and Davis ever worked and recorded together:

I was there at the studio when *Kind of Blue* was recorded. One of the Gil Evans sessions was done the same night. I remember seeing Ernie Royal and John Coltrane hanging around, waiting. I always loved Gil Evans. *The Birth of the Cool* with [Johnny] Carisi and Gerry Mulligan, I was all over that. I loved that whole school of writing.

That was my favorite music of all time. I had been thinking about doing it for a while. Dewey [Miles Davis] kept saying, 'I don't play that old shit.' But I was used to Miles huffing and puffing. So, I said, 'This is not old shit.' This was the greatest orchestration that ever happened in jazz, bar none. Frank Sinatra and Nelson Riddle and Miles and Gil Evans are the greatest collaborations ever.

[Miles] just resisted it. He resisted the idea of it, and it was part of being hip. Miles didn't want to do that. He didn't want to go back. Unfortunately, he was talking about some of the greatest music ever done. Finally, he got it. He knew how good the music was.

And I thought that night [of the concert], if I never, ever touch music again, this is as good as it gets for me. That and working with Sinatra, Basie, and Ray Charles. To conduct Miles.

We had a double orchestra that night. We had four oboes, two bassoons, ten French horns, and I was in heaven. And Miles, too. He just played soft, no vibrato. And it was like a beautiful pearl on a huge black velvet carpet. And Miles sat there during rehearsals and let Wallace Rooney play all the parts as they were written out because Miles didn't remember them. We only took two shots at it: rehearsal and then the sound check.

And he would increasingly say, holding up his hand to Wally, 'Oh, I got it.' And to see this beautiful man sit there at sixty-five challenging his twenty-four-year-old self! His only competition was himself. But he'd go after a note, miss it, and be absolutely fearless. Unapologetic. He just went for it! I have never experienced anything like that. Ever.

And he was so full of shit. I said, 'Ladies and Gentlemen, Miles Davis.' He's waving this flag—you know that's not him—and smiling at the audience, and I look over at him and said, 'Yeah, Dewey,' and he said, 'Fuck you! I'll take this shit all

over the world.' He loved it. Little did any of us know he was so sick. I just adored that man. I saw through his shell, and it was a shell.

I'll never forget the Chateau Montmartre when he was playing tough, and I had pleurisy and I was really sick. And he cooked my breakfast. He was as sweet as he could be.

Jones had just finished his autobiography, and he gave an assessment of Davis's controversial book: "Think Quincy [Troupe] let [Miles] go too far. It is a rough thing, but it is Miles. One hundred and forty motherfuckers on every page. But a lot of that shit he made up. He made up that shit about Quincy [Jones] and Marlon Brando giving Frances an engagement ring.[1] I said, 'Miles, you know that's bullshit.' 'Man, that fucking sounds good.' Miles was a serious dramatist, you know."

1   Frances Taylor, a dancer, was Davis's first wife. In *Miles: The Autobiography*, Davis mentions that Marlon Brando and Quincy Jones were in love with Taylor and that Jones had given her an engagement ring. (page 22)

Age 13, East St. Louis,
1939.

(In memory of Vernon Napoleon Davis—1929–1999—& with homage to Maestro Eugene Haynes, Miles's friend & classmate at Lincoln High & Juilliard.)

I. Prologue

(Prepping for the Maestro, the Prince, the Doyenne of Ballerinas & the Olympic Queen)

come aboard East Saint Jazz's cyclic jam session,
groove on its bluescentric elevations, splits & spins—
go *Walkin'* down 30s/40s/50s/60s 15th Street
while Blue n [East] *Boogie* ladles a *Bitches Brew*
of 1 part indigenous sun-people, 1 part Arkansippi Blues,
1 part 1917 Riot & 1 part killingfloor/river/railwaysong

> ("trumpet" Lincoln High's *Continuum* w/Charles Creath;
> "Prof" Elwood Buchanan & his proteges: Frank Gully, Harry Turner,
> Elbert "Red" Bonner, Miles Davis, Arthur Evans, Everett & Norvell
> Perry, Edgar & Greg Matthews, Roland Pulliam, Michael Bobbitt; &
> 80s/90s bellows Russell Gunn, Tony Wiggins, Delano Redmond . . .)

freefalling/free-rising/freefeeling—
& "let me blues ya fo I lose ya"—
in the "city with no pity,"
as barber/teacher/griot Tyrone Windett wails it,
though it's fair & square as the knife of life

> (croon, chronicle or finger its flatted thirds, fifths & sevenths
> w/George Hudson's "Apple Jack," Eddie Johnson's *Crackerjacks,*
> Flora Bush Smith's *Two Jacks & a Jill,* "Stumpy" Washington's *Caravan,*
> Fred Sample & Alvin Washington's *Tornadoes,*
> Garland Howard's *Canaries,* Ike/Tina's *first Ikettes* (from the projects),
> Bobby McClure's "Eight Days a Week," Phil Perry's *Montclairs*
> & Allen Merry's Young Disciples . . . take the *Third Flight to the Thirteenth
> Floor* w/YODIE's *Black Seed* & shock the judgefunky w/Bull Parks'
> Matadors while drinking Eddie Fisher's "Third Cup" w/Leo Gooden's
> Leo's Five . . . hook heels w/*Brown Sugar Connection,*
> share "shades" w/Ron Carter's *Infinity* & shoo-be-doos
> w/Prince Wells's Jazz Edge . . .)

"So What"(?) . . . It's "All Blues" Anyway:

An Anecdotal/ Jazzological Tour of Milesville

by Eugene B. Redmond

possessed by rail road legs & packing house hips
—& a river of tongues—its mid-section sashays & shape-shifts
—at mid-century—from all-white to all-black,
flirting with a litany of aliases . . . *Rivertown . . . Illinoistown*
Piggott's Town . . . Snootville. . . The Valley (s) . . . Hudlin's Villa . . .
Rush City . . . Goose Hill . . . East Boogie . . . Pollack Town . . .
Miles Davis Mecca . . . Habitation Dunham . . . Jackie's Junction

(snap to its trap, bongo, conga, bucket & djembe rim shots
w/Ben Thigpen & Jesse Brazier, Thurman Washington & James "Big
Thunder" Walls, Kenny Rice & Orlando Gray, Ricky Glasper & Papa
Justin, Errol Allen & Arthur Moore, Sylvester "Sunshine" Lee &
Jahi Bakari, James Belk & Charles Haynes, Eugene Johnson
& Wheetie Brimah, Bernard Long & . . .)

where you gotta bring "some" to get "some,"
& *so what* if you did it different
(in another-other-where),this is how you goom-bopped it *here*—
in yesteryarn's ruralurban/mackman ethos—
where everybody grew backyard gardens,
played homemade "axes" in frontyard orchestras,
crooned like Ecsktine—or voice-dripped like Lady Day—
into broom- & mop-handle microphones,
decked to the nines in cellophane shades, adrift
in dreams of Eugene Haynes, Raleigh McDonald
& M-i-l-l-e-s who'd forged footholds
in a country called *The Apple*

East Saint Indigene & Africa . . .
>of First Peoples' drum-filtered peace signals to sun gods
>& Middle Passage/bi-coastal arrivants in the Straits of Slavery
>climbing Deltas/UpRiver to Little Egypt ("Kayro") & East Boogie

East Saint Immigrant . . .
>of indentured lovers & explorers & Revolutionary/Civil War veterans,
>of Ellis Islanders & workers of the web of rivers—Ohio & Missouri
>& Mississippi—& Cahokia Creek—& lakes like Carondolet & Horseshoe

East Saint Patron Saint & Elder . . .
>of Patriarchs Piggott & Robinson, Lawyers Parden & Summers & Jones,
>of Matriarchs Maggie Freeman & the Turner Sisters (granddaughters of Prophet Nat),
>of William "Buffalo Soldier" Buchanan & Trumpetfather Charles Creath
>& Songsiren Daisy O. Westbrook, of Drs. Weathers & Davis & Eubanks,
>of Nonagenarian Pioneers Carrie Dawson & Scotia Calhoun & Katherine Dunham

East Saint FastSlowParadox . . .
>of the All American City of race riots & racial harmony & racial estrangement,
>of "conks" & "mobstars" & 3-card mollies & Bloody Island & living room *wakes*

East Saint Arkansippi . . .
>of the Second Middle Passage & migration & migraine, of North Star
>& guitar, foxtailed fenders & blues-bopping crawfish

East Saint Sixties . . .
>of Freedom Brigades of Homer Randolph (CORE's "core") & James Peak
>& Omar Canty & Taylor Jones III (& Katherine's "Ode to TJ") & Elmo Bush
>& Clyde C. Jordan & Will McGaughy & Ethele Scott's Blackbookstore
>& East Boogie's '63-March-on-Washington for Jobs & Dignity & Forty Acres;
>& Jeanne Allen Faulkner's NAACP Youth Council's "colorizing" Jones Park;
>& Dr. Miles Davis's SRO funeral at Lincoln High's Gymnasium
>backdropped by the bellows of Black Power: Black Liberators & Black Egyptians
>& Imperial War Lords & Black Culture, Incorporated; Harry Edwards
>& Rap Brown & Stokely Carmichael—also at Lincoln High—bellowing Black Powerites! . . .
>& Mrs. Sippi's debouchure meeting embouchure bellowing quietly
>as *autumn leaves* . . . introspective as a Miles-muted soulo . . . *round midnight* . . .

of Rush City, separated from the Southend by a river of tracks
but joined at sky-level by the "black bridge,"
pregnant with coal dust & chemical "spills,"
with streets like Liberty & Paradise that dead-end at railwayheaven,
ubiquitous radios blaring Joe Louis & Harry James,
overall-attired war-era sharpies,
bike brigades & backyard farmers,
johnnies marchin off to Germany & Japan & Korea
& Jail & Vietnam & Freedom & Million Man March,
neo-Moorish sailors returning from Mediterranean Cruises
with memory-splotched Sketches of Spain . . .
with Bucket of Blood & Cotton Club
Red Top & Sock Hop
slot machines & Lucky Strike rings,
white-washed tree-trunks & chain-strung porch swings,
apron-crisp grandmothers & women weighted with "family way"
& war-shipped coffins & GI brides,
train loads of Nazi POWs taking "stretch"
& "smoke" breaks on the Illinois Central,
mental "botherations" of survivors/escapees of Arkansippi Justice,
open-air ovens & red-peppered repasts,
"natural gas" & "copasetic"—& gutbucket—vernaculars,
chittlin-eating white hoboes & wheel-drivin black joes,
one-room school & one-way-out highway
(with interchangeable names: Eighth Street,
Mississippi Avenue, Interstate/Route #3),
a river of vomit & tub-fishing "holes,"
diddley daddies & spitfire mammas . . .

Rush City & Sister Southend, with Mrs. Sippi as midwife,
broke muddy water & gave birth to the "Cool"...

of Goose Hill, one-village-of-a-corner/pocket-island,
"ham"-strung & nostril-stung by live-stocking neighbors
in next-door National City, O Armour O Hunter O Swift,
poised around proud Garfield Elementary School,
w/its first hand-me-down classes for "colored" in "Illinoistown"
... Goose Hill, seduced by box cars & storefront sanctuaries,
& the Harlem Club (favorite of the Dukes of Ellington & Earl)—
a hip's hop/skip/jump/slip's-slide away in that pre-Emancipation Village
of Brooklyn, a.k.a. Lovejoy, ... Goose Hill, a bumping hive
of war-time humanity at the northern tip of East Boogie's head,
Goose Hill, where Miles walked—"duffed"—
sometimes with ace boon coon Millard Curtis—
to Winstanley Avenue to meet dance-sweet Irene
(& croon Ledbelly's "Good Night . . .") . . .

Goose Hill swiveled its packinghouse hips,
rotated its shoo-bee-doo shoulders, & said, "So What". . .

& "Pollack" Town, brooking Pole & Soul,
entered/exited via parallel sets of tracks & a perpendicular viaduct,
bass-lined w/barbeque/drinking holes/sauerkraut,
sooning on Sousa/John Lee Hooker/Ethel Waters/New Hope Baptists,
Billy Eckstine & the Drifters & "The Flight of the Bumble Bee,"
feisty/greasy-spoon entrepreneurs/jazzerati/poolhallgriots,
quarterbacks, halfbacks, sweetbacks & laser-leg *runners*,
prodigies—Eugene Haynes/Amos Leon Thomas/Sherman Fowler—
politicians & funeral parlors & oral epics & boy-*Miles* stories,
Missouri Avenue/Mason-Dixon line: black/south & white/north,
& railways yawning beneath the viaduct, dropping like a slide
into the playground of Crispus Attucks Elementary School
(sentry-stark like its namesake Boston ancestor)
where Dorothy & Miles & Vernon ate the bread of books . . .

"'So What' Back At Ya!" scatted "Lock" Town—
of the outhouse, slopjar, glass factory & indigenous geniuses,
steel foundry, Alcoa Aluminum & Slavic/Jewish/Black phonetic:

. . ."Lock" Town, last exit to Golden Garden & Leo's Blue Note,
Walter Gates's Country Club & Ida Lewis's Foxhole,
to Alorton & Centreville cum "Fireworks Station"
(& Ned Love's Tavern & Nick's Country Club) . . .
& Millstadt/"Germanville" (& Dr. Davis's 200-acre
hog/horse farm—summer "heaven" for Argean Sanlin's
Boy Scout Troop #75) . . . last exit . . .
to Belleville & Little Egypt en route back to ArkanSippi . . .

"Lock" Town, leaning like a hip steeple on one of Joe Preston's
edifices, scat-cooed, "Yeah, 'So What'. . . It's "All Blues" anyway". . .

so, come, s/whirl, & bop on this . . .
if rural-rich Rush City & Sister Southend co-birthed the "Cool". . .
while slaughter house-hips/Goose Hill wailed "So what". . .
& bass-lined "Pollack" Town intoned "It's 'All Blues' anyway,"
then 15th & Broadway, as pivotal "riffer,"
rhythm section & tone-setter, became the hipsofical nerve center—
a *Kind of Blue* metronome/polymetric/layering—
of citycentric ethnicities: African-Americans & Armenians & Germans
& Greeks & Jews & Poles . . . 15th & Broadway,
stationary like Ben Thigpen's "trap" set—and later,
in the 60s & 70s, like Rene Calvin's conga & Mor Thiam's djembe
—stationary, but spinning like a rim-shooting turret
keeping time & track of art & enterprise,
its spokes/streets shuttling intravenous "Toodle-oo's"
from "Lock" Town to Rush City to Goose Hill
to the Great White Way/way North across State Street . . .
to "booze cruises" to Chi-Town, KC, Memphis & Saint Blue . . .

join the Miles *stroll*:
sun-glassed, blues-suffused city of streetcars, barbeque & jazzerati,
anchored at 15th & Broadway (where 1960's JFK brought Boston Brogue
& New Frontier—& white-looking/"black" Commissioner Saverson
throng'd w/big shots that shook Jack's hand),
south-mackin/WWII–15th Street—running w/the river, Jesus & Elijah
toward the "black bridge"—mirrored in a succession of "on the corner"
hives: theaters/hat shops/classy greasy spoons/churches & schools
(beginning w/Washington Irving *cum* James Weldon Johnson)
& clubs (Sportsman & Peppermint lounges) & Chinese cuisine
& professional offices (Dr. Davis's dental art above Daut's Drugstore)
& a "netword" of "underground"/"hot traffic". . .
souljourning to Brady Avenue (& Saverson's Paramount Club),
Bond Avenue ([Davises & Turner Sisters' St. Paul Baptist Church]
& [Captain] John Robinson School/McDonald's Drugstore)
&—still-mackin southward—toward (Captain) Piggott Avenue
(& Lincoln Park's late 60s Mary Brown Center—
catty-corner to "Wink" Falconer's early 40s Vet's Club—
around the "corner" from Jackie-JK's 60s nurturing grounds) . . .
on to Tudor Avenue, marchin left/east to Teer's Castle
& a column of bright Gibraltars—Truelight/Friendship/Shiloh
—ending at Paul Laurence Dunbar Elementary School
(composed in 1910, four years following the great bard's death) . . .
& back/west/left to 15th Street, strollin south again to horses
& hogs & goats & chickens & sunflowers & cigar trees,
chemical plants & okra & O'connor's Hardware,
Town Talk Tavern & Holman's Hole & Colas Avenue "Canaries"
de-virginizing bobby-soxed divas under the "black bridge"
& prophets "on the corner" sayin Jesus is Comin Back Tomorrow . . .
& this time He's bringing yall "all blues". . .

now go *walkin* back upCity w/Miles:
north—reprising spit shined 15th Street—& plie at Broadway—
where stovepipe blonds give whistlers pieces of their mind
& hipsters laugh Miles out of Ringside Pool Room
sayin his Continental Suit is a waiter's jacket w/high-water pants . . .
fabled 15th Street's always "kinda blue" shades
of hipsters in Sportsman or Paramount Club or Vet's
(amen-cornering "Albino" Red &/or Grant Green, Lou Donaldson,
John Mixon, Ben Thigpen—flattening thirds, fifths & sevenths)
& dark (& "processed") couples strollin . . . *Round Midnight* . . .
eastward to Huff's Beer Garden or the Blue Flame
("they didn't even have locks," Vernon Davis verifies)
to joy-jump w/big-bang big bands
or bop w/George Hudson & Clark Terry,
Elwood Buchanan & Peanuts Whalum,
Percy James & Vernon Eugene Nashville & Clifford Basfield . . .
or westward/& destination: Manhattan Club, "juking" w/Johnny Taylor
& Ike (before/during/after Tina) & Jerry "Ice Man" Butler
& Bobby "Blue Boy" Bland . . .
or deeper—due-river—west to Bowman's/Judge's Chambers
for plush/elegant/intellectual evenings w/Ahmad Jamal
("Amie Jamie") & the Three Sounds & Oliver Nelson . . .
&/or round the "corner"/past Club 216 & the Southern (black) Hotel—
w/Leo Caldwell's electric feet & elocution at the Faust Club
conjuring 50s saxophonic "genie"—Jimmy "Night Train" Forrest
(joining Hank Crawford backing the vocal avalanches of teenager Leon Thomas)—
w/Jesse Brazier & Ben Thigpen & Miles & Flora Bush Smith sittin in—
sizzlin & sizin up the set like a seizmograph—
& another Miles mentor—Fred Teer—ballroominggggggggg . . .

II. Acoustical Sketches of Milesville: Excerpts from an Aural Innerview, September 9, 2000

During Miles Davis's youth, East St. Louis was a town of great vibrancy, creativity, and productivity. As you know, it was a railroad capital; it was a packing-house or slaughterhouse capital; and it was one of the nation's music capitals. It was also a vice capital, if you will, with a thriving red-light district and a lot of other underground activities going on.

A strong intellectual tradition that had begun in the latter quarter of the nineteenth century included Nat Turner's granddaughters—Fannie and Lucy—who came from Ohio to East St. Louis; a man named A. M. Jackson, who was a great sports coach but who could lecture in Latin; a woman named Irene King, who was a composer, painter, playwright, and poet; and Annette Officer, who recited her own poetry—and the works of other poets—on the circuit with Paul Laurence Dunbar. So you had quite a mix.

East St. Louis also was known as the Pittsburgh of the West, and I always liked to think of it as a rural-urban place. It was one of the fastest—one of the raciest—in the country, but it was also one of the slowest. Everybody grew something—in the South End in particular—something in a garden; or they raised livestock or chickens. So you had a kind of slow, rural ambiance right alongside the prostitutes, the mobsters, the gangsters, the conks, and the other elements of a very, very fast world. And that was the East St. Louis portraiture in the thirties, forties, and fifties.

The city started out in the 1870s with a black population of four hundred. But by 1960 it had thirty-six thousand black people. And between the 1870s and 1960, you had, of course, a number of upheavals, with the central or pivotal feature being the black population's presence due to the migrations from the South to the North: what I call the coming of the Arkansippians. Southern blacks came to East St. Louis in search of that fabled promised land: to work in the slaughter houses, to work in the railroads, in the chemical plants, the steel foundries.

Blacks replaced whites as inhabitants of those industrial parks around Monsanto; Armor, Swift, and Hunter Packing; Obernester Glass Company; and Aluminum Ore factories and the steel foundries. The Aluminum Ore strike in 1917 led directly to the infamous race riot. Generations of black communities grew up around those industries, which became the focal point of black life. And much of that activity was located in the South End. The black community that grew to become thirty-six thousand in 1960 was still, essentially, a hermetically sealed community, until the big "integration" pushes of the later sixties.

East St. Louis was a very segregated city at the time of Miles Davis's birth, and by the time Miles left East St. Louis it was still segregated, although there were pockets of integration. There were little UNs—United Nations, if you will—like Fifteenth and Broadway (site of the Davises first home) or what was called "Polack" Town, directly east of Fifteenth and Broadway and three or four blocks north. There were also pockets of black people in the middle of white communities, just as there were small pockets of white people in black communities, because many of the whites were unable or unwilling to leave the South End when the flight of the whites occurred after blacks moved up from the South.

East St. Louis, as it is situated today within the Bi-State metroplex, is both a pariah and a pioneer. And I say this because East St. Louis has often jump-started important happenings in the metro area. It has produced or nurtured what is arguably the most significant musician in history—at least on the level of popular jazz music—Miles Davis; what is arguably the greatest woman athlete in history, Jackie Joyner-Kersee; and what is arguably the most significant dancer, or doyenne of dance, in the world, if you take into consideration all of the contributions that Katherine Dunham has made. You might even be able to argue that the most influential vocal stylist in jazz came out of East St. Louis, and I speak of my high school classmate Amos Leon Thomas. Because, although there have been many great scatters, none of them actually added the yodel. And none of them went into the history or excavated the traditions that led to scatting and yodeling—in a very scholarly way—like Leon did.

Because of East St. Louis's position—historically, physically, intellectually, culturally—it is impossible for the Bi-State area to ignore it. You can't get away from it; you can't get around it. You've got to look at it. I was sitting in the clubhouse at Grand Marais Park recently, and someone said, "Look at the Arch." Now, Grand Marais is forty-six blocks east of the river. There's no place in St. Louis that you can see the Gateway Arch as vividly as I saw it during lunch from forty-six blocks away. There are so

many different reasons why East St. Louis's placement is important. When I was a kid, I read about bodies being dumped in East St. Louis by mobsters. Again, the pariah, the dumpyard. It has twenty-two toxic waste sites. Many of the physical structures are shells. The school board, the city government—they all have oversight committees. So, we are down for the count.

But the history is there, the potential is there—I mean, the track team that produced Jackie Joyner-Kersee and won something like seventeen straight state track championships. So the depth is there. The greatest football team in the United States resided for a long time at East St. Louis Senior High School. As the poet Jane Cortez says, "I ain't no fly by night. Check out my resumé." That's East St. Louis's very complex role and image. But it's complex *and* complicitous: because as goes East St. Louis, so goes the metroplex. If it goes down, then the metroplex will not survive; if it goes up, of course the metroplex rises. We see this right now: the St. Louis Rams have crossed the river. They're doing everything from tutoring to building

Habitats for Humanity. So it's beginning to click and tick.

As the largest black municipality in the United States, East St. Louis is beset with a lot of different problems, but it also is heir to the great legacies, the great names, and the great contributions to America that not enough people know about. It is currently going through some of its most difficult times. Economically, East St. Louis probably couldn't drop below where it is now. And as far as its "image" goes, it probably couldn't sink any further either. But East St. Louis has always been a very scrappy place, a very tough, resilient place with a lot of wherewithal and stick-to-it-iveness. The intellectual tradition that fed the community at the time of a Miles Davis, a Frank Gully, a Raleigh McDonald, an Elbert "Red" Bonner, a Eugene Haynes, a Barbara Ann Teer, a James Rosser, or a John Hicks (former deputy director of the United States Information Agency), still feeds the community today. That cultural, intellectual, and activist tradition that was established with John Robinson, who came to East St. Louis in 1878 from Harper's Ferry, where he had witnessed the execution of John Brown—and after whom we have named an elementary school and a housing project—that tradition continues to thrive.

Robinson was a plasterer, an interior decorator, and an excavator. He established the artist-as-activist-and-institution-builder tradition. And from that point—from his entry into East St. Louis—we've continued to produce those types of people. Miles Davis's father and mother followed that tradition of artistry, activism, and institution building. So did Leon Thomas and Barbara Ann Teer, who built the National Black Theatre in Harlem after growing up in the 1600 block of Tudor Avenue in East St. Louis. So that tradition is intact, and the people who are heirs to it are still around—if they're not in East St. Louis proper, they're in cities that ring East St. Louis, or they're somewhere else in the world and they are accessible.

So it seems to me that the hope of East St. Louis is its spine of creativity, activism, and institution building. You see it in Sylvester "Sunshine" Lee and Katherine Dunham coming to East St. Louis in the 1960s to jumpstart her career as an institution builder, a teacher, and an artist in residence. I think that is the face of East St. Louis today, a city that clearly is going to have to rely on its cultural traditions, on its cultural history, and on its creativity to come back in this age of high tech. It's clear to me that East St. Louis is not going to survive in the mode of a traditional city, that industry is not going to rush back,

and that people are not going to rush back into the city. East St. Louis today, as Harry Belafonte and Danny Glover said during a recent visit, is looking at its cultural heirlooms and its cultural strengths and its artistic and intellectual resources. And that's what's going to be the savior of East St. Louis; that's what's going to revive and stabilize the city.

Miles Davis is emblematic of East St. Louis. He symbolizes East St. Louis. He actualizes East St. Louis. Miles is both a literal and figurative person or event—a phenomenon. Miles is also the tip of the iceberg. If you were to do an anatomy of the Lincoln High School band between 1940 and 1945, where Willie Walker was first-trombone at the same time that Miles was first-trumpet, after Frank Gully held that seat; if you look at all those people who were on the same level with Miles—Red Bonner; Raleigh McDonald, who later toured Europe with the *Porgy and Bess* cast; Harry Turner, and all those trumpet players that came behind, thinking, "I'm just a trumpet player"—you see that Miles is, again, the tip of the iceberg. And so it was happenstance— and of course Miles had great talent—but

happenstance that got Miles to where he was. He could have been taken out by drugs; he could've been taken out by a jealous lover; he could've had an accident; he could have died earlier on. Miles is the apex, but there is a foundation beneath him. Check out the resumé.

I think Miles means that East St. Louis will never go away. That East St. Louis will never disappear. That a man, William Washington Buchanan, born in 1871, who sent his son Elwood a telegram in 1933—while Elwood was playing on a riverboat in New Orleans—saying, "Come home, there's a job teaching music here," began a chain of activity that changed the face of music in the world and altered how people defined and related to music forever. That man, who produced Elwood Buchanan and was a Buffalo Soldier; who was on San Juan Hill with Teddy Roosevelt; who played trombone in the famed Eighth Illinois Band, one of the greatest state-sponsored bands in the country—that's what Miles means. Miles came out of William Washington Buchanan, who gave us Miles's first "great" teacher, Elwood Buchanan, and his brother William, who graduated from Lincoln High in 1930 when Miles would have been four. William, the surviving brother, still goes to work at his pharmacy about three days a week in East St. Louis, at Seventeenth and Central. So that's what Miles means. He says, "Thank you. I respect that tradition; I'm part of that tradition."

At the end of his autobiography—the one that Quincy Troupe helped him with—Miles says he never felt as comfortable around anybody as when he was with his old buddies in East St. Louis. And so that's what Miles means to East St. Louis: he's the peak; he's how we strut our stuff. 'Cause everybody couldn't go to the Apple; everybody couldn't go through what he went through. Even the rites of passage, the most nefarious ones he experienced, were representative of who we are as a people, human beings in general, specifically East St. Louisans, and black East St. Louisans even more specifically. That's what Miles represents for East St. Louis: a luminous and sacrificial native son, a cultural ambassador, a crown jewel of culture—into perpetuity.

III. Milestone: The Birth of an Ancestor

For Miles Dewey Davis III
(1926–1991)
In Memoriam, In Futuriam

("Prologue" to poem read at Miles's
Memorial, October 13, 1991, at
Lincoln High School in East St. Louis, Illinois)

Dressed up in pain
the flatted fifth began its funereal climb
up the tribal stairwell:

grief-radiant as it
bulged and gleamed with moans
spread like laughter or Ethiopia's wings
mourned its own percussive rise
became blues-borne
in the hoarse East Saint Louis Air:

bore witness to the roaring calm
the garrulous silence
the caskets of tears
the gushing stillness:

the death of the Cool
became the birth of an Ancestor . . .

death of the Cool
birth of an Ancestor

With George Avakian,
New York, 1957.
Photograph by
Carole Reiff.

George Avakian is a living history book of the modern record industry, having played important roles at several major record labels in developing popular recorded music in the middle of the twentieth century. Avakian is the man who signed Miles Davis to Columbia Records and who produced his first albums on the label, including the orchestral *Miles Ahead* collaboration with Gil Evans.

Born in 1919 in Armavir, Soviet Union, Avakian's Armenian family moved to the United States in 1923. Early in life, Avakian "started out like so many people did in those days, as being a fan" of American jazz. The music "reminded me of my parents' Aremenian records," he recalls. In high school he wrote letters to record companies advocating the reissue of important records, such as the Louis Armstrong *Hot Fives*. While at Yale, he began writing "Collector's Corner" columns for *Tempo* magazine, taking over for his friend, the jazz collector Marshall Stearns. In 1940, he began working at Columbia Records in the first jazz reissue program. At the end of the world war, he helped develop

Columbia's ambitious popular album program using the new long-playing format, and he began producing a variety of new music as well as supervising significant reissues.

Avakian's first love always remained jazz, and his efforts to increase the Columbia label's roster of jazz artists led him to sign Miles Davis eighteen months before Davis's contract with the smaller Prestige Records terminated. The move paid off; Davis's association with Columbia made him an international star, and he remained with the label for thirty years.

Avakian left the music business decades ago, adopting a globetrotting life in his family's oriental rug business, but he remains an important resource for a remarkable period in American music.

BC: The development of the LP after the war seemed to change everything in the record business, didn't it?

GA: It sure did. At the same time I was working on the first 33 rpm albums, I was also asked to be the new director of the international department. It didn't amount to much because there wasn't much to do. But lo and behold, the LP got bigger and bigger and greatly overshadowed the single business. Same thing happened with the international market, because abroad people didn't care about a specific song.

"He's Miles Ahead": George Avakian

interview by Benjamin Cawthra

They cared about people they'd seen in the movies, like Frank Sinatra and Doris Day. So as the LP got ahold of the market in Europe, the department got to be so big that more income came in through pop albums abroad than even in the United States. Eventually, by the late 1950s it got to be so big that I thought I was going to kill myself because I was working so hard. So I left and eventually helped develop the Warner Bros. catalog.

BC: So at Columbia in the forties and fifties, there was really no distinction between jazz and pop—it was all treated and marketed as pop?

GA: The pop album department was developing a jazz volume because the idea of the department was to have something for every possible customer, and I mean every possible. Somebody pointed out that nobody in the history of the industry has ever recorded as many different types of repertoire as I did because of the position I was in with a company that had a very wide catalog. I did cantorial music, I did gypsy music, even the first recordings of Ravi Shankar when he came to America. The complete German operas of Kurt Weill. Country music. Rhythm and blues, even rock and roll, and so on. People, especially from Europe, thought I was in charge of jazz, but the sign on my door said, "Mr. Avakian—Popular Album Department." But nevertheless, the jazz part of course was very dear to my heart. One of the things I wanted to do in the fifties at Columbia was to have a selective catalog of the better bop artists, and that wasn't too easy because most of them had been signed to smaller labels. But a couple of them got loose at the right moment, like Art Blakey. One who almost did was Miles Davis.

BC: You knew Miles well in advance of signing him, right?

GA: Miles and I had become very good friends, in an odd way, and years after I had signed him and he was a big star, he started to tell people, "You know, I was after George for four years before he would record me." And then the next time there was a party at his house or something he would say, "I kept after George for six years and he wouldn't pay attention to me." When he got up to eight years, I said to him one day—because I used to drop in at his house a lot, he was a neighbor you know, and a lonesome man actually—he kept saying this so much I told him, "Look, you've got to stop this, because I didn't know you really, eight, ten years before." He said, "Oh, I can prove it to you." I said, "Okay." He said, "But not today. The next time you come to the house." So the next time I came to the house, we had been chatting for about an hour. He jumped up and said, "Wait!" He ran up the stairs—it was a two-story house—and I heard this banging of drawers and everything. And he came down waving something and he said, "See, here's the proof." And I looked and it was one of those fold-out albums with a photograph inside from a nightclub. It was from the Three Deuces on Fifty-second Street.

And he said, "Remember this?" and I said, "Sure." It was a picture of Dizzy, Miles, Sterling Brown—who had been my guest at the lecture series I had started at NYU in 1947—and me, and we were at a table and a female photographer had come along and said, "Gentlemen, would you like a souvenir picture?" I felt very expansive. I said, "Sure." So she took a picture of us, and she said, "How many?" I said, "One for everybody." They cost seventy-five cents a piece. And Miles had kept his; I hadn't. I said, "Miles, that's great, but you know, this wasn't really when it began." He said it was close to it.

BC: So you knew Miles in the late 1940s but didn't sign him until 1955.

GA: I knew him even before then. That picture had to have been taken in the winter of 1946–47 or 1947–48. I can't remember which. But it doesn't matter. Miles really had been after me starting in 1952, certainly, to record him. And I was reluctant because he was a junkie at the time, and I had enough experience with junkies that I didn't want to mess around. And of course he was under contract to Prestige. Finally in the spring of 1954, Miles came up with an idea. What he said was, "George, you know Bob Weinstock who runs Prestige. Talk to him and tell him, "'Look, I'm going to sign Miles anyway when the contract expires in 1956. Why don't you let Miles record now, and I'll keep the master.'" That way Columbia could release the first Miles Davis recording on Columbia immediately after his Prestige contract ran out without having to wait six months to go into production, and meanwhile, Prestige, knowing what's going to happen, could build up a catalog and coast in on the publicity and advertising, which Columbia would pay for, but which will be even more profitable at first to Prestige because they would have their own catalog of recordings to release over time.

Well, it was a brilliant idea, but so crazy that I thought, "Nah, that's a little too bizarre." But my brother Aram, who was a terrific photographer and filmmaker, he had become a good friend of Miles also, of course. At the 1955 Newport Jazz Festival, he said, "Look, why don't you record him because somebody else will do it if you don't because he's the head of the festival."

BC: And he was right. But Miles couldn't release anything on Columbia until 1957.

GA: Right. So that takes us into the whole business of the planning of what we could do to make it worthwhile to sign Miles a year and a half before he could be released from his Prestige contract. And that worked out through Jack Whittemore, my good friend who was with the Shaw Artists Agency, and just about the only agent willing to put up with Miles at the time. And when I outlined the plan to him and told him, "Look, it would only work if you can keep Miles working steadily with a group that he's organized," which fortunately was damn good. Everything fell in place, the right time, you know. And so Jack did that, and the idea of something more elaborate and more commercially attractive than the quintet worked out also. All of a sudden Miles was taking off like crazy.

BC: What did you hear in Miles that steered you toward the signing?

GA: Well, I already felt that Miles could be commercially saleable without any compromise, because he had a beautiful soft tone when he played ballads like "But Not for Me" or "My Funny Valentine." I thought to myself, "Hell, nobody in the pop music business is selling these songs the way Miles sells them, and he doesn't even realize that he's selling these songs." That's one thing. I thought that maybe he might come fairly close to, say, Dizzy Gillespie as being a spectacular trumpet player in terms of up-tempo things and all, but I also thought he could be much more than a great ballad player in what we were already calling the cool style. But that was the first attraction. Then the other was the mystique of Miles having hung around as a young man—age eighteen, age nineteen—hanging around Parker and all that, was building to the point that he was getting publicity on that score—nothing big yet. But that too gave him an entrée into an area where he wasn't really so highly accepted, you see.

BC: What do you mean?

GA: I don't like to talk about it, because people don't realize that Miles was not a highly respected musician at the time. I mean, he appealed to people enough that he won the *Metronome* and *Down Beat* polls, but the musicians didn't respect him that much. They thought of him, I guess, as one of the lesser lights who had a commercial appeal, which better jazz musicians of that style and era didn't have. It wasn't much talked about, but it was in the air. Although Miles played with Parker and was inspired by Parker and of course Dizzy, he wasn't in their class in terms of being a thorough, across-the-board musician with technique as well as ideas. So that was one of the things that forced Miles, in a way, into being more than a hotshot bop musician. I don't want people to think that Miles was anything less than a great genius artist. Miles was also an ordinary guy who was out to make himself better known. And the best way he knew, and he was right, was to sign a contract with Columbia Records, because he knew that as his friend and admirer I would spend money on advertising and promotion and make him a star, because I wanted to make a star of every artist that I had.

BC: I wanted to ask you about Gil Evans. How did you first become aware of his work?

GA: Gil was one of the arrangers used by Claude Thornhill in the 1940s. As the very junior new member of the A-and-R staff—we weren't called artists and repertoire people then, it was just "recording director"—I got to learn and be an apprentice to the engineers and the senior producers by going to their sessions and then being given assignments on my own, and among them were the artists that weren't so important to the company, of course. That's how I got to produce Claude Thornhill, and Elliott Lawrence, who had people in his band like Gerry Mulligan. Of course I had no idea that Gerry Mulligan was going to be important. He was just a funny-looking kid with very short hair. So that's the way that all began.

BC: What did you notice about Gil's work?

GA: Gil impressed the hell out of me because I was always very interested in contemporary classical music. In high school I became aware of Debussy and Ravel and Shostakovich and Stravinsky and Alban Berg and so on, and I started buying their records when I was in college. And so Gil's arrangements reminded me certainly of the French impressionists, or even more so Delius, for example. If you love jazz, you've got to get into this, and so few people did. Although some of the bop musicians after the war were getting into Stravinsky. So the friendship with Gil didn't lead anywhere except that I admired his work and we hit it off pretty well. He was a very shy, retiring sort of guy. And when I heard that he had gotten together with Miles and was sort of the principal force behind the rehearsals that took place in his apartment and the arranging that was done by Gil and others for Miles's little nine-piece band, that became a natural possibility for the idea that I had of expanding the nine-piece orchestra, inspired a good deal, of course, by the Gunther Schuller *Music for Brass* album on which Miles had been a featured soloist. So in effect, that was the godmother, I guess, of the Gil Evans collaboration with Miles on *Miles Ahead*. Gil already had taught himself the elements that would be necessary for the project I had in mind.

BC: You were aware at the time that he was self-taught?

GA: As far as I know—I never talked to him about it. But I think he simply picked up arranging by working with jazz bands in California, especially the Skinny Ennis band. He certainly had the ability, and I had no worry about saying to Miles when the time came, "Only two people can do this: Gunther Schuller or Gil." And he chose Gil, as I expected, because they were so close and he had done all the rehearsals for his nine-piece band with Gil a few years before.

BC: So you have Miles, you have Gil, and a concept. How did it all come together to produce *Miles Ahead*?

GA: It developed out of all these sources, and I thought that if my feeling was correct, this would expand Miles's appeal far, far beyond what he could ever do just working as a "jazz" musician. It was a jazz album, but at the same time it had a sound and a texture that hadn't been heard before except in the music that had touches of French impressionism in it, because that is, I think, the key element to the success of the Gil Evans collaboration. And the more up-tempo, more spectacular performances, again it had touches that really came out of classical music. You can hear bits of Stravinsky and Shostakovich in Gil's arranging, for example. It's not very close, but I think that's one reason why people who liked classical music and didn't think much about jazz ended up buying the *Miles Ahead* album. That was the first album, I would say, that we could tell appealed to Masterworks or Columbia classical record buyers.

BC: In thinking about the *Miles Ahead* record, one of the things that's appealing about it is the sense of it being a continuous suite using the works of several composers. Was that idea there from the beginning?

GA: The idea of continuity on *Miles Ahead* was entirely Gil's conception, and he hadn't told me about it. He told me as we were recording that "I'm going to end this piece in such a way that you might think 'where's the ending?' but it'll go into the next track because I want it to be continuous." And I said, "Sure, that's no problem." And that's what we did. Later on I found out that he got the idea from an album that I had done in the *Piano Moods* series, which was a series of twenty or twenty-five piano albums—all ten-inchers because there was no twelve inch pop line at the time—and this one, all the pieces were bridged together because the pianist had the idea that he'd like to make it sound as though he's in a cocktail lounge and he's just playing continuously as background for the customers. Which was fine with me. The *Piano Moods* series gave me a great excuse to record favorites of mine, like Earl Hines and Eddie Haywood. Erroll Garner's first record for Columbia was a *Piano Moods* record.

BC: Of course, you could only make this happen with the new popularity of the LP format.

GA: Oh absolutely. You had to have LP as a separate concept, which was exactly what I had in mind when I got into the idea of creating product for this new style of recording. The inspiration for it was very simple: the broadcasts that I heard as a child in the 1930s, like the Casa Loma Orchestra playing on a program called the *Camel Caravan*. The format was partly set up by the fact that these were broadcasts that had to be recorded and planned in such a way that the discs could be shipped out to the central and west coast areas and played a week later because you couldn't broadcast coast-to-coast. The telephone wires weren't able to transmit the music

faithfully at that time. And these discs were cut as sixteen-inch discs with the turntables revolving at 33 rpm, and one side at 33 rpm would play for fourteen and a half minutes, and then you turn it over and the second side is the second half of a half-hour show. Now, this gave me the formula for the ten-inch pop LP. Those broadcasts started with, "Bang! Let's grab the audience." So I always tried to make the first track of every pop LP something that would grab you. Usually it was a bright up-tempo tune. Not always; the first Miles Davis LP [*Round About Midnight*] has a ballad starting it.

BC: That leads us to "Springsville" on *Miles Ahead*.

GA: That's right. On the second album, "Springsville" starts it off with a bang, you know. I'd not said to Gil, "Be sure that 'Springsville' is the first track," because I didn't know that "Springsville" existed, you see. I'd left the repertoire entirely up to Gil and Miles, and essentially it became Gil even more than Miles, with only one proviso, which was, "Make sure that I have one original tune that I can call 'Miles Ahead' because that's going to be the title of the album, the thrust of the entire promotion." Miles is ahead of everybody else, he's miles ahead of the competition, he's moving ahead, Miles is ahead, ahead, ahead, ahead.

BC: Miles told the story of Gil calling him in the middle of the night and saying, "Miles, if you're ever depressed, listen to 'Springsville.'"

GA: You know, I've heard that, too. And I always wondered if he just meant that it's such a lively grabber that you can't stay down. You have to go up. And I'm sure that's it, because it's the philosophy that I discussed with Gil. "We have to grab people right away. I don't know what you're going to do afterwards, but I trust you." And that was it.

BC: What did you think of some of Miles's later records, especially when he went electric?

GA: I didn't like them, because I thought, "This is a distortion of Miles. Miles does not need this." And as you probably know, he deliberately set out to do something about the fact that he bitterly resented all these nothing musicians making huge fortunes and getting great reputations out of nothing. And so he bought up tons of rock records of all kinds, and decided, "I can do this better than they can, and I'm going to."

BC: But the music didn't sound pop.

GA: No, that's true. It didn't. But whatever it was, I didn't care much for it because Miles himself, as the musician that he is, as the personality that he is, I felt was somewhat lost in it. It was something else, but it wasn't Miles. Now, what does that make me, a stick-in-the-mud traditionalist, I suppose? But Miles to me—the Miles Davis I carry in my head and heart—it will always be that earlier Miles. Now that's a very big Miles, because that's a broad, broad range. Go too far away from it and it becomes something else.

BC: You were essentially neighbors with Miles for many years in Manhattan. What kind of a person was he?

GA: He was a very nice, sweet person, I thought, with of course a driving force inside to make himself more everything—more money, more prestige, more this and more that. But basically he was almost a shy person, I thought. That's why I think a great deal of this brashness was put on in order to attract attention for himself. He did set an agenda for himself, I'm convinced. Just as he himself said, he set an agenda with me, because once we got to be friends, and he saw that I was becoming an important force in the record business, he wanted very much to record with me. Because he felt that that was his passport to fame and fortune on phonograph records, which would translate into everything else, and it did.

BC: How should Miles be remembered?

GA: I think he'll be remembered more than anything else for the personality that he created. But he also created a musical personality that to me is the real Miles Davis musically, not the later electronic Miles Davis. And that will stand forever.

At Columbia's Thirtieth Street Studios,
New York, 1957.
Photograph by
Don Hunstein.

In February 1961, in Miles Davis's apartment on West Seventy-seventh Street in New York, a group of jazz musicians reveled in a mock-revenge fantasy. Under a table-turning "press conference in reverse" contrived by publicist Pete Long, jazz writers Nat Hentoff, Ira Gitler, John Wilson, Martin Williams, Stanley Dance, Robert Reisner, and Dan Morgenstern submitted themselves to a post–cocktail-party interrogation by musicians Cannonball Adderley, Gerry Mulligan, J. J. Johnson, Philly Joe Jones, Horace Silver, Billy Taylor, and Gil Evans. As host, Miles Davis cut an understated, slightly mysterious profile. Press coverage of the event said very little about the famous trumpeter and bandleader himself, focusing instead on the stylish ambiance of his upscale dwelling. *New York Post* reporter Gene Grove took note of the "walnut coffee tables" in Davis's "white-walled, book-lined living room," while Morgenstern's dispatch in *Metronome* mentioned the chauffeured Rolls Royce lurking on the street in front of the apartment, a special touch that Davis—well known to favor Italian sports cars—had leased for the occasion.[1]

As if applying his less-is-more musical credo in his approach to hospitality, Davis relegated his participation in the hour-long inquisition to a few concise interjections—and not one of them was laced with the creative obscenity that was as much his signature as the vibrato-free sound he seduced out of his horn. Cannonball Adderley assumed the role of moderator, leading with a question that affably but piercingly hoisted the writers on their own petards: "What is Jazz?" the stumper fed to musicians for years, often to their bafflement. ("If you have to ask, you'll never know," ran Louis Armstrong's classic retort.) After Hentoff spent a few minutes dissembling, Davis mumbled something and walked out of the room. Horace Silver jumped in with a question that had the musicians and onlookers licking their chops: "What qualification does a jazz critic need?" Hentoff, still reeling from the first question, confessed, "Anybody can be a jazz critic. The standards are very low."

The ever-earnest Martin Williams tried to defend the craft, arguing that not everyone who writes about jazz qualifies as a "real" critic. Hentoff agreed, saying that while there were a number of Europeans with the requisite musical knowledge, here in the U.S. there were only a handful, namely Williams, Louis Gottlieb, and Gunther Schuller. Just then Davis reappeared and said that he'd be willing to include Hentoff himself on that

Miles and the Jazz Critics

by John Gennari

list, but only if Hentoff acknowledged the debt he owed his questioners. "Now Nat, when did he become a critic?" Davis asked. "You remember, J. J.," he said, turning to trombonist J. J. Johnson. "We gave Nat his first gig."[2]

That Miles Davis would host an event where critics got their comeuppance—but in a manner that suggested a certain rough rapport and intimacy with the musicians—illustrates the complexities of the man, the time, and the jazz world itself. In 1961, Miles Davis was no mere jazz musician; he was jazz's version of a pop star. His last several Columbia LPs (including *Kind of Blue, Sketches of Spain,* and *Someday My Prince Will Come*) sold in massive quantities, allowing him to expand significantly his real estate holdings and indulge his love for fine wood and fast cars. *Esquire* magazine had anointed him one of the best-dressed men in America. As a highly visible black man, Davis was no stranger to racism—the most notable instance being the vicious clubbing he received by a white policeman in front of a New York City club in which he was performing in 1959. But at a time when the black freedom struggle in the United States and Africa focused public attention on poverty, injustice, and white supremacy, Miles Davis reigned as an African American symbol of artistic genius, bourgeois comfort, and sovereign cool.

For jazz, too, this was a flush moment. A burgeoning LP trade, college concert bookings, jazz festivals and schools, new jazz magazines and books, and jazz-themed movies gave the music a strutting, triumphal presence in the expanded postwar cultural marketplace. State Department–sponsored tours used the music as a tool of cultural diplomacy in Cold War hot spots across the globe. Mainstream jazz—a classification first introduced by jazz critics in their canon-building efforts but then appropriated by marketers as a commercial label—had become part of the mainstream of American culture. In line with the consensus, end-of-ideology politics of the 1950s, mainstream commentators and gatekeepers evangelized the music as a force of racial harmony and bourgeois normalcy, cleansing jazz of its affiliations with political radicalism and bohemian subcultures. Noting jazz's appeal to everyone from "a pneumatic drill operator to a little old grandma knitting in a rocking chair," the *New York Post* claimed that one did not have to be a "rootless drifter of the Beat generation," a "boozer," or a "weedhead" to appreciate "America's only true native art." Contrasting jazz with "such popular lunacies as rock and roll," the *Post* counted among the jazz listening public "doctors, lawyers, housewives, and even Congressmen." *Good Housekeeping* characterized jazz musicians as "no longer murky characters with short beards and berets on their heads, or hopped-up fellows who sleep all day and crawl forth at 4 A.M.," likening jazz's transformation in the public mind to "the boy with dirty hands whom you wouldn't let into your house" becoming one with "clean hands . . . found in the concert halls, the music conservatories, and by way of respectable and carefully produced LP records, in the nicest living rooms."[3]

Miles Davis, raised in a solid black middle-class family in East St. Louis and once enrolled at Juilliard School of Music before becoming smitten with bebop and a fast lifestyle that eventually included a heroin addiction, was a walking and breathing symbol of this purifying transformation. In his 1961 book *The Jazz Life*, Nat Hentoff took issue with Eric Hobsbawn, who, writing under his jazz nom de plum, Francis Davis, in the *New Statesman*, claimed that Davis's introverted, melancholic sound revealed an "uncompromising hostility to the outer world." Hentoff portrayed Davis instead as a happy, well-adjusted professional who "invests successfully in the stock market and in real estate" and "characteristically, makes his own decisions on what stocks to buy, often based on his own empirical testing of a company's product or his observance of current supply-and-demand balances in the various areas through which he travels."[4]

Hentoff and the other critics who sipped cocktails in Miles Davis's living room that afternoon in 1961 were both agents and beneficiaries of jazz's hyped-up middle-class respectability. But they also knew how airbrushed the picture was that showed the jazz world as a harmonious village. A year earlier at the Newport Jazz Festival—founded in 1954 by promoter George Wein, who favored big names and all-star bands that brought together musicians from different generations and schools, fostering the impression of a jazz family happily reunited after the painful 1940s modernist-fundamentalist rupture—a group of musicians led by Charles Mingus and Max Roach organized an alternative or "rebel" festival in another part of town. Claiming that the main festival reeked of Jim Crow, finding its supporters' embrace of jazz suffocating rather than liberating, the rebels—an intergenerational group that included swing-era titans Coleman Hawkins and Jo Jones, hard bop trumpeter Kenny Dorham, and free jazz pioneer Ornette Coleman—literally constructed their own bandstand, printed their own handbills,

and erected tents on their own guerrilla concert site. Seizing the rhetoric and imagery of the *salon de refuses*, the rebel festival fancied itself a virtuous self-governing republic of artists pitted against a corrupt empire of profiteering booking agents, promoters, and hoteliers.

Roach characterized the event as an effort to "prove that the musician can produce, present, and participate [by and for] himself"—an idea that Roach and Mingus had attempted to carry out through owning and managing their own recording company, Debut Records. Such initiatives for self-determination intersected with, and were crucially inspired by, domestic civil rights and international anticolonial freedom

struggles, pan-Africanism, and African American cultural traditions. These jazz musicians were not pushing for racial separatism, but rather for greater influence and control over the making of the music, its public dissemination, and its use as a symbol of American culture. Mingus, Roach, Hawkins and the other Newport "rebels" were not just registering their impatience with a Jim Crow patronage arrangement; they were trying to find a serious interracial audience for an artistically adventurous and intellectually challenging music. Told that he would have to be briefed by the State Department before going abroad on a jazz tour, Dizzy Gillespie sharply responded: "I've got three hundred years of briefing. I know what they've done to us, and I'm not going to make any excuses." Gillespie later said in his memoirs, "I sort've liked the idea of representing America, but I wasn't going to apologize for the racist policies of America." These paradoxical gestures of affiliation and repudiation underscored the ambivalent position of the black jazz musician, who sought to take advantage of the opportunities engendered by jazz's status as a booming American art while simultaneously asserting jazz's significance as a crucible of black cultural memory, agency, and autonomy.[5]

In his superb eulogy for Miles Davis, Greg Tate suggests that Amiri Baraka was wrong in saying that black music "implores us to sing and fight." Black people would "do that anyway,"

Tate says, "just out of human necessity." What the black music tradition, and Davis in particular, instead teach "is more Joycean in tenor: silence, exile, and cunning." Davis didn't completely exile himself from the public side of the black freedom movement; in 1964, his quintet did an important benefit concert to raise money for voter registration efforts by SNCC, CORE, and the NAACP. But Davis was not the kind of organizer or protester who manned the ramparts, waved a banner, or worked at the grass-roots level to challenge and transform institutions. For one, Davis, as many who knew him could attest, was actually a shy man behind all the flamboyance. Shyness was a quality he prized, and when he saw it in James Baldwin when they first met, he recognized a kindred soul. "He was a very shy person and I was too," Davis said. "I thought we both looked like brothers. When I say both of us have a shyness I mean an artistic kind of shyness, where you are wary of people taking up your time."[6]

Like Baldwin, Davis also intuitively understood the power of white privilege; sometimes he seemed obsessed about it. The black critic Stanley Crouch, Davis's sternest critic, has argued that Davis was "a man of monumental insecurity who, for all his protests about white power and prejudice, is often controlled by his fear of it." Crouch writes, "Davis asserts that he never listens to white music critics, and blames many of the woes of the music business on them, but then he

admits that once they had him worried that he sounded inferior to [white trumpeter] Chet Baker, who was his imitator." This argument has some validity, but it obscures one of the subtle ways Davis struggled against the racial asymmetry of the jazz world, with most of the critics and gatekeepers being white and most of the important innovators being black. This asymmetry had characterized the marketplace for black art at least since the Harlem Renaissance, when the white critic, fiction writer, and photographer Carl Van Vechten emerged as a crucial patron and proselytizer for Bessie Smith, Langston Hughes, Zora Neale Hurston, and others. As literary scholar Emily Bernard suggests, the contradictory effort of black artists and intellectuals to "locate a purely black art *and* invest in cross-cultural exchange were not *failings* of the Harlem Renaissance; they constituted the Harlem Renaissance." This contradictory impulse, Bernard argues, "is almost always at work in black cultural production: a simultaneous promotion of black cultural independence, as well as an effort—sometimes hostile, sometimes hopeful—to naturalize white influence as a feature of black experience."[7]

One of the hallmarks of Miles Davis's power as a black artist was his facility at absorbing, managing, and manipulating his white influences, both in the sound of his music and in the shaping of his career. Davis was deeply rooted in the blues and an heir to a

tradition of black trumpeters that included Louis Armstrong, Freddie Webster, Ray Nance, Clark Terry, Rex Stewart, Harry Edison, Buck Clayton, Fats Navarro, and Dizzy Gillespie. From the 1960s on, he turned his ear to the black soul and rock of James Brown, Motown, Jimi Hendrix, Sly Stone, and Prince. Yet, Davis was not afraid to soak in the influence of white artists as various as Harry James, Benny Goodman, Frank Sinatra, Doris Day, Claude Thornhill, Orson Welles, Humphrey Bogart, Fred Astaire, and Karlheinz Stockhausen. One of his major artistic collaborations and friendships was with the Canadian-born white arranger Gil Evans. Throughout the years, many of his bands were interracial. For Davis—and this is the crucial point—interracial exchange was not motivated out of a strong commitment to racial integration for its *own* sake, but was part and parcel of black art and black cultural independence. This carried over into his relationships with the few white critics he saw as exceptions to the racist norm. These critics he challenged, provoked, titillated, humiliated—and used to secure the cachet and cultural capital he needed to triumph in the white-dominated marketplace.

The 1961 "press conference in reverse" and other key instances of Davis's relationships with white jazz critics do not appear in *Miles: The Autobiography*, the 1989 tell-all book Davis crafted with black poet Quincy Troupe. Nor do these interracial relationships square very easily with the unambiguous, summary dismissal of white critics that Davis delivered to Amiri Baraka in their interview for a *New York Times Magazine* profile in 1985. "I don't pay no attention to these white critics about my music," Davis said. "Be like somebody from Europe coming criticizing Chinese music. They don't know about that. I've lived what I've played."[8] In truth, Davis's relationships with critics, both black and white, were cunningly personal, usually self-serving, sometimes cruel, and always full of intrigue. For all of his shyness, his wariness of people taking up his time, his defensiveness and bluntness, it is remarkable how intimate he could become with those writers whom he invited into his home and his life. This intimacy comes through in the language and feeling of *Miles: The Autobiography*. But it also surfaced in the 1950s and '60s with the white writers Leonard Feather, Nat Hentoff, Ralph Gleason, and Dan Morgenstern, and in the late 1970s with Eric Nisenson. It was with Feather and Hentoff, in particular, that Davis emerged as a highly articulate jazz critic in his own right, offering acute and strongly opinionated assessments of other jazz musicians.

When the "New Journalism"—with its emphasis on visual detail and the subjective presence of the writer—worked its way into popular music criticism in the late 1960s, Davis proved to be an alluring subject. Rock writer Stephen Davis, interviewing Miles in 1973, was astonished when Davis, to show the effects of thirty years of playing the horn, took the writer's hand and guided his fingertip over his scarred lip. Profiles of Miles Davis in this period dwelled on the private details of a life that seem scripted by the *Playboy Advisor*. Stephen Davis was quite taken by Miles's extensive wardrobe and ten-foot bathtub. Morgenstern wrote in *Down Beat* in 1970 that he found Davis's bedroom "so groovy that if it were mine, I might never leave it." Morgenstern's article went on to detail his experience watching Davis work out at Bobby Gleason's gym and having Davis drive him around Manhattan in his new Lamborghini. When physical problems and a nasty cocaine habit overtook Davis in the late '70s and early '80s, some of these scenes played out as bad pornography. Eric Nisenson, by his own account, found himself in a kind of "indentured servitude," servicing Davis's drug needs and witnessing firsthand his appalling violence against women. Eventually, Nisenson reports, Davis "cut me off very sharply," and the writer's hopes of coauthoring Davis's autobiography vanished. Deeply hurt, Nisenson tried to assuage himself with the knowledge that "sooner or later Miles did this to almost everyone close to him; for some reason I thought that I was the exception."[9]

Davis's vexed posture toward jazz critics dates to the outset of his professional career. In 1945, less than a year after arriving in New York from East St. Louis, Davis appeared on Charlie

Parker's first session as a leader, *Charlie Parker's Reboppers*, recorded for the Savoy label. Dizzy Gillespie played trumpet on "Warmin' Up a Riff," "Meandering," and the harmonically complex, bristling up-tempo "Ko-Ko." Davis took solos on two tunes, "Billie's Bounce" and "Now's The Time," as Gillespie switched over to piano. *Down Beat*'s review of the record unfavorably compared Davis to Gillespie, demeaning Davis as a greenhorn, a pretender with no sound of his own, desperate to copy the more seasoned bebop pioneer. Dan Morgenstern, among other critics, retrospectively has offered a different view of Davis's performance on that session, saying that his solos "reveal a more than budding originality, a

personal sound, and that rare thing, musical intelligence." In a highly influential series of articles on bebop for *Record Changer* in 1948, critic and Dial Records owner/producer Ross Russell wrote: "Miles Davis may be said to belong to the new generation of musicians. There is now a mounting body of evidence that Davis is leading the way to, or even founding, the next school of trumpet playing." The prescience of Russell's statement appeared borne out by *The Birth of the Cool* nonet sessions for Capitol in 1949 and 1950, recordings on which Davis's lyrical, introspective sound cut against the grain of bebop's angular edges. As Morgenstern has pointed out, these sessions were well received in *Down Beat* and *Metronome*, "if not as enthusiastically as hindsight might demand."[10]

Such positive critical attention did little to assuage Davis, still smarting from the *Down Beat* review of the 1945 recording. In *Miles*, Davis says: "I don't pay any attention to critics, but back then that [review] kind of hurt me, because I was so young and all, and playing on the record and doing good

was very important to me. But Bird and Dizzy told me not to pay that shit critics said no mind, and I didn't; I respected what *they*—Bird and Dizzy—had to say about how good I played."[11] This experience becomes a template, and it resurfaces in Davis's discussion of the cool reception many critics gave to the young musicians he employed during his comeback in the early 1980s:

The guys in the band played so well and they were great to be around. The only problems I had with them was that they were reading the critics, who were saying that the music we were playing wasn't happening. They were young musicians, trying to make their reputations and they thought they were playing with someone that everyone would love. They expected the critics to say everything we played was great. But the critics didn't, and that disturbed them. I had to hip them to how critics felt about me—at least some of them. I told them that so-called critics had done the same thing to Bird when he first started playing that great music he was playing, and that they had also criticized Trane and Philly Joe when they were in my band. I hadn't listened to them then and I wasn't going to listen to them now. After this, me and the guys in my band got closer than ever, and they stopped paying attention to the critics.[12]

Davis makes exceptions in the autobiography for Hentoff, Leonard Feather, and the San Francisco–based critic Ralph Gleason, "the only music critics who didn't write like fools." He notes that Feather and Barry Ulanov, as coeditors of *Metronome* in the 1940s, "understood what was going on with bebop . . . liked it, and wrote good things. But the rest of those white motherfucking critics hated what we were doing. They didn't understand the music. They didn't understand, and hated, the musicians."[13]

Jazz lore is filled with stories about Miles Davis giving writers his backside (though trombonist-turned-writer Mike Zwerin, who as a wet-behind-the-ears college student in 1948 was tapped by Davis to play in *The Birth of the Cool* band, says that later when he interviewed Davis "he always greeted me with a hug"). Writers told many of these stories about themselves willingly, as if a blunt rebuke by Davis were a masochistic hazing ritual required to maintain good standing in the jazz critic fraternity. Ralph Gleason may have been one of the few writers Davis trusted, but this didn't preclude him from confirming that he, too, had been firmly put in his place. Gleason wrote in his liner notes to the Columbia LP of Davis's live date at the Blackhawk club in San Francisco in 1961: "Once [Miles] told me that he had been [past myself] that afternoon en route to Dave Brubeck's. 'Why didn't you stop in?' I asked in a stereotyped social response. 'What for?' he answered with

shattering frankness." In 1969, Martin Williams went to the Columbia studios in New York to watch a recording session where the young guitarist George Benson joined Davis and his celebrated 1960s quintet with saxophonist Wayne Shorter, pianist Herbie Hancock, bassist Ron Carter, and drummer Tony Williams. In his article on the session for *Stereo Review*, Williams portrayed Davis as a careful craftsman, intensely attentive to musical details, but also adroitly working the room with a stream of dialogue by turns friendly, humorous, and wickedly sardonic. Williams himself was targeted: producer Teo Macero told Davis that Williams liked a take of one of his solos that the trumpeter himself found unsatisfactory. What the **** has Martin got to do with it," Davis sneered.[14]

Black writers haven't had any easier a time dealing with Davis. In his essay "Up Close and Personal: Miles Davis and Me," Quincy Troupe notes his trepidation when Davis first granted him an interview in 1985: "I don't know what I expected of Miles, but I had heard of the cavalier and unresponsive way he has treated writers over the

years. Miles was reputed to hate journalists, so I [was] surprised that he [didn't] just bite my head off from the giddiup." Davis was at work on a painting when Troupe entered his home; he kept at it, silent, while Troupe waited nervously. Finally, Davis turned to him, squinted for a closer look at Troupe's dreadlocked hair, and said, "Man, you're a funny lookin' motherfucker." Troupe says he didn't take offense, interpreting the greeting as the sort of "straight to the point and kind of 'country'" social intercourse he knew from growing up in St. Louis, just across the river from Davis's East St. Louis breeding ground. But Troupe soon learned that even homeboy status didn't exempt him from the Davis treatment. "He can be cold on a motherfucker if you come off wrong," Troupe says, recounting a time when Davis dressed him down for not knowing that pianist McCoy Tyner—in Davis's view—"can't play shit." "If you're with Miles and you come off wrong, you will suffer one of three things. First, he might just ignore you altogether. Two, he might turn those ray-gun eyes on you as if he were trying to execute you with a mere stare. Third, he might just curse you out and put you down verbally in such an unbelievably cruel manner that you would never repeat what you have just done."[15]

Amiri Baraka remembers the night in 1960 "when I was a little boy of 25 trying to be a jazz critic. I had gone without benefit of a sponsor to the Village Vanguard where Davis was playing." Baraka—then LeRoi Jones—wandered into the dressing room, hoping to get an interview with the man he had idolized in his youth in Newark as a fledgling trumpeter and bebop aficionado. He was left high and dry. "He waved off my request, mumbling something, I guess, about how he didn't want to be bothered." The disappointed but daring Jones shot back at Davis: "I'd bet you'd do it if I was Nat Hentoff!"[16]

Hentoff—who with Martin Williams, coeditors of the short-lived journal the *Jazz Review*, published LeRoi Jones's first jazz writings in 1960—did succeed in gaining access to Davis in the 1950s, and this proved beneficial to both of their careers. In 1955, Davis was trying to regain his perch at the top of the jazz world after a lackluster period marred by his struggle with heroin addiction. His performance with Thelonious Monk at the Newport Jazz Festival that summer garnered rave reviews, and a new contract with Columbia Records promised better distribution than the smaller Prestige label had given him. That fall, Davis gave Hentoff—then the New York editor of *Down Beat*—an interview in which he spoke enthusiastically about his new band members, Sonny Rollins, Red Garland, Paul Chambers, and Philly Jo Jones. He also surveyed the current jazz scene and offered some pointed opinions:

Saxophonist Jimmy Guiffre and drummer Shelley Manne can really play, but in general the west coast music "gets pretty monotonous even if it's skillfully done." Dave Brubeck has wonderful harmonic ideas, but has no sense of touch and can't swing. Saxophonist Lee Konitz does swing, but relies a bit too much on off-center 7- or 11-note phrases. Richie Powell plays too much comp piano behind Max Roach and Clifford Brown. Charles Mingus's composition "The Mingus Fingers" performed with Lionel Hampton is "one of the best big band records I ever heard," but some of the pieces Mingus and Teo Macero have written for small groups "are like tired modern pictures." Singer Billy Eckstine "needs somebody like Sinatra to tell him what kind of tunes to sing and what kind of background to use." The best drummers are Max Roach, Kenny Clarke, Philly Jo Jones, Art Blakey, and Roy Haynes, though Haynes "has almost destroyed himself working with Sarah [Vaughan]."[17]

Hentoff, meditating on the relationship between jazz musicians and critics, wrote in *The Jazz Life*:

The jazzman, particularly the Negro, is proud of what he has developed by himself. Because of the huge emotional investment he has made in his music, the jazz musician generally respects only the opinions of other musicians who have also worked out their problems and styles by themselves and does not always respect theirs. In addition, the Negro player frequently does not believe that the critics—nearly all of whom are white—have paid the emotional "dues" he has been assessed from the time he was born. Therefore, he reasons, not always with justice, how can the critics possibly understand his message, which is so much more than the notes he plays?[18]

With these serious concerns in mind, Hentoff and Martin Williams, in the *Jazz Review*, encouraged musicians, both in interviews and in their own writing, to air their own critical assessments and meditate on the music's larger social meanings. One of Hentoff's ideas was to hatch a better version of the "Blindfold Test" that Leonard Feather had started in the 1940s in *Metronome* and continued to publish in *Down Beat*. Calling Feather's tests "adventures in skeet shooting," Hentoff aimed to create a more relaxed and mutually enriching atmosphere by identifying the recordings beforehand, transcribing the musicians' reactions, and encouraging them to elaborate on stories about the jazz life. The plan was to engage Miles Davis in a series of these encounters to be published over the course of several issues. Hentoff ended up with only one session, but that one, published in the December 1958 *Jazz Review* under the title "An Afternoon with Miles Davis," turned out to be a classic in the history of jazz letters.

The interview airs a few of Davis's trademark acid dissections ("Oscar [Peterson] makes me sick because he copies everybody. He even had to *learn* how to play the blues. Everybody knows that if you flat a third, you're going to get a blues sound. He learned that and runs it into the ground worse than Billy Taylor. . . .") and dyspeptic asides ("I usually don't buy jazz records. They make me tired and depressed."), but the dominant tone is one of reverence and deep feeling for the accomplishments of his forebearers and the innovations of his contemporaries. Part of the editorial mission of the *Jazz Review* was to combat the sectarian impulse in jazz criticism, to make the case for a jazz "tradition" that transcended any one particular style. Davis did just this in his interview, and with an understated elegance and feeling for the humanity of the music found only rarely in the work of the best critics themselves. Responding to a Bessie Smith record, Davis says, "She affects me the way Leadbelly did, the way some of Paul Laurence Dunbar's

poetry did. I read him once and I almost cried. The Negro Southern speech." On Louis Armstrong's "Potato Head Blues": "You know you can't play anything on a horn that Louis hasn't played—I mean even modern." On Coleman Hawkins: "I learned how to play ballads from Coleman Hawkins. He plays all the chords and you can still hear the ballad." On Ahmad Jamal: "Listen to the way Jamal uses space. He lets it go so you can feel the rhythm section and the rhythm section can feel you." On Thelonious Monk: "A main influence he has been through the years has to do with giving musicians more freedom. They feel that if Monk can do what he does, they can. Monk has been using space for a long time." On the future of

jazz: "I think a movement in jazz is beginning away from the conventional string of chords, and a return to emphasis on melodic rather than harmonic variation. There will be fewer chords but infinite possibilities as to what to do with them."[19]

When Davis focuses on the late 1950s–early 1960s period in *Miles: The Autobiography*, he argues that a conspiracy exists among white jazz critics who, because they feel threatened by Davis (in his opinion), champion avant-garde free players like Archie Shepp, Eric Dolphy, Albert Ayler, Cecil Taylor, and Ornette Coleman. Davis had been an outspoken critic of the "new thing" from the beginning. In a "Blindfold Test" published in *Down Beat* in 1964, among the records Leonard Feather asked Davis to discuss were recent releases by saxophonist Dolphy and pianist Taylor. "That's got to be Eric Dolphy—nobody else could sound that bad!" Davis snorts at Dolphy's tune "Mary Ann," adding, "The next time I see him I'm going to step on his foot." He was even more annoyed by Taylor's "Lena": "Take it off! That's some sad ****, man. In the first place, I hear some Charlie Parker clichés. . . . They don't even fit. Is that what the critics are digging? Them critics better stop having coffee. If there ain't nothing to listen to, they might as well admit it. Just to take something like that and say it's great, because there ain't nothing to listen to, that's like going out and getting a prostitute." In *Miles*, Davis says, "I think some of pushing the free thing among a lot of white music critics was intentional because a lot of them thought that people like me were just getting too popular and too powerful in the music industry. They had to find a way to clip my wings. They loved the melodic, lyrical thing we were doing in *Kind of Blue*, but the popularity of it and the influence we got from doing it scared them."[20]

As a strictly empirical matter, this statement is highly misleading. It is true that the influential white critics Williams, Schuller, Hentoff, Gitler, Morgenstern, and Whitney Balliett, in varying ways and to different degrees, had taken up the cause of the avant-garde. It is also true that these critics remained deeply invested in shaping and propagandizing a jazz canon rooted in blues-based tonalities and timbres, swing rhythm, and improvised solos tethered to the chord structures of American popular songs— so much so, that at a certain point in the 1960s, each of these critics came under attack for being insufficiently supportive of the most radical creative and political impulses of the free jazz movement. The history of American jazz criticism—from debates in the 1930s about big band swing's relationship to the New Orleans and Chicago jazz of the 1920s, down to the fierce polemics over the neo-classical movement of the 1980s and 1990s—is made up of a succession of these kinds of sectarian wars. When Williams and Hentoff argued that Ornette Coleman's polytonality and fourteen-bar blues or John Coltrane's

scalar modalism were legitimate expressions of jazz, they incurred the wrath of traditionalist critics and fans, white and black, who continued to define jazz as the dance-oriented swing style pioneered by Fletcher Henderson, Duke Ellington, Louis Armstrong, Count Basie, Benny Goodman, and Jimmy Lunceford.

The racial dynamics of these jazz culture wars were not nearly as obvious as Davis's umbrella label "the white critics" might suggest. If Davis had been more reflective and honest about the 1960s, he would have noted that the critics who emerged as the most forceful and important advocates of the free jazz music that he despised were the black writers Amiri Baraka and A. B. Spellman. While both of these writers were passionate Davis devotees, the trumpeter's interracial affiliations and influences, huge popularity, and celebrity lifestyle made it difficult to give him top billing in the radical critique of mainstream American culture that accompanied their loyalty to a proto-black cultural nationalist sensibility. In his 1963 book *Blues People*, Baraka

squirmed and shuffled to try to keep Davis tucked inside his concept of an authentic black aesthetic, but Davis kept pushing against the boundaries. "For all his deep commitment to the blues," Baraka wrote, "[Davis] often seems to predicate his playing on the fabrication of some discernible object. And in this he seems closer to Bix Beiderbecke than Louis Armstrong." (Later, Stanley Crouch would note instances of Davis's "removal from the world of Negro trumpet tone," rue his disavowal of "the Afro-American approach to sound and rhythm" in *The Birth of the Cool*, and viciously chastise his late 1960s turn to electronic fusion as a betrayal of jazz authenticity and African American cultural standards.) Davis may have been "an unreconstructed black man," in Quincy Troupe's keen phrase, but he was not the sort who met the purity demands of the Black Arts Movement. Ornette Coleman once called Miles a black man who lives like a white man—a statement that ignores the racism Davis encountered throughout his life but captures an important difference between Davis's experience and that of the 1960s black avant-garde players and older, less recognized bebop veterans who struggled mightily to make ends meet. Davis lived out his own version of the blues, but he sounded different notes than the ones of "alienation, frustration, humiliation and deprivation" that Spellman uncovered in the work and lives of Cecil Taylor, Ornette Coleman, Herbie Nichols, and Jackie McLean in his 1966 book *Four Lives in the Bebop Business*.[21]

Miles Davis was one of the singular artistic voices of the twentieth century; a bandleader who cultivated the talents of three generations of cutting-edge jazz innovators; a fashion symbol who defined cool, elegant, dark-skinned masculinity for the post–World War II generation; and, on a less heroic but perhaps more enduring note, an inveterate woman-beater who serves as a deeply disturbing symbol of misogyny. Can he also be a reliable historian who provides a sober, unbiased guide to the vagaries and racial dynamics of jazz criticism? Of course not. But Davis's intense focus on jazz critics and perspective on jazz criticism—revealed in *Miles: The Autobiography*—is one of the more intriguing aspects of his career. In the end, one gets the sense that Davis tried to assume the role of super–jazz critic, the final arbiter on who one should listen to and why.

1   Dan Morgenstern, "Sippin' at Miles' or a Press Conference in Reverse," *Metronome* (May 1961): 8, 46. Gene Grove, "Jazz: The Authors Meet the Critics," *New York Post* (February 21, 1961).

2   In my re-creation of the "press conference in reverse," the dialogue quoted comes from Dan Morgenstern's account of the event in his 1961 *Metronome* dispatch. Nat Hentoff vouched for the accuracy of Morgenstern's account in a telephone discussion with me in April 2000.

3   Don Nelson, "Cool But Not Crazy," *New York Post* (April 13, 1958). George Marek, "From the Dive to the Dean, Jazz Becomes Respectable," *Good Housekeeping* (June 1956): 120.

4   Nat Hentoff, *The Jazz Life* (New York: Da Capo, 1975 [1961]), 205–6.

5   The Dizzy Gillespie quote comes from his memoir (with Al Fraser), *To Be, or Not to Bop* (New York: Da Capo, 1985 [1979]), 315. The 1960 Newport festival riot and musicians' rebellion were extensively covered in the jazz and general press. See Gene Lees, "The Trouble," *Down Beat* (August 18, 1960): 20–24; Thomasina Norford, "Newport Freezes Jazz Festival," *New York Amsterdam News* (July 23, 1960): 1, 34; Nat Hentoff, "Bringing Dignity to Jazz," in *The Jazz Life* (New York: Da Capo, 1961 [1975]): 98–116; "The Wild Newport Stomp," *Life* (July 18, 1960); Hsio Wen Shih, "Jazz in Print," *The Jazz Review* (September/October, 1960): 32, 34–35; Whitney Balliett, "Musical Events," *New Yorker* (July 16, 1960): 84–88; Robert Reisner, "The Newport Blues," *Village Voice* (July 7, 1960); and Ken Sobol, "Beatnik, Stay Home," *Village Voice* (July 14, 1960): 7, 12.

6   Greg Tate, "Silence, Exile, and Cunning: Miles Davis in Memoriam," in *Flyboy in the Buttermilk: Essays on Contemporary America* (New York: Simon and Schuster, 1992), 89. Miles Davis with Quincy Troupe, *Miles: The Autobiography* (New York: Simon and Schuster, 1989), 280–81.

7   Stanley Crouch, "Play the Right Thing," *The New Republic* (February 12, 1990), reprinted in Gary Carner, ed., *The Miles Davis Companion: Four Decades of Commentary* (New York: Schirmer Books, 1996), 39.

Emily Bernard, "Black Anxiety, White Influence: Carl Van Vechten and the Harlem Renaissance" (Ph.D. dissertation, Yale University, 1998).

8   Amiri Baraka, "Homage to Miles Davis," reprinted in Carner, 50.

9   Stephen Davis, "My Ego Only Needs a Good Rhythm Section," *The Real Paper* (March 21, 1973), reprinted in Carner, 161; Dan Morgenstern, "Miles in Motion," *Down Beat* (September 3, 1970), reprinted in Carner, 113; Eric Nisensen, "Hangin' Out With Daffy Davis," introduction to '*Round About Midnight: A Portrait of Miles Davis*, reprinted in Carner, 172–84.

10   Dan Morgenstern, "The Complete Prestige Recordings," reprinted in Carner, 8–9.

11   *Miles: The Autobiography*, 76.

12   *Miles: The Autobiography*, 356.

13   *Miles: The Autobiography*, 67, 353.

14   Mike Zwerin, liner notes for *The Complete Birth of the Cool* (Capitol Records, 1998). Ralph Gleason, "At the Blackhawk," reprinted in Carner, 84. Martin Williams, *Jazz Masters in Transition: 1957–1969* (New York: Da Capo, 1970,: 276.

15   Quincy Troupe, *Miles and Me* (Berkeley: University of California Press, 2000): 27, 63.

16   Carner, 41.

17   Nat Hentoff interview with Miles Davis, *Down Beat* (November 2, 1955), reprinted in Carner, 58–64.

18   Hentoff, *The Jazz Life*, 251.

19   Nat Hentoff, "An Afternoon with Miles Davis," *Jazz Review* (December 1958), reprinted in Carner, 86–92.

20   *Miles: The Autobiography*, 271–72. Leonard Feather, "Blindfold Test (Miles Davis)," *Down Beat* (June 18, 1964).

21   LeRoi Jones (Amiri Baraka), *Blues People: Negro Music in White America* (New York: William Morrow and Company, 1963), 210. Stanley Crouch, "Play the Right Thing," and "Miles in the Sky," in Carner, 21–40, 98–102. Quincy Troupe, "Up Close and Personal: Miles Davis and Me," *Conjunctions* 16 (1991): 88. A. B. Spellman, *Four Lives in the Bebop Business* (New York: Limelight Editions 1985 [1966]).

Birdland, New York, 1960.
Photograph by
Beuford Smith.

Pianist Ahmad Jamal, born in Pittsburgh in 1930, has been one of the most commercially successful small-group leaders in jazz for five decades. Known for a light right-hand touch and steadily flowing improvisations, Jamal began playing with older musicians in Pittsburgh at age eleven. At the beginning of his professional career, he was a member of St. Louisan George Hudson's touring band, a group that earlier had included the young Clark Terry (the teenaged Miles had sat in on occasion with the Hudson band in St. Louis).

Working out of Chicago by the 1950s, Jamal's small groups became some of the most popular in jazz, recording such albums as the live *Ahmad's Blues* (1958) with his trio of bassist Israel Crosby and influential New Orleans drummer Vernell Fournier. During this period, Miles Davis recorded several tunes after Jamal had recorded them, from standards such as "But Not For Me" and "Autumn Leaves" to Jamal originals such as "Ahmad's Blues" and "New Rhumba," the latter in a Gil Evans orchestral arrangement for the *Miles Ahead* album in 1957. Davis was impressed by the rhythmic sense in Jamal's music, and with what Davis later called Jamal's "concept of space, his lightness of touch, his understatement. . . ."

Jamal credits Pittsburgh's musical tradition in his own work. "Pittsburgh meant everything to me and it still does," he said, citing Pittsburgh pianists Earl Hines, Billy Strayhorn, Mary Lou Williams, and especially Erroll Garner as important colleagues and influences. He has led working bands since 1951, mainly leading small ensembles (he finds the term "trio" to be misleading and limiting). Jamal produced a string of excellent recordings in the 1990s, including the live *Chicago Revisited* (1992) and remains a top draw in clubs around the world.

"Sensational Pulse": Ahmad Jamal

interview by Benjamin Cawthra

BC: You are from Pittsburgh, but you have a connection to St. Louis.

AJ: The man that made me leave my happy home, George Hudson, was originally from Pittsburgh, but he became a St. Louis personality, because he worked there. In fact, the majority of my colleagues I worked with in the Hudson band were from St. Louis. Out of that band came Clark Terry, Ernie Wilkins, myself, and that band made me leave Pittsburgh when I was only seventeen, and it was an East St. Louis/St. Louis band.

BC: When did you first become aware of a trumpeter who was three or four years older than you named Miles Davis?

AJ: Well, Miles has always been one of the great influences in music, and I was aware of Miles early on when he was making those records with Gerry Mulligan, those 78s on Capitol Records. I think I had heard of him even before then, but I remember really focusing in on Miles when he did those. They were spectacular records, spectacular arrangements, and he always had a very successful career, and deservedly so. But I think that was my first awareness of Miles as a great contributing factor in twentieth-century music.

BC: How did it feel a few years later when Miles Davis, who was also very popular, kept citing you in interviews as a major influence and kept recording tunes you had done?

AJ: I was in a panic, because I hadn't copywritten "New Rhumba." I got the word that Columbia wanted to get licensing for "New Rhumba," which I had written back in '48 but never had it copywritten. It was a panic when I got a call saying, "Send us a license." I had to run out and get the thing copywritten. That's what it was like at first, when I discovered that Gil Evans had taken note-for-note the things we had done with the small ensemble and adapted it for big band. So it was a panic. I didn't

want to lose any time there [laughs]. But it was complimentary, of course. Miles began to do a lot of my things. One was a Red Garland recording of "Ahmad's Blues."

BC: Did you become friends at that point?

AJ: Miles was a great supporter of mine, his entire life. A great supporter of mine. He always came to see me. And I remember a great occasion during a festival in Finland. I was the first person he saw when he came out of a car with throngs of people around him, because he was a charismatic person. Came out of the car and came right to me. And I remember he came to the Smiling Dog Saloon in Cleveland. A very nondescript place. And he pops in because he knew I was there. The last time I talked to Miles I was in George Butler's office [at Columbia] doing some business and Miles happened to call at that time, and George said, "You know who's here?" And Miles said, "Who?" "Mr. Jamal is here." That's the last time I talked to Miles, although we lived just

a block and a half from each other. I was on Seventy-fifth Street on the West Side and he was on Seventy-seventh. So Miles was a great supporter of mine.

BC: Here is a quote from Miles: "Listen to the way Jamal uses space. He lets it go so that you can feel the rhythm section, and the rhythm section can feel you. It's not crowded. Ahmad is one of my favorites. I live until he makes another record."

AJ: That's a great statement, isn't it? What better compliment, what better thing to say about a peer than emulation and that kind of compliment. We all revel in that and love that. I think he was talking about my discipline as opposed to my space. People call it space, but I call it discipline. That's my answer to the people who try to analyze what I'm doing. I'm a very disciplined person musically, and I think it's important in music to be aware of the fact that in music you can't overdo, you can't be excessive in anything in life. You have to sometimes be a minimalist.

BC: When you heard a Miles Davis record or had a chance to hear him live, did you hear some of the same musical values in his music? What might you have heard that you related to?

AJ: We're contemporaries, number one. There's not that much age difference. Number two, we both grew up in several eras: we were both around in the days of the big bands—Jimmie Lunceford, Duke Ellington. Then there was the revolutionary period of Charlie Parker and Dizzy Gillespie. And then here comes the electronic age. Three eras. So when you have people that have embraced all three eras, you have many things in common.

BC: Such as?

AJ: A pulse, a sensation, a body of work that is very selective. You're going to have certain compositions that you do. I grew up with a wealth of music from my aunt in North Carolina, and I learned a lot of the standards. So at eleven years old in Pittsburgh I was playing with guys sixty years old.

That's what we have in common, those three eras. Gil Evans, Thad Jones—the same way. Thad wrote in such a way that it made your hair stand on end because he was drawing on three eras. Very few people can write like Thad Jones. Jimmy Heath, the Heath Brothers, they are also prodigies. So all of us had many things in common. Sensational pulse. As Milt Jackson said, "knowing where 'one' is." Miles loved all of those musicians. Sometimes the "one" is lost now. The pulse is lost because we have a departure from reality in some of the music that's being played today, in spite of the great skill that is out there.

BC: How did you understand Miles from the perspective of being a band leader?

AJ: We were both leaders. People ask me, "Did you ever work with Miles?" Well, no, I couldn't work with Miles. I was busy working with my own thing like he was. And I've had people that I have fostered that have done great things, and he has that parallel. If you look at his roster of sidemen, they have all gone and done great things. Cannonball, Ron Carter. With my group I had the great bass player Israel Crosby, who was working between me and Benny Goodman, and many others who were imitated and sought after. People are still playing Israel's lines. I also had Ray Crawford, who was the first one to

come up with the bongo effect on the frets of his guitar. On one of my early records "Billy Boy," that's Ray Crawford. He was the one that started it. Barney Kessler, Herb Ellis . . . Oscar Peterson used to come in and listen to us at the 115 Club on Forty-seventh Street. Vern Fournier is the most imitated—plagiarized—drummer in the world, to this day. And then Miles came along and he heard what we were doing with "New Rhumba" and the medley, "I Don't Want to Be Kissed," all that kind of stuff. Miles was not the only one who emulated what we were doing. That's a misconception. So I've had groups that have been influential. And part of that has been the players I've been associated with, just like Miles. We've had the fortune to pick the right people at the right time.

BC: What do you remember about Miles's first band, which played so many of your compositions and standards you had recorded? What made that group connect with audiences?

AJ: What made that group so popular? Miles Davis. He made any group popular. His whole demeanor, his whole approach. You know, Miles did a lot of things. Like Dizzy said, Miles was the one that stopped musicians from playing 40/20. When we did the Showboat in Philadelphia and all those rooms that we all were doing, we'd do forty minutes on, twenty minutes off, five sets a night. Forty minutes on, twenty minutes off. You know who stopped doing that? Miles. And later, he was the one who was also more animated on stage. Some people took issue with him walking around, but then that became part of the decorum to be animated on stage, not to be at one spot. So he did many things that are still sticking today. And that group you're talking about was one of the spectacular groups. Why? Because you had John Coltrane, you had all the other players. But still, everything depends on the leader. I don't care who you have. You can have great musicians. But if your whole demeanor, your whole image is weak, you're going to have a weak group. So you have to be strong. And Miles was a strong personality. And you must be that way. You must almost be tyrannical.

BC: No question, he had a strong personality.

AJ: The first chair of a symphony is not going to respect any conductor who isn't a dominating force. That's why they loved Toscanini. All these great conductors are respected because of their tyrannical attitudes. If you don't have that dominating personality, I don't care who you have, it's not going to work. The group falls apart. He had many great groups. Tony Williams, Ron Carter, and Herbie Hancock, that was another fabulous group. He didn't ever have a weak group. Even in the electronic age, he had the fabulous Marcus Miller. Marcus is a brilliant young musician. So he never stopped. He had that uncanny knack of selecting those people that complemented him to the utmost. But here again, the reason why those groups were successful was because of Miles.

BC: What kind of a musician was Red Garland, and what contribution do you think he made to the Miles Davis sound?

AJ: Well, one thing about Red, be careful, because he could knock you out with one punch. That's for sure [laughs]! One would never know it, but he was not an exhibitionist when it came to his physical abilities. He was an exhibitionist on piano. I liked Red. In fact, the last tour he made, my ex-bassist Jamil Nasser took him to Tokyo. He had a big, big following. Jamil was the only one who could get Red on a plane, and I think that was Red's last field of work, in Tokyo. But Red was one of the Philadelphia personalities, and certainly was sought after a great deal. He and Philly Jo Jones worked together a lot. And we shared the stage, shared the billing a couple of times, too. That group wasn't Miles's group then, it was a group composed of local Philadelphians. And Red was a very interesting player. He did two things of mine, "Billy Boy" and "Ahmad's Blues," of course. I was always fascinated by Red and his approach, because he did the different chordal structures. He did different chordal structures completely. Very good player. Fascinating player.

BC: What do you think of the suggestion that Miles Davis saw him as someone with the "Ahmad Jamal" sound?

AJ: I think he saw Red Garland the same way he saw Bill Evans, the same way he saw Herbie Hancock, and all of his players. I think he saw them as individuals. At certain times they had reference to me, but certainly not one that would impose my personality on them completely. I think he sought those people for what they were worth within themselves.

BC: What did you think of the direction Miles went in the late sixties?

AJ: I thought it was great. I laughed. Because Miles could just about accomplish anything musically, and he did. The electronic things he did were great, fascinating to me. Completely fascinating and funny because people took exception. And he got flak. He didn't care one iota. He just went ahead and made the money, made the mark, and in the eighties he was doing everything

from Prince to since. And it worked. He had some great writers. He had Marcus Miller doing that stuff, and it came off great. I enjoyed it. I didn't have a chance to engage my ears to everything he was doing, but it was funny to me, and it was even funnier because it was phenomenally successful.

BC: So you found the response of the jazz world to be humorous?

AJ: Oh, sure. We don't care anything about what critics and these people say. The point is that he was doing something that people liked. He loved it, and everybody who had any musical sense knew what Miles was doing. If you had the experience that we have been fortunate to have had, living through all those eras, you knew exactly what Miles was doing. He was smart. Very clever. He was his best PR person, musically, clotheswise, the whole thing. And a good investor, too [laughs].

BC: What made Miles Davis the force that he was in music?

AJ: Well, Miles was very fortunate. He was very gifted, very blessed. He was in the right places at the right times, musically. He had the type of parentage that allowed him to go to Juilliard, a place that I wanted to go. That part of my career was aborted, and sometimes I regret that because I think that the young mind should always be buffered. We lose a lot of our greats because they aren't buffered enough. Charlie Parker, Fats Navarro, Tadd Dameron, Billie Holiday. A lot of people we lose, because at eleven years old you shouldn't be in nightclubs. You don't know the difference between yes and no. You're a body of clay, you're absorbing everything, and Miles was fortunate to have exposure in Juilliard and some of the other benefits of his background. So number one, he was in the right place in the right time. Number two, he was extremely talented. And number three, he had the camaraderie of people like Charlie Parker and Dizzy Gillespie. It doesn't get much better than that, you see? And that's what's missing now. You have this great age of technology, a wonderful age of technology. The youngsters are playing their butts off. Phenomenal players. But what's missing now is camaraderie. And the spirit of the music. You don't have the revolutionary spirit of Charlie Parker or Dizzy Gillespie. The camaraderie is missing.

BC: Thinking back on your friendship with Miles, what stands out?

AJ: The thing that I think about is his place on Seventy-seventh Street. If you didn't belong there, don't go in there [laughs]. I had a couple of occasions of going over there during that period when he was off, when he didn't work for six or seven years. Interesting times for me and interesting times for him. Those are the close encounters I had with him. They were brief but close encounters with Miles. And I lived on Seventy-fifth Street. We were only a block and a half from each other. So I remember those two occasions on which I went to his house. Interesting place. Interesting man [laughs]. Interesting man. He came running downstairs, and of course he was delighted to see me. And I was delighted to see him, because at that time, I needed him.

BC: He probably needed you.

AJ: I think so. He used to come down to the Village Gate, because I was the artist in residence there for a long time. We used to pack the place. Unbelievable. And it was a big, big, cavernous place. And Miles was off during that period. He used to limousine himself. He could afford it, too. He'd go down to the Village Gate to see his contemporary, Mr. Jamal. A quality but not quantitative relationship. And that's the important thing, to have a quality relationship, not one of quantity. Because to me, familiarity breeds contempt, and we didn't have one of contempt, and that I appreciate. That's the main thing. We had a quality relationship, but not a contemptuous one. Because I'm very private, and I think Miles was private to a great extent. And it worked. It worked for me, it worked for him.

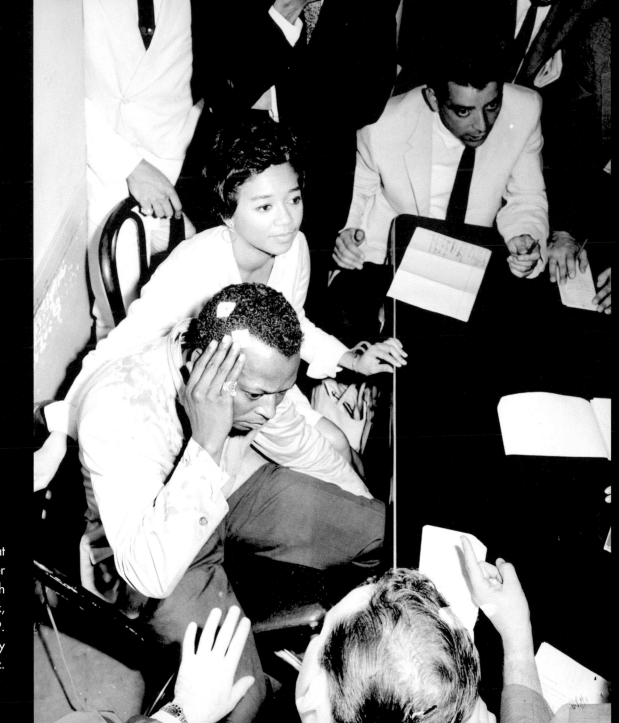

With wife Frances at press briefing after Birdland incident, 54th Precinct, New York, 1959. Photograph by Vincent Lopez.

Miles is just a brand new Negro in his thinking.

—Harold Lovett[1]

Nothing seemed to cause more consternation in the late 1950s than Miles Davis's stage demeanor. Davis's refusal to announce tunes or introduce his band members and his habit of leaving the stage during the solos of his sidemen were, for some, signs of malice and hostility, and for others, the utter embodiment of hipness. Those who admired Davis's attitude found it political in nature, the ultimate refusal of the Jim Crow expectation that African Americans smile, grin, and entertain for the pleasure of white folks. Miles's style— that confluence of sonic beauty, timing, introspection, sartorial elegance, masculine swagger, and utter contempt for racism—projected an attitude of "unabashed *badness*" that filled in the symbolic hole left by Charlie Parker's untimely death in 1955.[2]

For his fans, Davis's music justified all. The poignant lyricism of his ballads (including "Round About Midnight," "My Funny Valentine," and "Nature Boy"), with their scooped, shaded, shaped lines defining a three-dimensional space of sonic experience, belied the "meanness" Miles projected in interviews and on-stage behavior. As a musician who spoke with *Ebony* noted, "Nobody in the world can play music as beautifully as he does and not be a beautiful person inside."[3]

Writings of the late fifties and early sixties offered many explanations for Miles's "enigmatic" behavior. His father speculated that Miles's experiences with racism in East St. Louis as well as drug addiction had put a "hard crust" on him. An unnamed musician insisted that his aloofness was an "extreme defense mechanism" that covered a shy, sensitive person who easily could be hurt.[4] Miles himself insisted that everything he did on stage had a reason. He didn't announce the titles to pieces because he only decided at the last moment what he was going to play next. As for walking offstage during the solos of other musicians: "I ain't going to just stand up there and be detracting from him. What am I going to stand up there *for*? I ain't no model, and I don't sing or dance, and I damn sure ain't no Uncle Tom just to be up there grinning."[5]

Miles, Politics, and Image

by Ingrid Monson

Others viewed such anti-showmanship as a calculated pose, a position most elegantly articulated by Ralph Ellison:

The result was a grim comedy of racial manners; with the musicians employing a calculated surliness and rudeness, treating the audience very much as many white merchants in poor Negro neighborhoods treat their customers, and the white audiences were shocked at first but learned quickly to accept such treatment as evidence of "artistic" temperament. Then comes a comic reversal. Today the white audience expects the rudeness as part of the entertainment. If it fails to appear the audience is disappointed.[6]

If Charlie Parker was the quintessential jazz hero for the bebop generation, Miles Davis, through his combination of musical mastery, attitude, and visual style provided an image of defiance suitable for the civil rights years. His sound was lyrical, with infinite grace, intensity, and excitement, yet also indelibly shaped by the historical moment when it appeared, that is, in the midst of the civil rights movement, African nationalism, and the Cold War.

If Miles Davis's stage demeanor and disdainful treatment of fawning fans has been interpreted widely as overt resistance to racism, the particular trajectory of Davis's relationship to the historical moment of the civil rights movement is less widely known. The task of this article is to examine three politically marked moments in Davis's career—the beating he suffered at the hands of New York City police outside Birdland in August 1959, the benefit concert for the African Research Foundation performed in May 1961, and the fundraising concert undertaken in February 1964 on behalf of the

Student Nonviolent Coordinating Committee (SNCC), Congress of Racial Equality (CORE), and the National Association for the Advancement of Colored People (NAACP) Legal Defense Fund. Like so many musicians in his peer group, Miles, in the early 1960s, demonstrated an interest in both Africa and the civil rights struggle. The powerful interplay between Davis's stormy personality, the politics of the world around him, and the symbolics of sound made the trumpeter one of the great heroes of modern jazz.

The Birdland Incident

Miles Davis offered the following account of the Birdland beating, which took place on August 26, 1959:

I had just finished doing an Armed Forces Day, you know, Voice of America and all that bullshit. I had just walked this pretty white girl named Judy out to get a cab. She got in the cab, and I'm standing there in front of Birdland wringing wet because it's a hot, steaming, muggy night in August. This white policeman comes up to me and tells me to move on. At the time I was doing a lot of boxing and so I thought to myself, I ought to hit this motherfucker because I knew what he was doing. But instead I said, "Move on, for what? I'm working downstairs. That's my name up there,

Miles Davis," and I pointed up to my name on the marquee all up in lights. He said, "I don't care where you work, I said move on! If you don't move on I'm going to arrest you." I just looked at his face real straight and hard, and I didn't move. Then he said, "You're under arrest!"[7]

When Davis refused to allow Officer Gerald Kilduff to arrest him, a struggle ensued during which Miles was beaten about the head with a billy club by a detective named Donald Rolker, who had rushed to the scene to assist Kilduff. Davis was arrested, his cabaret card confiscated, and he required from two to five stitches in his head according to newspaper accounts.[8] The struggle was so noisy that members of the Hodges-Robbins orchestra who were rehearsing across the street put their mike booms out of the window and captured on tape New York City's finest calling Miles Davis the n-word. *Down Beat* received a letter suggesting that Davis's attitude was to blame for the incident, but, in general, the jazz community, domestic and international, was indignant.[9]

In October 1959, after a two-day trial, Davis was acquitted of the disorderly conduct charge. Judge Kenneth Phipps noted that taking a breath of fresh air between sets was perfectly normal behavior for musicians at nightclub engagements.[10] Davis was tried a second time on the charge of third-degree assault and was acquitted in January 1960. Although a suit against the New York City Police Department was announced, the attorney retained to file the claim missed the deadline and Davis consequently lost the $500,000 damage suit.[11] As Miles recounted in *Miles: The Autobiography*, "That changed my whole life and whole attitude again, made me bitter and cynical again when I was starting to feel good about the things that had changed in this country."[12]

The year 1960 proved significant in both political and musical terms: the student lunch counter sit-ins began, the controversy over Ornette Coleman raged within the jazz community, several African nations became independent, Charles Mingus and Max Roach organized the Newport Rebel Festival, the *Original Faubus Fables* and *Freedom Now Suite* were recorded, Fidel Castro took up temporary residence in Harlem, and Martin Luther King, Jr., was arrested shortly before the 1960 presidential election. Several benefit concerts and sit-ins for civil rights organizations and African independence took place at New York nightspots, especially the Village Gate.[13] Max Roach's *Freedom Now Suite* included a piece dedicated to the

victims of the Sharpeville massacre in South Africa, and Randy Weston's *Uhuru Afrika* (Freedom Africa) was dedicated to the emerging African nations.[14]

Miles's personal experience with racially biased law enforcement, thus, had taken place at a time of considerable political and musical controversy. Davis's next major project, *Sketches of Spain*, was at least partly motivated by an interest in Africa. As he explained in his autobiography:

In the Andalusian area you have a lot of African influence in the music, architecture, and in the whole culture, and a lot of African blood in the people. So you had a black African thing up in the feeling of the music, in the bag pipes and trumpets and drums.[15]

The Moors, who conquered Spain in the eighth century and brought an Islamic influence to Andalusia, lived north of the Senegal River in present-day Mauritania.[16] Davis's interest in the African element in Spain was shared by a broader segment of the African American community in the mid to late 1950s. Charles Walker, for example, ran a story in 1955 titled "The African Imprint in Spain." Walker had a regular column on Africa published in the *Amsterdam News*.[17] When *Sketches of Spain* was released, a press announcement proudly advertised that a diplomat from Ghana's mission to the UN had attended Miles Davis's press conference to celebrate the occasion.[18]

Benefit for the African Research Foundation

On May 19, 1961, Miles Davis performed a benefit concert for the African Research Foundation at Carnegie Hall.[19] Featuring Gil Evans's orchestra and Davis's quintet with Wynton Kelly, Hank Mobley, Paul Chambers, and Jimmy Cobb, the concert is better known by its recording, *Miles Davis at Carnegie Hall*.[20]

The African Research Foundation (now the African Medical and Research Foundation) was founded in 1957 by a group of three white doctors concerned about making health care services available in post-independence Africa. Known as the "flying doctors" they developed mobile units (first on trucks, then on planes) that took primary health care services to remote regions of sub-Saharan Africa.[21] By 1961 they constituted a multiracial organization committed to the goal of leaving black Africans in charge wherever they operated. Julius Nyerere, head of the

TANU (Tanganyika African National Union) and soon to be the first president of independent Tanganyika (now Tanzania), was a frequent visitor to the African Research Foundation (ARF) office in New York, something that may have interested Miles.[22]

Davis became aware of the organization through Jean Bach, a friend of founder Thomas Rees and someone whom Miles dated briefly.[23] According to Dr. Ronald Moss, those most heavily involved with the organization were "all jazz nuts," regularly attending concerts and performances in New York. Davis had been reluctant to accept a concert hall engagement in New York, but his interest in the organization apparently tipped the balance. Carnegie Hall was booked, Gil Evans's orchestra engaged, and plans were made to record the concert. Joe Eula's poster for the concert, also the basis for the album cover, featured Davis's signature 'S' posture emerging from the mouth of an elephant. The concert sold out and raised $25,000 toward a mobile medical unit.[24]

The concert nevertheless was picketed by Max Roach and several demonstrators, who questioned the politics of the African Research Foundation. During Davis's performance of "Someday My Prince Will Come" (the opener for the second half), Roach and a companion emerged, sat down on stage, and held up placards reading "Africa or the Africans," "Freedom Now," and "Medicine without Murrow Please." Davis left the stage angered and returned only

after guards had removed Roach from the stage. According to George Simon, who reviewed the concert for *The Herald Tribune*, "Davis, who till then had been playing his usual fine, cool trumpet, returned and began blowing some of the wildest, free-swinging jazz this reviewer has heard from his horn in many a moon."[25] Roach's protest, it seemed, had a beneficial effect on Davis's performance. Afterward, Max apologized for interrupting the concert.[26]

The demonstrators accused the liberal, predominantly white organization of having connections with CIA front groups and, consequently, of playing into the hands of colonialism. According to Ronald Moss, Max had been misled into thinking that the ARF was a "white supremacist organization in league with South Africa" when, in fact, the organization had no contact with South Africa until after Nelson Mandela became president. Nevertheless, the ARF was a liberal rather than revolutionary nationalist organization.[27]

African nationalist sentiment, it should be remembered, was at a fever pitch in the spring of 1961 in the wake of the assassination of the Congo's Patrice Lumumba. Max Roach and Abbey Lincoln had participated in the demonstrations at the United Nations that included members of the United African Nationalist Movement, the Liberation Committee for Africa, and On Guard. Other musicians, like Dizzy Gillespie, also were interested in events in Africa. Dizzy premiered a work dedicated to the newly independent African nations at Carnegie Hall on March 3 and participated in a celebration of African Freedom Day in April.[28]

The demonstration was not the only source of conflict affecting the May 19 concert. Earlier in the day Davis had angered Teo Macero by canceling the scheduled recording of the concert, despite the fact that arrangements for moving Columbia's recording equipment already had been made. When Macero arrived at the hall he asked a hall employee if he had any recording equipment. A small monaural 1/4 track deck (a Webcor) that recorded at 7 1/2 rps, a mixing pot, and four microphones were found; Macero recorded surreptitiously and illegally from the front

left of the house. After the concert Macero threw the tape at Davis, exclaiming, This could have been a great record!" A few hours later, in the middle of the night, Davis called Macero and asked him to arrange for the release of the tape. To secure permission from Carnegie Hall, Macero talked the shop steward into helping him comply retroactively with union rules.[29]

What should have been a stereo recording, consequently, is a mono recording made under technically challenging circumstances. The selections with the Gil Evans orchestra suffer most from the inadequate recording equipment. In addition, the deletion of several small group tunes from the original release has obscured the strength of the quintet's performance that evening.[30] Indeed, on "Walkin'," "Teo," "Oleo," "No Blues," and "I Thought About You," the rhythm section of Wynton Kelly, Paul Chambers, and Jimmy Cobb is truly impressive, anticipating aspects of the open, adventurous, accompanimental style that Ron Carter, Herbie Hancock, and Tony Williams would perfect a few years later. Miles scoops, slides, and soars over the top.

A Civil Rights Benefit

Benefit concerts were the most obvious form of political participation by jazz musicians in the early 1960s. Such events came in many different varieties, from small club-hosted events to gala concerts at concert halls and stadiums, and they benefited many different causes including civil rights, African independence, and black labor organizations. At many of these events jazz musicians appeared alongside gospel singers and folk musicians, or on the same bill with more mainstream entertainers such as Frank Sinatra and Sammy Davis, Jr. Actors and writers also were among those drafted for these fundraising events, including Sidney Poitier, Ruby Dee, Ossie Davis, Peter Lawford, Marlon Brando, and Lorraine Hansberry.

Among those who participated in fundraising events were proponents of a full range of jazz styles including Count Basie, Louis Armstrong, Miles Davis, Duke Ellington, Cannonball Adderley, Thelonious Monk, Dizzy Gillespie, Dave Brubeck, John Coltrane, Sarah Vaughan, Prince Lasha, Ella Fitzgerald, Paul Bley, Don Friedman, Max Roach, Abbey Lincoln, Eric Dolphy, Charles Mingus, and many more. For jazz fans born after 1960, the number of fundraising concerts done by well-known jazz musicians in the early sixties, as well as the diverse jazz styles represented, likely will surprise. Ever since Frank Kofsky's *Black Nationalism and the Revolution in*

Music, free jazz commonly is associated with the raging politics of the sixties. Relatively few are aware of the aesthetically broad range of African and non–African American musicians who regularly lent their names to civil rights organizations in the years between Greensboro and Black Power.[31]

Although socially minded concerts had been a feature of the jazz landscape since the 1930s when Duke Ellington, Benny Carter, and many others played for a variety of causes including the Scottsboro Boys and the NAACP, a threshold was crossed on February 1, 1960, when the student lunch counter sit-ins began in Greensboro, North Carolina.[32] The speed with which these protests spread across the South announced a new period of direct mass action whose symbolism, events, and ideologies deeply affected not only the jazz world, but American society as a whole.

Benefit concerts occurred in response to major events in the civil rights movement, including the Greensboro sit-ins, the Freedom Rides of 1961, the Birmingham movement and March on Washington in 1963, and the Mississippi voter registration projects of 1964. Although benefit concerts generated considerable amounts of money for civil rights organizations, their purpose and popularity cannot be fully explained by the economic dimension alone. Many of these events offered a dramatic forum in which northern audiences could hear directly from southern activists about day-to-day life on the front lines of the movement. They also created social spaces in which musicians and audiences could feel like they were "doing something" to aid the southern struggle.

It is important to keep in mind that participation in fundraising events did not always indicate full endorsement of a particular organization's political ideology. As Clark Terry recalled, "All of the organizations SNCC, CORE, NAACP—all of them were very, very important organizations, as far as we were concerned. And we supported them all." In the early 1960s Terry performed at benefits for CORE, SNCC, the Southern Christian Leadership Conference (SCLC), and the A. Philip Randolph's Negro American Labor Council (NALC). Many other musicians performed benefits for multiple political organizations, including Dizzy Gillespie (CORE, National Urban League [NUL], NALC, SCLC), Dave Brubeck (SCLC, NAACP, SNCC, CORE), and Max Roach and Abbey Lincoln (CORE, SNCC, NAACP, SCLC, Malcolm X). Musicians seemed to respond to particular events in the civil rights movement rather than show exclusive loyalty to particular organizations. After the passage of the Civil Rights Act of 1964 and the Voting Rights Act of 1965, the number of events sponsored by well-known civil rights organizations decreased, as politically related concerts shifted to black nationalist arts organizations, where the explicitly political and spiritual force of black music, dance, and art was celebrated. Among the best known of these organizations was Amiri Baraka's Black Arts Repertory Theatre/School (BARTS), whose regulars in 1965 included Sun Ra, Albert Ayler, Milford Graves, and Andrew Hill.[33]

The most aesthetically celebrated civil rights benefit concert is undoubtedly Miles Davis's Lincoln's birthday (February 12, 1964) concert for Mississippi and Louisiana Voter Registration, which benefited SNCC, CORE, and the NAACP Legal Defense fund. We probably owe the live recording of the Lincoln's birthday concert to another dispute Davis had with producer Teo Macero, this time over the release of *Quiet Nights* in 1963. Davis was so angry over the premature release of this unfinished work with Gil Evans that he refused to record in Columbia studios for most of 1963 and all of 1964. To keep up their catalog, Columbia was forced to make live recordings.[34]

A coalition of civil rights organizations benefited from the concert, but this collaboration was not a voluntary arrangement entered into freely, but a condition forced on the groups by Steven Currier, the principal financier of the

Voter Education Project (VEP). Currier's Taconic foundation had been instrumental in launching the VEP after the Freedom Rides in 1961. After the March on Washington, an event that required a great deal of compromise on the part of individual organizations, movement unity received considerable emphasis. The Taconic foundation insisted on a joint fundraising effort to support the voter registration initiative. As Marvin Rich, principal fundraiser for CORE, recalled: "None of the groups liked it, but we couldn't quite say no to him because he had big bucks which he would give to each of us." A year earlier Davis had been asked to participate in a gala SNCC fund raising event at Carnegie Hall, but his rhythm section had just resigned.[35]

Miles Davis allowed his personal stationery to be used in a letter advertising the Lincoln's birthday benefit concert. Its introduction outlined the principal aims of the voter registration efforts:

The civil rights movement is launching an all-out drive to register Negro citizens in Mississippi and Louisiana. Hundreds of field workers are pouring into these states at this moment, setting up registration clinics, preparing potential voters for registration tests, transporting citizens to the registrars' offices. All of this costs money—and the most urgent need is for cars—durable automobiles that can transport our people into and out of the widespread rural areas of both states.[36]

A handwritten note to Julia Prettyman, the administrative secretary of the New York SNCC office, explained the purpose of the letter: "This is the so-called 'rich folks letter,' so titled and written by Val Coleman [a CORE organizer]. We're typing individual copies for people we hope will buy—like Nelson Rockefeller, etc. We're using this stationery rather than CORE, SNCC, or NAACP paper, hoping it will catch their attention as something different." They also telephoned people directly to urge attendance of the concert.[37]

Although the benefit had been planned a few weeks in advance, Miles didn't tell his band that they would be waiving their customary fees until the night of the performance. Since the band hadn't worked for several months some of the sidemen were not happy about Davis having committed their earnings without their consent. Miles, who made a six-figure salary at the time, was, after all, in a much better position to forego income than they were. Ron Carter was particularly annoyed; he wanted to be paid and also to decide how much he wanted to give and to which organization. Carter felt he already had done his part, since he had recently played at a benefit for CORE held at the Five Spot. Miles ultimately insisted that they *all* waive their fees as a condition of any further employment in his group. Consequently, as Davis explained in his autobiography, "When we came out to play everybody was madder than a motherfucker with each other and so I think that anger created a fire, a tension that got into everybody's playing."[38]

It is interesting to speculate on Miles's advance strategy for the concert. Perhaps he deliberately avoided telling the band that the concert was a benefit to make sure they would show up for the gig; perhaps he counted on making the band angry to provoke a particularly intense performance from them; perhaps both these results were inadvertent. In any case, although Davis used his role as a bandleader to do the right thing from a political point of view, he did so by running a typically Milesian power trip—using his status and prestige as an employer to secure compliance. Did the sidemen wish to be associated with him in the future? If so, they had better do as he wished.

Some musicians, it is important to note, were paid for participating in civil rights benefit concerts, although at a rate far below their customary fees. Organizers of civil rights benefits had to observe union rules requiring that a minimum number of musicians be paid scale before the union would grant permission for a benefit event. Local 802, the New York chapter of the American Federation of Musicians, was remarkably consistent on this point. As long as the required minimum number of musicians for a particular venue was

paid scale, the union did not care whether additional musicians played for free. If the minimum was not met, the union rejected the event.[39] In many cases, the musicians who received pay turned it over to the sponsoring organization—as did the musicians who played for an SNCC fundraising dinner in 1965. The African Research Foundation received clearance from the union for the Carnegie Hall benefit, but no such permission was secured for the Lincoln's birthday concert.[40]

Two albums were issued from the February 12, 1964, performance, *My Funny Valentine* and *"Four" and More*. Both albums have been celebrated as among the greatest live performances in jazz.[41] Subsequent generations of jazz musicians and scholars have studied closely the inspired playing of the entire quintet, with its innovative rhythm section, subtle metric transformations, deep emotional pathos, and blistering up-tempo intensity.

Reading about Miles Davis is never enough. Some moments not to miss in the performance are:

1 The transition from a slow ballad feel to double time during Miles Davis's solo on "My Funny Valentine" (2:02–2:56). (Listen to how Ron Carter's bass work leads the transition.)
2 The opening to George Coleman's tenor solo on "My Funny Valentine" (5:29–5:58).
3 Miles's V-shaped phrase in "Stella by Starlight" that sends the audience into applause (2:14–2:30).
4 The way the rhythm section punctuates the top of each chorus on Miles Davis's solo on "So What" (1:26–2:55).
5 Herbie Hancock's riffed chorus on "So What," followed by an elegantly free-flowing chorus (6:11–6:59). Listen to how Tony Williams's drums intensify the flow.
6 The interplay between Herbie Hancock and Tony Williams underneath George Coleman's solo on "Seven Steps to Heaven" (2:27–3:20).

Although the music from this concert has become canonic, on the night of the concert the band wasn't so sure they'd been successful. Herbie Hancock remembers that "we all felt dejected and disappointed. We thought we had really bombed! . . . but then we listened to the record—it sounded fantastic!"[42]

The concert generated six thousand dollars in proceeds, but according to the *Amsterdam News* the house was only a quarter full. Perhaps insufficient publicity or the high ticket prices— ranging from three dollars to fifty dollars (considerable for the time)— accounted for the sparse attendance. A few weeks after the event Davis received a letter reporting that CORE had been able to send a thousand dollars to voter registration efforts in Iberville, Louisiana, and the same amount to help rebuild the Plymouth Rock Baptist Church in Plaquemine. SNCC also sent a thank you note, reporting that the concert had enabled them to contribute two thousand dollars to support voter registration in Mississippi's fifth congressional district.[43]

Unlike most benefit concerts, the Lincoln's birthday concert did not include speeches or direct testimony from veterans of the movement's front lines, nor did Miles play any selections specifically dedicated to civil rights events. Rather, he played his usual repertory with inspired excellence. And unlike other fundraising concerts, Miles's were recorded for posterity. In benefit concerts as in other aspects of his career, Miles Davis didn't do exactly what everybody else did.

So What?

What do these detailed accounts of Davis's participation in benefit concerts during the civil rights years add to our understanding of Miles as a historical figure? The jazz world has been so wedded to the modernist notion of the artist as a transcendent genius to whom nothing matters but the music that the historical particularity of how the icons of jazz achieved greatness often has been lost. Such narratives of individual greatness—that presume the source of the excellence to be simply talent—have missed the fundamentally social processes by which a musical voice becomes heard, evaluated, identified with, and ultimately takes on symbolic force. I am arguing here that in addition to the time-honored attributes of talent and greatness, Miles Davis improvised his musical voice, attitude, and image against the turbulent backdrop of the civil rights movement and African nationalism, two political forces that most musicians in the early 1960s felt compelled to address in some way.

One of the principal ways that the civil rights movement affected the world of jazz was in persistent demand that people take a stand, put their bodies on the line for their convictions. Heated arguments took place both within movement organizations and between different groups about not only political principles and ideologies, but also about putting them into practice. As the Birdland incident demonstrates, Miles put his body on the line, when it would have been much easier to capitulate to police authority. A certain defiant swagger— and a willingness to go to jail—also went hand in hand with the civil rights movement. Benefit concerts, in many ways, offered an easy way out. Musicians could contribute to the cause by allowing the civil rights movement to capitalize on the cultural prestige of their music, but they didn't have to leave the communicative medium where they were most comfortable.

Politics as an additional accompanimental track for Davis's development, I would like to conclude, was also deeply important in shaping the reception of his sound and attitude. Miles's voice became larger than itself, not simply because he always chose the right notes, but because large numbers of people have wanted to sing along with his most poignant, militant, and uncompromising moments. Miles's voice was not disembodied, after all, but delivered by a complex human being prodded by the same social forces as everyone else. If contemporary audiences perceived Miles as a "brand new Negro," it wasn't, after all, because he came "out of nowhere."

1   Mark Crawford, "Miles Davis: Evil Genius of Jazz," *Ebony* (January 1961): 71.

2   I borrow Houston Baker's phrase. Houston A. Baker, Jr., *Modernism and the Harlem Renaissance* (Chicago: University of Chicago Press, 1987), 50.

3   Crawford, "Evil Genius," 72.

4   Ibid.

5   "Alex Haley, *The Playboy Interviews* (New York: Ballantine, 1993), 4.

6   Ralph Ellison, *Shadow and Act* (New York: Vintage, 1964), 225.

7   Miles Davis with Quincy Troupe, *Miles: The Autobiography* (New York: Simon and Schuster, 1989), 238.

8   The incident was extensively covered in New York newspapers as well as in the jazz and African American presses. See Martin Burden and Ernest Tidyman, "Jazzman Miles Davis Battles Two Cops Outside Birdland," *New York Post* (August 26, 1959); "Jazz Man Free on Bail," *New York Times*, (August 27, 1959); "Police Club Miles Davis for 'Chivalry'," *Pittsburgh Courier* (September 5, 1959): 2; "This Is What They Did to Miles," *Melody Maker* (September 12, 1959): 1; "The Slugging of Miles Davis," *Down Beat* (October 1,1959): 11.

9   Irving Kolodin, "'Miles Ahead,'" or Miles' Head?" *Saturday Review*, no. 12 (September 1959); "Of Men and Miles," *Down Beat* 26, no. 24 (November 26, 1959): 6.

10 Les Matthews, "Free Miles Davis of Cop's Charge," *New York Amsterdam News* (October 17, 1959): 1; "Charge Dismissed," *Down Beat* (November 12,1959): 11; "Aftermath of Miles," *Down Beat* (October 29,1959): 11.

11 "Judges Dig Baker the Most: Free Miles Davis With Some Cool Sounds!" *New York Amsterdam News* 50, (January 16,1960): 1, 15, "Miles Files," *Down Beat* (March 31, 1960): 13; "Miles Exonerated," (February 18, 1960): 12; "To Sue NYC, for $1 Million," *Baltimore Afro-American* (December 15, 1959): 15.

12 *Miles: The Autobiography*, 238.

13 Duckett, Alfred. "Why Castro Fled To Harlem," *Chicago Defender* weekend ed. (October 1, 1960): 1; "Sit-in for CORE," Jimmy McDonald to George Haefer [sic], July 25, 1960, Institute for Jazz Studies, Topics Files, Race Problems; "'Cabaret for Freedom,' New Theatre Movement," *New York Amsterdam News* (November 19, 1960): 18

14 Max Roach, *We Insist! Freedom Now Suite* (New York: Candid CCD 9002, 1960); Randy Weston, *Uhuru Africa* (New York: Roulette R 65001, 1960).

15 *Miles: The Autobiography*, 241.

16 The Almoravid and Almohad dynasties brought significant numbers of black Africans to Spain in the 11th and 12th centuries, especially to Andalusia. See, "Spain," www.africana.com/tt_338.htm.

17 Charles Walker "The African Imprint in Spain," *New York Amsterdam News* (August 6, 1955): 17.

18 The diplomat was Kenneth K. S. Dadzie, who later became Secretary General of the United Nations Conference on Trade and Development (UNCTAD). The press conference, held in early August 1960 celebrated both the release of *Sketches of Spain* and the Randall's Island Jazz Festival at which Davis appeared. "Miles Davis Holds Press Conference," press release from Henry O. Dormann, Institute for Jazz Studies, Clippings Files, "Miles Davis."

19 The name of the organization has been incorrectly reported as the African Relief Foundation in both *Miles: The Autobiography* (page 253) and Jack Chambers, *Milestones II: The Music and Times of Miles Davis Since 1960* (Toronto: University of Toronto Press, 1985), 36.

20 Miles Davis, *Miles Davis at Carnegie Hall* (New York: Columbia CL 1812, May 19, 1961). The original LP included only part of the concert. The complete performance was released in 1998 as *Miles Davis at Carnegie Hall—The Complete Concert* (New York: Columbia C2K 65027, May 19, 1961).

21 The African Medical and Research Foundation headquarters is located in Nairobi. They have a web page: http://www.amref.org.

22 Nyerere supported a version of African socialism that stressed self-reliance and communalism. His notion of *Ujamaa* (cooperative villages, cooperative economics) is celebrated as one of the seven principles of the Kwaanza holiday season. See, Julius Nyerere, *Ujamaa—Essays on Socialism* (London: Oxford University Press, 1977).

23 Ronald Moss, interview with author, April 21, 1995. Moss co-founded the organization with Thomas Rees. *Miles: The Autobiography*, 238, reports the name as "Jean Bock." Jean Bach later directed the film *A Great Day in Harlem*, Image Entertainment, 1995.

24 The mobile unit may have been named for Davis, Moss, interview with author.

25 "Roach Interrupts Davis Concert," *New York Amsterdam News* (May 27, 1961): 17; George T. Simon, "Miles Davis Plays Trumpet

in Carnegie Hall Concert," *New York Herald Tribune*, May 20, 1961; Institute for Jazz Studies, Clippings Files, "Miles Davis." *Someday My Prince Will Come* was cut short. When Miles returned he began with *Oleo*, not *No Blues* as Chambers reports. See *Milestones II*, 36.

26   Ian Carr, *Miles Davis: A Biography* (New York: William Morrow and Company, 1982), 128.

27   Moss, interview with author; Carr, *Miles Davis*, 127–28. Carr reports that African nationalist groups accused the ARF of being in league with African diamond interests.

28   "Riot in Gallery Halts U.N. Debate," *New York Times* (February 16 ,1961): 1, 10; "Dizzy to Present New African Work," *New York Amsterdam News* (February 18, 1961): 13; "Africa Freedom Day," *New York Amsterdam News* (March 25,1961): 17.

29   Teo Macero, interview with author, May 15, 1995.

30   The LP (Columbia 1812) deleted *Teo, Walkin', I Thought About You*, and *Concierto de Aranjuez*. These selections were released on a separate issue, *Live Miles: More Music from the Legendary Carnegie Hall Concert*, CS 8612 (LP); Columbia CK 40609 (CD).

31   Frank Kofsky, *Black Nationalism and the Revolution in Music* (New York: Pathfinder Press, 1970). For more information on benefit concerts, see Ingrid Monson, *Freedom Sounds: Jazz, Civil Rights, and Africa, 1950–1967*. Forthcoming, Oxford University Press.

32   Stanley Dance, *The World of Duke Ellington* (New York: Charles Scribner's Sons, 1970), 21.

33   Clark Terry, Interview with author, March 27,1997; Amiri Baraka, *The Autobiography of LeRoi Jones* (Chicago: Lawrence Hill Books, 1997), 298–99; Roswell Rudd, interview with author, June 28, 1998.

34   Jack Chambers, *Milestones II*, 60, 47–48.

35   Meier, *CORE*, 172–74, 222–24; Rich, interview with author; Charles Mingus and Thelonious Monk appeared at the SNCC benefit concert on February 1, 1963, "A Salute to Southern Students," *SNCC Papers*, Subgroup B, series I, reel 45:1097.

36   Miles Davis, appeal letter, January 27, 1964, *SNCC Papers*, 1959–1972 (micro-

film), subgroup B, series I, reel 45, frame 995.

37   Ibid.

38   Ron Carter, conversation with author, New York: April 23, 1995; *Miles: The Autobiography*, 266.

39   In 1960 union scale for a five-piece band for one night at a class A nightclub in New York was $121.64 for three hours. "Adjusted Scales for Single Engagement Club Jobs," *Allegro* 34, no. 4 (February 1960): 23.

40   "April 25th Dinner, Financial Report," May 11, 1965, *SNCC Papers* Subgroup B, series I, reel 46: 1234; "Executive Board Minutes," *Allegro* 36, no. 8 (June 1961): 16.

41   Miles Davis, *My Funny Valentine* (New York: February 12, 1964) Columbia CL 2306; *"Four" and More* (New York: February 12, 1964) Columbia CL 2453. The CD reissue provides the complete performance. *The Complete Concert 1964: My Funny Valentine + "Four" and More* (New York: February 12, 1964) Columbia CK 40609. For an analysis of a Davis solo on *My Funny Valentine*, see Robert Walser, "'Out of Notes': Signification, Interpretation, and the Problem of Miles Davis," *Musical Quarterly* 77, no. 2 (summer 1993): 343–65.

42   Carr, *Miles Davis*, 138.

43   Raymond Robinson, "Miles Davis Appears at Philharmonic," *New York Amsterdam News* (February 22, 1964). Marvin Rich to Miles Davis, March 13, 1964, *Congress of Racial Equality Records, 1941–1967*, series 5, box 28, folder 8; Jim Monsonis, "To Miles Davis." *SNCC Papers, 1959–1972* (Microfilm), 1964, Subgroup B, series I, reel 45:1009. The remaining funds went to the NAACP Legal Defense Fund.

Copenhagen, 1964.
Photograph by
Jan Persson.

Ron Carter is one of jazz's most accomplished string players. Born in Michigan in 1937, Carter began receiving instruction on the cello at the age of ten and, when his family moved to Detroit during his teen years, hoped for a classical career.

"At the time I was seventeen in high school, I was made aware that the classical world was not ready to accept talented African American musicians, and they made it pretty well known to me," he said. "So I switched to string bass—there were no African American string bass players in the orchestra—to make them have to hire a talented person. And then when I got to college at the Eastman School of Music I found that nothing had changed other than my age and the calendar date. Orchestras still were not willing to accept in their ranks an African American player who may have been more talented than the players that they had in the orchestras. So, having worked as a jazz musician through college, I said, 'Well, they don't seem to be biased. If you can play, you get the job.'"

He switched to the bass in 1954.

Before joining Miles Davis's quintet in 1963, Carter played with the Chico Hamilton quintet that featured reedman Eric Dolphy. He also played with Thelonious Monk, Jaki Byard, Bobby Timmons, and Cannonball Adderley.

Carter remained with Davis until 1968, playing with a group that included pianist Herbie Hancock, drummer Tony Williams, and saxophonist Wayne Shorter. It was not only one of the finest jazz groups of its day, but one of the best in the history of jazz. He was also the bassist on Herbie Hancock's *Maiden Voyage* album (1965), considered one of the landmark albums of jazz.

After leaving Davis, Carter went on to a successful career as a studio musician, playing on literally more than a thousand records, from jazz to rap. He has also led his own small groups, playing either the double bass or the piccolo bass. He has participated in several super-group reunions including VSOP, which first came together in 1976/1977 as a re-gathering of the Davis quintet—with Freddie Hubbard standing in for Davis (it has been reunited several times since)—and the Milestone Jazzstars with pianist McCoy Tyner, drummer Al Foster, and saxophonist Sonny Rollins.

BC: When did you first become aware of Miles Davis?
RC: Well, everyone in my age group at the time, in the fifties, knew those

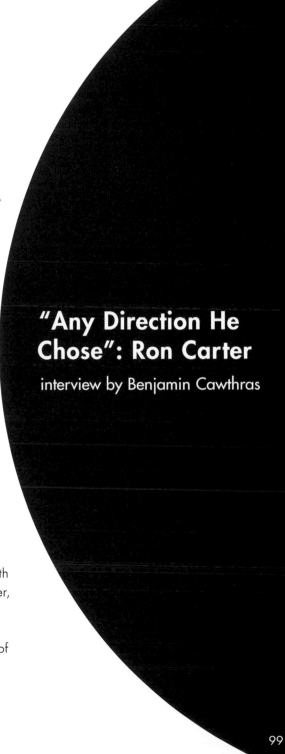

"Any Direction He Chose": Ron Carter

interview by Benjamin Cawthras

records he had made with Bird. As I got in college, '57, '58, the Red Garland, Paul Chambers, Philly Joe Jones rhythm section was all anyone talked about and played like. So my awareness of him goes back to high school and all through college.

BC: What did you like about that rhythm section, with Paul Chambers, the man who preceded you?

RC: Well, they just played like a group. They made the rhythm section sound like a big band. They knew the songs, they knew the forms, they understood the changes. They were all, in their own way, individually creating on their instrument, but they sounded like one.

BC: You had played a little with Herbie Hancock and Tony Williams before Miles, right?

RC: Well, I probably had made a couple of recordings, but when you're at a date it's a lot different than making a gig, you know. At the date you've got seven tunes, which makes maybe thirty-five or forty minutes, and

maybe rehearsal, so your focus is more on how to get the music done in this small space of time, not necessarily nor solely how you can evolve to the next recording session, because you might not be on the next recording session. When you've got a gig, you've got two sets a night, five or six nights a week, and four sets on Friday and Saturday—a whole week of a lifetime in music to see if you can take it somewhere else in the next set or the next evening.

BC: How did you get the gig with Miles?

RC: I was working with Art Farmer at a club called the Admiral, that has long since been gone. Art Farmer, Jim Hall, and I think Walter Perkins. Miles came in during the second night of the gig and said he was forming a new band, and he was leaving for California the next week to do a six-week tour and he wanted to know whether I'd be able to go. I said to him, "Well, I have a job. I'm working with Art Farmer for the next two weeks. But if you ask Art, and if Art says it's okay to leave after this week, I'm happy to go. If Art says I can't go, then I won't be going to California." So he called Art over, and they had a talk. Art told me he understood what Miles's band was all about and he gave me permission to leave. But he also told me that he was very pleased that I held him in such high esteem, that I would make sure he said I could go rather than

just leave the gig that next night. And that showed the level of respect in our relationship, mine and Art's. I might add that because Miles had to ask him before I could go, that kind of gave Miles another view of what kind of values I placed on relationships and friendships. It was a hot band, and everyone wanted to join it, but that didn't necessarily supersede my commitment to Art. And the fact that I understood that, and that Miles had to deal with it, put us in a different relationship than most people at an early stage.

BC: Why do you think he chose you, Hancock, and Williams?

RC: I have no idea. My general sense of it is that he picked three guys who he thought could help him make some "new" music. He seemed to have the ability to always put together the kind of groups that would make it easier to do the kind of music he was looking to do, whether it was Paul, Wynton, and Jimmy Cobb, or Paul, Bill Evans, and Jimmy Cobb, or Philly, and Paul, and Red. He seemed to find the combination of rhythm section players to make whatever he was looking for more easily found. In those five years none of us looked at him as a guy who put together these three people for this music. We just knew he'd hired us. And I think not until many years later would we have sat down and said, "Wow, this is the reason why we were chosen." And it worked out as best it could.

BC: It was a composer's band, and all of you wrote. Did it start out that way? Did he ask you to bring new music?

RC: Once we started making records, yeah. Before, we were just playing the old library. As we got more studio work, more dates with him, he would suggest that we bring in songs and we'd try them out at the date and see if it worked, and we'd work on them in the studio and make the record. Unfortunately, most of those tunes never got a chance to be developed on the bandstand, for whatever reason. Most of them were very difficult. Since we were not a real rehearsal band in that we didn't go to a studio and rehearse the songs in a closed environment, our next performance of those tunes was always in the club or the concert. There was really not a chance to dig out in private time what those tunes meant and then try them out on the bandstand, and I think because of that the library wasn't as extensive live as it could have been. But

composition was part of the band's personality.

BC: The late Tony Williams seemed to be a very powerful force in that band. What did he do musically that seemed to appeal to Miles and the rest of you?

RC: I don't know what appealed to Miles, so I couldn't really speak to that point, but for me the sound of the drums and how he pitched them was really important for me, because I played with no amplifiers and no bass mikes. The clubs usually had an antiquated house system at best, and more often than not, there were only two mikes: one with the piano and one for the horn. So basically I was playing an unmiked instrument. Tony had a great sense of dynamics, and because his drums were tuned in such a fashion, he allowed the bass to speak through all that stuff he was playing. That was important for me. One of the important factors.

BC: It was a time of musical activism, lots of benefit concerts, such as the Lincoln Center program in 1964.

RC: Miles played a lot of those kind of benefit things. Max Roach did a lot of them. I'm not sure if Mingus did many, but he was certainly aware of the sociological situation. We had been off maybe two or three months before that concert came up, and we all showed up backstage and Miles told us it was a benefit for CORE or

SNCC or one of those kind of groups, and that we were doing it as a benefit. I was always the guy who spoke up first. I said, "Wait a minute, now. We've been off three months and you're telling me we're playing this for free, and you're giving our money away? Don't give our money away. I'll tell what you do, you tell them to give me my check, and if I want to give them all of it, part of it, I'll write them my check after the check clears. Just seems reasonable to me that we do it like that. I resent you determining that you want to give my money to this group. I don't know who they are, man." Of course I knew who they were. "What they stand for?"

I knew what they stood for. But I just thought it was a big assumption on his part to take the stance that what's good for him to do should be good for everybody else. He said, "What are you going to do?" I said, "I'm going to go home, man." He said, "You can't go home." I said, "Why?" "Because you got a concert." I told him, "No, you got a concert. You signed up for it; I didn't sign up for it." I said, "The solution is not complicated. Just tell them to give me my share, whoever is going to get paid tonight, and I will write them my check for that amount. That way, they have my check for their funds and I have a receipt that my accountant will love as a tax benefit. A tax gift. Charity." He said, "Okay. We can do that." And we just did the concert. But again, you know, we would do them all the time. We would do them individually for the fundraisers without him being there because people knew who we were and we would draw a larger crowd for this benefit than if it was someone else who was not with the Miles Davis band, or the local guy, whoever he was, who had friends but couldn't pull in the kind of money these benefits were hoping to raise for their various causes. We were active in our own way in that situation.

BC: The role of the bass seemed to change through the years. In his autobiography, Miles keeps talking about wanting to get a deeper bass sound, more bass, doubling the bass. What were the implications for you?

RC: Well, he never discussed that with me, so I wasn't aware that he was looking for a different kind of bass quality. When he started doing the electric stuff, I was playing electric bass on some jingles anyway. I had already played it in college just so I could have money to stay in school because it was getting expensive. Those early electric dates we made, I told him I didn't like the electric bass because it wasn't really my kind of sound. I had worked a long time to get a sound quality that I wouldn't mind being held accountable for, and this instrument, for all it could do, it wasn't a sound I wanted to be held responsible for. Besides, there were guys who played it better, and there were guys who spend as much time playing that as I had spent playing acoustic. I just thought I didn't want to spend a second lifetime trying to play this instrument. He told me, "Well, just play it like you do the upright." And I just thought that was a joke, because they're so different. But, given all that, I made of it the best I could and brought some musicality to the instrument that maybe wasn't available at that time.

BC: It's an odd moment; he was at a divide that seems cultural as well as musical in terms of what kind of bass to use.

RC: I think had there been the kind of pickups and bass amplifiers then that there are now, he probably would have felt less of a need to use an electric bass. But times were changing and things were becoming more amplified, and they were becoming quality amplifications. They weren't just playing loud. They had some good equipment. They were inventing the pickups, they were inventing the pianos, they were inventing new microphones, they were inventing portable mikes where you could walk around the stage. The electronic revolution was really taking place then. By the time they were really jumping off, I was out of the band, doing a different kind of situation. But I think if those electronic developments had started maybe with the same force in '68 that they did in '70, maybe I would have stayed in the band a little bit longer, I don't know, just to see how those things worked.

BC: What did you think of the direction Miles went in 1969–70?

RC: I appreciated it because of the musical value, but it was nothing that I wanted to spend an equal amount of time being able to do. I had something else I wanted to do. I was still trying to learn how to play the acoustic bass. I had some things in my mind that I thought I could best do in a different kind of environment. But I liked all those guys' playing. They played real well, and they were good musicians. It just wasn't a direction that I personally wanted to spend as much time in as they did.

BC: When Miles laid out in the late seventies, did you have any contact with him?

RC: I went by a couple of times. He lived over on Seventy-seventh Street. We talked about politics and sports and on occasion he would want to eat something and I would go out to this restaurant on Seventy-seventh and Broadway and get some Cuban food for him, and he would eat and I would say, "Okay, you're straight for the day and I've got to go about my business." I had to leave then. He would call and thank me for stopping by. A real friendship, relationship, that continued throughout the years.

BC: Did you feel that he was lonely?

RC: [Pause.] I knew he was by himself. "Lonely" is a word that's hard to put on somebody if you don't know their psychological makeup. I would say he was by himself, and I knew that he had my phone number, and if he wanted me to come by, I was three blocks away; I would have come by. So I felt that if he wanted company, he sure could have had me for a companion for as long as my time would allow or our relationship could tolerate. So, lonely I don't know, but by himself, yes.

BC: Then he comes back in the early eighties. There's a lot of attention being paid to two trumpet players. You're in the unique position of having played with both: Miles Davis and the young Wynton Marsalis; you played and recorded with him at the beginning of his career. What did you think of all the controversy surrounding that situation?

RC: I thought Wynton was speaking through his hat. And I thought the comments he made were not very knowledgeable and ill-tempered. That's the only way I can think of it. To have him make those comments about Miles and his commercializing the music and later make a Christmas record wearing a Santa Claus suit, that's pretty fucking bizarre. I think he owed the jazz community an apology or an explanation as to how this person could take any opportunity to put Miles and his music down for what he calls selling out, then later make an album of Charlie Brown tunes. I mean, that's pretty outrageous. He hasn't seen fit to comment, and no one else has seen fit to comment. If someone had asked me, I would have commented on it. Just pretty bizarre.

As far as the controversy, there really wasn't one. Wynton wasn't in Miles's class, so how could there be a controversy, as far as I was concerned. I think one of the sad parts of that event was that Columbia showed, the recording industry showed, that if they are willing to make someone popular or famous in the jazz community, they have the machines to do it. They haven't decided to do it since. The label's been cut. It doesn't even exist now as it stands. The old story that jazz can't be sold or doesn't sell has been proven many times false by those same people who say it doesn't sell. That is the tragedy of that scene. Not so much Wynton against Miles or vice versa, but the fact that the industry showed that they could sell if they wanted to and other times, they chose not to. But as far as comparing those two? I was so appalled, you know, "How dare you compare the two?" It's just not part of my mentality.

BC: Miles passed ten years ago. Do you remember what you were doing?

RC: I was having dinner with my wife in the kitchen out there, and they made the announcement on the station. Actually, Tony had called, and I was at work on a record date and I got word on my machine, that I didn't get until after. Then Herbie called, and he left word on my machine. Again I was at work. When I got home, my wife said that she thought she heard on the television that Miles had passed away, and it was in fact true. So I was at work making a record, came home to dinner, and found out he'd passed.

BC: The four of you got together soon after for the tour?

RC: It was decided that we would do a tour. It wasn't a quick thing; we all had our own projects. It was a chance, a legitimate chance, to work together under an important banner: the Miles Davis tribute band. I think we all felt that his last Montreux event was him getting ready to reform that quintet to do a series of concerts. Unfortunately, he didn't live long enough for us to see if our prediction was true. But it was a chance to kind of help keep this view of music alive, and for us to acknowledge that he was an important factor in our lives, the fact that he was an important person who brought us together. More than anything else, I think, it was a chance to acknowledge that relationship and that friendship.

BC: You've accomplished so many things; yet you will be principally remembered by many people for playing with Miles. How does that feel?

RC: It depends on how it's said, who says it, and how I feel about me at that time. If the wrong person says it I take great offense because they haven't seen my career past 1968. If the right person says it I will add, "Yes, it's true, and I've done other things subsequent to that." I've done things before that. I made the first jazz cello record where the cello was tuned like a cello. My career is full of things I'm happy to say that I was a part of. I still haven't heard all those records we made, because I just haven't, one, taken the time, and two, it hasn't been important to my day to have that kind of reminder that I helped make this music. But teaching school for all these years, that music comes in and out of fashion. I've been forced to listen to one or two tracks just to answer some students' questions as best I could. So I sit down and listen to it and say, "Oh, my. I missed that. How did that get by me? Check that out. How'd we get to that?" So I listen to those records only from that point of view for those specific questions in classes I have been involved in. I guess fate's going to do what it's going to do and if that happens to be my contribution to the broad world of music as music history is analyzed, it's not a bad way to be thought of.

BC: How should Miles be remembered?
RC: As one of the few who was able to turn the world of music in any direction he chose.

BC: Period?
RC: Period.

Backstage, Monterey Jazz Festival, 1969.
Photograph by
Ray Avery.

> *. . . the Sorcerer, the Prince of Darkness, charisma incarnate, trendsetter, and talent scout supreme. At that intersection of aesthetics and hype, substance and stylishness, brash innovation and mass appeal—a junction most jazz musicians never approach—Miles Davis remains a monolith.*[1]

By 1960, at age thirty-four, trumpeter extraordinaire Miles Dewey Davis, II, had become the most acclaimed jazz musician of his generation. Miles vividly personified the popular perception of the jazz avant-garde. His status as a popular exemplar of the jazz avant-garde derived principally from his signal contributions to the major jazz developments from the mid-1940s on. That exceptional body of music gave him impeccable avant-garde credentials and was vital to his expanding avant-garde and modernist capital.[2] This was especially the case in the popular mind, if not always in the minds of the jazz establishment, especially jazz critics.

His public persona as a major figure in the American artistic and cultural avant-garde early on grew in stature with increasing recognition and fame. A highly stylish and flamboyant lifestyle only enhanced his avant-garde credentials. Most important, however, aesthetically and musically his avant-gardism consisted largely of his lifelong quest to discover something new to say in jazz. That quest featured critical breaks with his musical past that were critical markers of the sea changes and striking discontinuities over time characteristic of modern cultural avant-gardism.

From forties bebop to fifties cool jazz, hard bop, and modalism, Davis was at the center of the action. While neither a technical virtuoso nor the key innovator within these jazz movements, he was a highly committed and very influential modern artist who transgressed boundaries in jazz and other areas of his life. Deep exploration of the music as a way to push it forward, nonetheless, remained his touchstone. The hallmarks of his modernist jazz aesthetic were commitments to order, progress, and creativity. In fact, his entire

Miles Davis and the 1960s Avant-Garde

by Waldo E. Martin, Jr.

jazz career embodied the creative tension between the imperatives of improvisation and change, on the one hand, and the imperatives of understanding and building upon jazz tradition, on the other. His modernism and his avant-gardism thus dynamically played off of one another.

Miles's steady development as a distinctive soloist, as a powerful group leader and talent scout, and as an artist committed to the ongoing expansion of his musical horizons earmarked Davis as the pre-eminent jazz force in the 1950s. Barely out of his teens, he had played in several of Charlie Parker's key mid-forties bebop combos. Crafting a spare, some say fragile, vibrato-less, yet emotion-laden style featuring the middle registers of his instrument, Miles created a sound at once bold and evocative. Miles's trumpet approach offered an arresting counterpoint to the furious and aggressive style of his bebop mentors.

Characterized as sounding "like a man walking on eggshells" or "a little boy crying in a closet," Miles charted a very unique and highly influential trumpet sound: ethereal, romantic, and vulnerable. In gendered terms, the sound drew upon feminine as well as masculine impulses; it often veered toward androgyny. That the public and private Miles exuded a virile and uncompromising brand of black masculinity only intensified the complexity of his sound and its broad appeal. Walter Bishop, Jr., labeled it "this haunting kind of a sound." During this especially fertile period, then, Miles fixed upon a singularly gripping style. Bob Blumenthal writes that Miles's style was "less focused by necessity on technique while giving heightened emphasis to lyricism, economy and an intriguing mix of strength and vulnerability."[3]

As a soloist, Miles was especially enamored with the use of space, silences, and various tones, notably the mute, to create desired musical effects. Rather than the technical wizardry, high notes, and rapid-fire delivery associated with his one-time mentor, friend and bebop innovator Dizzy Gillespie, Miles created a trumpet style representative of that of his St. Louis hometown, like that of "homeboys" Clark Terry and Lester

Bowie. Quincy Troupe perceptively has described that style as "generally cooler, more subtle and conversational," say, than the "hotter, bigger, brassier" New Orleans style of Louis Armstrong and Wynton Marsalis.[4] Of course, when the music demanded it, Davis could blow hot, big, brassy, even high and fast.

Miles quickly became identified as a superb musician deeply interested in and comfortable playing different styles of jazz. He was clearly an immensely creative musician evolving a distinctive musical language and voice. His eclecticism and experimentalism—additional elements of his modernism and avant-gardism—was apparent early on in what came to be known as *The Birth of the Cool* sessions. With kindred spirits arranger Gil Evans, trumpeter and composer John Carisi, saxophonist Gerry Mulligan, and pianist John Lewis, Miles brought together a short-term nonet playing a style of jazz which artfully combined the mellow, minimalist side of Parker's music with the "soft, dense, and static" music of the Claude Thornhill Orchestra, a significant white society band.[5] By 1950 these musical interactions had spawned the highly influential, very popular, and white-dominated "West Coast School" of cool jazz, featuring players like trumpeter Chet Baker (heavily influenced by Davis), alto saxophonist Lee Konitz, and Gerry Mulligan.

For most of the fifties, however, the best of Davis's live and recorded music increasingly explored several directions. In one sphere, he explored orchestral jazz with European classical inflections, as in the critically acclaimed and popular series of albums arranged by his good friend Gil Evans. Particularly noteworthy were *Porgy and Bess* and *Sketches of Spain*. His most influential work in this period, however, was the music of his mid-to-late fifties groups, especially those with the pulsating saxophone work of John Coltrane, which explored two major styles. One was the soul-inflected, and more rhythmically-based, idiom of hard bop popularized by the groups of Art Blakey. By the decade's end, he was deeply into the second major style, demonstrated by his influential forays into modalism, a music structured around scales or modes rather than the chordal progressions of bop. The very influential *Milestones* as well as *Kind of Blue*, one of the most significant and popular jazz albums ever, epitomized Miles's modal phase.

II

At this peak in Miles's musical career, the rapidly evolving free jazz movement soon mounted a powerful challenge to his status as the exemplar of the jazz avant-garde, notably within the jazz establishment. This powerful jazz insurgency came both from within and without his musical circle. Within his circle, the insurgency came from the music and personality of John Coltrane. Outside of it, the insurgency came primarily from the music and personalities of alto saxophonist Ornette Coleman, pianist Cecil Taylor, saxophonist Albert Ayler, and multi-instrumentalist Eric Dolphy. Playing a jazz increasingly operating to varying degrees outside traditional parameters of solo and group improvisation as well as harmony, melody, and rhythm, adherents of the "new thing" soon divided audiences and critics alike.

When Coleman's quartet arrived in New York, the atmosphere was thick with electricity and anticipation. An early evening press conference to publicize the new music only added to the intensity of the expectations. Thus "on a chilly autumn evening, the New York jazz establishment faced its most serious challenger since Charlie Parker came out of Kansas City in 1939," A. B. Spellman has observed. [6] A series of important albums—*Something Else* (1958), *Tomorrow Is the Question* (1959), *The Shape of Jazz to Come* (1959), and *Change of the Century* (1959)—provided listeners in the know with an impressive view of this innovative musical vision. The successful yet controversial New York debut of Coleman's group at the Five Spot in November and December 1959, and several weeks in January 1960 heralded an advancing frontier in jazz. Not surprisingly, it also sparked an acrimonious debate about the new music. Trumpeter Don Cherry, bassist Charlie Haden, and drummer Billy Higgins together had played Ornette's music for several years now and made musical waves out in Los Angeles. New York, however, was the center of the jazz world and American avant-garde culture generally.

Spellman has provided a revealing cross-section of immediate responses among musicians, critics, and jazz lovers alike to the music of Coleman's group. Of Coleman, they maintained:

He'll change the entire course of jazz." "He's a fake." "He's a genius." "I can't say, I'll have to hear him a lot more times." "He has no form." "He swings like hell." "I'm going home to listen to my Benny Goodman trios and quartets." "He's out, real far out." "I like him, but I don't have any idea of what he's doing.

In his autobiography, Miles recalled the Five Spot performances by Coleman's group "turning the jazz world all the way around. He just came and fucked up everybody."[7]

Miles apparently claimed early on that he liked Ornette "because he doesn't play clichés." Soon, however, he began to express an argument that he elaborated upon in his autobiography. The free-form qualities of Coleman's music were important, Miles contended, but neither particularly new nor revolutionary. Unimpressed with the group's musical aesthetic, he had been equally unimpressed with its artistry. While he admitted to liking some of Ornette's later music, he found the early free jazz of Coleman's group, especially that created during the famous Five Spot stint, interesting but not exciting. He heard them several times during that epochal engagement and even sat in with them a few times. He explained that "what they were doing back in the beginning was just being spontaneous in their playing, playing 'free form,' bouncing off what each other was doing. That's cool, but it had been done before, only they were doing it with no kind of form or structure and that's the thing that was important about what they did, not their playing."[8]

Soon, however, Miles's dislike for free jazz became more pronounced, and he came to be associated publicly with the opposition of the jazz traditionalists to the "new thing." While the critical move away from chord changes found in the modalism of Miles and others went in the direction of free jazz, it did not venture very far. The late-fifties music of Miles clearly had made modalism acceptable. Still, many in the jazz world increasingly understood that its possibilities as a new direction for the music were limited. Indeed, Miles's performed and recorded music during much of the 1960s covered very familiar territory. In fact, it was not until the latter sixties, when he began his jazz fusion phase, that the play list for his concerts ventured significantly outside his fifties body of work.

For the exemplar of jazz innovation in the popular mind, this fallow sixties period represented a serious musical crisis. As he sought to come up with a fresh direction for his own music, he also had to think seriously about the shift in musical tastes, notably the declining popularity of jazz and the expanding popularity of white rock and black rhythm and blues. Clearly he, too, like so many others who disliked the "new thing" saw that it contributed to the declining popularity of jazz, including his own music. The question arose, What kind of fresh direction in jazz would jibe not only and most importantly with his own taste, but also with that of the jazz public? Could these now be brought into sync as they had been during his earlier moments of musical achievement and peak popularity?

Concurrently, the Black Freedom Struggle shifted from an insistence on civil rights to a radical demand for Black Power. Many in the free jazz movement, including musicians, critics, and supporters, increasingly tended to see the "new thing" and the increasingly militant Black Freedom Struggle as interrelated. This intensifying black nationalist context rendered Miles's signal music, created in the fifties and reflecting that decade in crucial ways, as less politically and aesthetically relevant. If the often-furious free jazz of John Coltrane signified autonomy and Black Power, the far more restrained late-fifties and early-sixties work of Miles signified integrationism and civil rights.

Several free jazz artists, especially those in the mid-sixties' second wave, like saxophonists Albert Ayler and Archie Shepp, publicly and politically linked the expanding musical insurgency with the expanding African American Liberation Insurgency. The increasingly racialized and nationalistic posture of this wing of the jazz avant-garde had a very influential spokesman in the person of poet, dramatist, and cultural critic LeRoi Jones, soon to become Amiri Baraka. Miles understood this black radical cultural politics, but he did not wholly embrace it. His own cultural politics were more mixed and hybrid, as opposed to sectarian or essentialist. Craig Werner has observed that in their creative and personal milieu, those he calls the "jazz impulse musicians," especially Jimi Hendrix and Miles, had more complex ideas about race and music. "In contrast to political discussions that assumed blackness as an answer to the most fundamental questions confronting black people, jazz impulse musicians understood racial identity as part of a larger, more complicated mix."[9]

Musically speaking, Miles perceived that the avant-garde jazz associated with this brand of black nationalist cultural politics did not square with his own more tradition-centered, eclectic, and far less racialistic approach to musical innovation. In fact, the dissonant, atonal, and relatively unstructured avant-garde jazz that Davis seemed to dislike strongly spoke pointedly to the profound challenge it represented for those modernists and avant-gardists like Miles far more grounded in jazz tradition. It must be understood that for all of his iconoclasm, trendsetting, and stylistic shifts, Miles deeply identified with and was deeply enmeshed within the jazz past.

Throughout his career, however, Miles consistently spoke of his deep-seated need to break away from the fetters of the jazz past, of his continuing and related search for the new sound. In the late sixties he explained in an interview that "I have to change. It's like a curse." Biographer Ian Carr has agreed. He perceptively argues that the whole of Miles's musical life is not just about changing musical styles, or change for the sake of change. Instead, that musical life strikingly illustrates the awesome achievement, and in jazz a particularly unique achievement, of "sustained conceptual development" over four decades.[10] Still, unlike the most "out-there" explorers in the sixties avant-garde such as Coleman and Ayler, who did much of their most innovative work musically working from outside, or moved from outside further outward, Miles was different. He essentially worked musically outward from within.

In addition to finding most of the music of the 1960s jazz avant-garde unsatisfying, Miles also found unpalatable the rigid ideological strictures of the most radical elements of the black nationalist wing of the jazz avant-garde. Still, he fully understood and accepted the complex ways that both the Civil Rights (1945–1965) and Black Power (1966–1975) movements suffused American culture and jazz. He was a partisan of the Black Freedom Struggle in its entirety.

In 1959 Miles was part of an outstanding lineup, including Dizzy Gillespie, Count Basie, and Dave Brubeck, at a jazz festival on behalf of the Chicago Urban League. A May 19, 1961, benefit concert in New York for the African Research Foundation featured not only some inspired music by Miles Davis and his group, but also a stunning protest by Max Roach and a cohort who disrupted the concert by coming on-stage with protest placards.

They wanted to make visible their objection to the foundation's alleged white conservative ties. A benefit concert for the NAACP in the 3,200-seat Masonic Temple in October 1961 caused a mild furor because some objected to jazz being played in such a venue. Nevertheless, the concert was a success. A February 12, 1964, concert at New York's Philharmonic Hall in support of the voter registration work of the NAACP, CORE, and SNCC was likewise a big hit. Miles, who also dedicated the last mentioned concert to the memory of the recently assassinated President John F. Kennedy, obviously contributed formally to The Movement.[11]

Miles was admired widely as an uncompromising and proud black man who had beaten the odds and fashioned a highly successful jazz career financially as well as artistically. In many ways he personified the kind of hard work and success that the Black Freedom Struggle trumpeted. For many he became a symbol for that very struggle precisely because of his uncommon personal and racial pride, combined necessarily with his uncommon achievements as a jazz musician. Gerald Early has emphasized that Miles "was a man who was not afraid to be himself." Similarly, Troupe notes that Miles—an "unreconstructed black man"—was "amazing as a role model of black pride and defiance." Miles, according to Troupe, was "completely independent, amazingly creative, fiercely proud." Eric Porter

perceptively has noted the broader cultural importance of Miles as an exemplar of a strong, proud, and uncompromising representation of black manhood. This image of Miles resonated with particular force within the interrelated Black Power and Black Arts movements.[12]

In addition, though Miles made it clear that he strongly identified with his people's ongoing liberation insurgency, he also understood the need to work with sympathetic nonblacks, especially whites. This also carried over into his willingness to work with white musicians and to employ them in his groups. He was not a racial chauvinist, and he refused to bow to nationalist bigotry. As a vigorous opponent of Jim Crow, he refused to succumb to what some at the time called Crow Jim: the understandable refusal of some black artists to work with and to employ white musicians because of the racism against black musicians. "I think prejudice one way is just as bad as the other way," he once explained. Speaking of the white composer-arranger Gil Evans, Miles maintained that "we couldn't be much closer if he was my

brother." Continuing in this vein, Miles claimed a kind of color-blind hiring policy:

And I remember one time when I hired Lee Konitz, some colored cats bitched about me hiring an ofay in my band when Negroes didn't have work. I said if a cat could play like Lee, I would hire him, I didn't give a damn if he was green and had red breath.[13]

Miles was a harsh and often subtle critic of American cultural and racial mores. In the popular and critical white enthusiasm for "free jazz," Miles saw and therefore lambasted the hyped, faddish, and racist arrogance and condescension. Even more pointedly, he roundly criticized the continuing efforts of influential white critics to frame and control the production, interpretation, and reception of black music. If, as he and many others believed, "free jazz" contributed significantly to the declining popularity of jazz, these powerful white critical voices, like that of Gunther Schuller, were partly to blame.[14]

Miles also found highly distasteful the ideological tendency among some within the radical black nationalist avant-garde, like Shepp and Ayler, to conflate the music with a separatist and chauvinistic black politics. This move led to a kind of unimaginative protest music that Miles decried as music, on one hand, and politics on the other. As Early has observed, Miles "never saw jazz as a kind of protest music, for the protest was implicit in the act of a black person making this art under the conditions he or she was making it in the United States."[15] Thus while Miles aptly perceived an intrinsic interpenetration of art and politics, his vision of cultural politics demanded far more insight into the art, the politics, and the interrelationship between them. This was especially the case in the work, heard by Miles, of some of the most influential elements within the radical black jazz avant-garde.

John Coltrane was different. Since their fine work together between 1955 and 1960, Miles knew Coltrane to be an extraordinary, uncompromising, and evolving artist whose peerless technique, searching and highly inventive extended solos, and improvisational ingenuity made him a principal jazz innovator. Coltrane is perhaps best known for his "sheets of sound. " John Litweiler aptly has described them as "broken scales or arpeggios played so fast that he seems to be trying to give the impression of chords." In fact, Coltrane had developed this sound in his work with Miles, and he

subsequently expanded upon it throughout his all-too-brief career as a bandleader (1960–1967).

Even when Coltrane's own music pushed the free jazz idiom into areas Miles found disagreeable—especially Coltrane's mid-to-late sixties sonic assault on rhythm, harmony, and tempo—Miles always acknowledged Coltrane's superior musicianship and aesthetic sensibilities. Miles also appreciated the larger symbolic as well as iconic resonances of Coltrane's music. While Coltrane's most "out-there" music reflected the symbiosis between him and the likes of Albert Ayler, Coltrane never articulated the black nationalist ideology of those like Ayler. Instead, Coltrane's rhetoric, like his music, became more

intensely spiritual and inclusive. Still, because of the unusual power of Coltrane's music, its larger cultural meanings and influences and its symbolic resonances were widespread, complex, and ultimately beyond Coltrane's control.[16]

In a remarkably revealing passage in his autobiography, Miles spoke movingly and thoughtfully about the complicated resonances of Coltrane's later music (1964–1967) for the Black Freedom Struggle, notably its early Black Power phase:

> Trane's music and what he was playing during the last two or three years of his life represented, for many blacks, the fire and passion and rage and anger and rebellion and love that they felt, especially among the young black intellectuals and revolutionaries of that time. He was expressing through music what H. Rap Brown and Stokely Carmichael and the Black Panthers and Huey Newton were saying with their words, what the Last Poets and Amiri Baraka were saying in poetry. He was their torchbearer in jazz, now ahead of me. He played what they felt inside and were expressing through riots—"burn, baby, burn"—that were taking place everywhere in this country during the 1960s. It was all about revolution for a lot of young black people—Afro hairdos, dashikis, black power, fists raised in the air. Coltrane was their symbol,

their pride—their beautiful, black, revolutionary pride. I had been it a few years back, now he was it, and that was cool with me.

Miles both accepted and personified the important role of jazz artists as "a self-conscious cultural vanguard." According to Brian Ward, "modern jazz artists tended to emerge from, and work mostly within, a self-conscious cultural vanguard, where music and racial, personal and collective politics were expected to mix."[17] Such was certainly the case with Miles, and mix they did. With Miles, however, the results were often idiosyncratic and unpredictable.

Nonetheless, Miles's self-conscious self-representation as a symbol of black pride reflected his highly developed self-perception as a cultural leader and icon for African Americans, in particular, and untold numbers worldwide. This strong sense of self and of his broad cultural influence contributed significantly to Miles's avant-gardism, notably his lifelong commitment to artistic (and personal) renewal and re-invention. "The greatest single thing about Miles Davis," Ralph Gleason once observed, "is that he does not stand still. He is forever being born."[18]

Not surprisingly, in this exceedingly complicated context, Miles's castigations of free jazz became more ill-tempered. In a 1964 "Blindfold Test" for the pre-eminent jazz magazine *Down Beat*, conducted by Leonard Feather, Miles was asked to listen to a series of recordings, try to identify the musician, and comment on the music and musician. Of a selection by the important free jazz player multi-instrumentalist Eric Dolphy, Miles exclaimed: "That's got to be Eric Dolphy—nobody else could sound that bad! The next time I see him I'm going to step on his foot. You print that. I think he's ridiculous." On hearing a piece by avant-garde pianist Cecil Taylor, Miles demanded: "Take it off!" He continued: "I hear some Charlie Parker clichés. . . . They don't even fit. Is this what the critics are digging? Them critics better stop having coffee." Upon identifying Taylor as the pianist in the piece, Miles explained that Taylor lacked "the way you touch a piano. He doesn't have the touch that would make the sound of whatever he thinks to come off."[19]

At this time, in the context of the debate about free jazz as the "New Thing," Miles had difficulty acknowledging publicly the new music as the cutting-edge. When asked in 1964 about the future of jazz, he claimed not to hear a forthcoming "really new thing." "There is no next trend," he explained. "If there's another trend, then we're going backwards. . . . There's not going to be another trend unless it's the walking-off-the-stage trend."

Indeed, his hostility to the playing of Shepp was firm. In 1967, when Shepp sat in for a set with Miles's group at the urging of the drummer, Tony Williams, Miles simply walked off the bandstand because he argued Shepp "couldn't play." In a 1968 "Blindfold Test," he blasted a recording by Shepp accompanied by fellow avant-gardists Don Cherry and alto saxophonist John Tchicai. After mistaking the work for the music of Coleman, Miles explained: "Ornette sounds the same way. That's where Archie and them got that ___ from; there sure ain't nothing there."[20]

It was clear to Miles that to reposition himself as an innovator, to restore the cutting-edge quality of his music, and to revive his popularity, a change was imperative. To borrow a line from Soul Brother Number One James Brown, Miles desperately needed a "Brand New Bag." He got one in his stellar mid-sixties quintet featuring Williams, Herbie Hancock on piano, Wayne Shorter on sax, and Ron Carter on bass. Working at his eclectic best with a first-rate crew, Miles emerged from the creative doldrums with a steadily developing music. Building upon his earlier hard bop and modal work and melding the often more contemporary compositional influences of the new group members, Miles's new quintet blazed a fresh and influential musical path. This evolving music necessarily included influences drawn from free jazz, especially the Coltranesque touches of Shorter.

Ironically, then, in spite of Miles's professed intense dislike for free jazz, both free jazz and other contemporary musical currents, which he obviously liked much more, transformed his own subsequent jazz-fusion explorations.

While much has been made of the impact of rock, soul, and funk on his fusion career, far less has been made of the very important impact of free jazz on those musical explorations.[21]

In crucial ways, free jazz offered a kind of postmodernist cornucopia—openness, indeterminacy, ambiguity, hybridity, and diversity—that propelled much of Miles's later music, and his fusion period represented a postmodern updating of his music, with both positive and negative results. One way of thinking about the impact of the free jazz avant-garde on the trajectory of Miles's music, then, is to see free jazz as a crucial element in his final major musical shift. Free jazz was vital to the musical mix, pushing Miles, the quintessential jazz modernist, headlong into an increasingly postmodern musical world. As Miles's politics necessarily responded to the challenge of the Black Power moment, he wittingly and unwittingly made music that, in turn, responded to the challenge of the corresponding free jazz moment. Indeed, his music had to respond to the challenge of the sixties jazz avant-garde, if only to go in a different yet related musical direction.

Even as the debates over the merits of Miles's fusion music of the late sixties and beyond raged on, his stature as the popular personification of the jazz avant-garde, as the "Prince of Jazz," persisted. In fact, Miles and his music have remained pivotal to debates around the very meaning of a jazz avant-garde. As Gary Giddins observed of Miles in

1981, "Every time he comes up with a new answer, the whole music shifts in its seat. He didn't originate all the directions that became associated with his records, but he found ways to make them palatable, even popular. His popularity probably accounts for the frequent omission of Davis's name from discussions of jazz radicals."[22]

The narrow view of the jazz avant-garde rejected here is patently insufficient. In addition to the major innovators—the virtuosi—the jazz avant-garde of necessity must include the principal long-term makers and shapers of the expanding jazz tradition like Miles Davis. Free jazz in the 1960s represented one way of thinking about the jazz avant-garde: "the new thing." Miles Davis represented another: an avant-garde jazz life, both culturally and musically, of almost fifty years.

As Giddens concluded, Miles was "a terribly conscientious avant-gardist, continuously remaking jazz in his own image, and often remaking himself in the process."[23] Jazz, especially given the depth and complexity of its history, demands a flexible and inclusive notion of avant-gardism. Such a notion of the jazz avant-garde must highlight the cutting-edge work and profoundly influential iconic stature of Miles Davis. Equally important, it must put into proper context the less impressive though nonetheless valuable parts of his massive body of work, notably that work created amid and beyond the turbulent free jazz insurgency.

1 Bob Blumenthal, "Miles Gloriosus," *Boston Phoenix*, July 7, 1981, reprinted in Bill Kirchner, ed., *A Miles Davis Reader* (Washington, D.C.: Smithsonian Institution Press, 1997), 213.

2 I must acknowledge the insight of Eric Porter, who pointed out to me the salience of "avant-garde capital" as a way to represent and to gauge Miles Davis's avant-gardism.

3 Bob Blumenthal, *Miles Davis and John Coltrane: The Complete Columbia Recordings, 1955–1961* (2000), 46.

4 Quincy Troupe, *Miles and Me* (Berkeley: University of California Press, 2000), 5–6.

5 This characterization of the Claude Thornhill Orchestra's music is drawn from Ian Carr, *Miles Davis; A Biography* (New York: William Morrow and Co., 1982), 32.

6 A. B. Spellman, *Black Music: Four Lives—Cecil Taylor, Ornette Coleman, Herbie Nichols, Jackie McLean* (New York: Schocken, 1970), 81. [Originally published as *Four Lives in the Bebop Business* by Pantheon in 1966]

7 Ibid., 81–82; Miles Davis with Quincy Troupe, *Miles: The Autobiography* (New York: Simon and Shuster, 1989), 249.

8 *Miles: The Autobiography*, 249–51, cited on page 251.

9 Craig Werner, *A Change Is Gonna Come: Music, Race, and the Soul of America* (New York: Plume, 1998), 137.

10 Miles Davis quoted in Hollie I. West, "Black Tune," *The Washington Post*, March 13, 1969, cited in Carr, *Miles Davis*, 148.

11 Brian Ward, *Just My Soul Responding: Rhythm and Blues, Black Consciousness, and Race Relations* (Berkeley: University of California Press, 1998), 306; Carr, *Miles Davis*, 127–28, 130, 137–38.

12 Gerald Early, "Miles Davis as Ahab and the Whale," *The American Poetry Review* (January/February 1997): 31: Troupe, *Miles and Me*, 117, 166–67; Eric Porter, "'It's About That Time': The Response to Miles Davis's Electric Turn."

13 "The *Playboy* Interview: Miles Davis," *Playboy* 9, no. 9 (September 1960): 62.

14 Leonard Feather, "Miles Davis: Blindfold Tests," Part I, *Downbeat* (June 13, 1968). Carr, *Miles Davis*, 151–53.

15 Early, "Miles Davis," 31.

16 John Litweiler, *The Freedom Principle: Jazz After 1958* (New York: Da Capo Press, 1984), 86; *Miles: The Autobiography*, 222–24, 396; Frank Kofsky, *Black Nationalism and the Revolution in Black Music* (New York: Pathfinder Press, 1970); Litweiler, *The Freedom Principle*, 80–104; Gerald Early, "Ode to John Coltrane: A Jazz Musician's Influence on African American Culture," *Antioch Review 57*, no. 3 (Summer 1999): 371–85.

17 Ward, *Just My Soul Responding*, 306.

18 Ralph Gleason cited in Troupe, *Miles and Me*, 166.

19 Leonard Feather, "Blindfold Test: Miles Davis," *Down Beat*, (June 18, 1964): 31.

20 Leonard Feather, "Miles and the Fifties," *Down Beat*, 31:20 (July 2, 1964): 98; *Miles: The Autobiography*, 268; "Blindfold Test: Miles Davis," *Down Beat* (June 13, 1968).

21 *Miles, The Autobiography*, especially 271–332; Amiri Baraka, "Miles Davis: 'One of the Great Mother Fuckers,'" in Kirchner, *A Miles Davis Reader*, 63–73; Harvey Pekar, "Miles Davis: 1964–69 Recordings," in ibid., 164–83: Peter Keepnews, "The Lost Quintet," in ibid., 184–89; Blumenthal, "Miles Gloriosus," in ibid., 212–16; Gary Giddens, "Miles Wiles," in ibid., 217–23;

22 For thoughtful treatments of this debate, see Gary Tomlinson, "Miles Davis, Musical Dialogician," in Kirchner, *A Miles Davis Reader*, 234–49; Porter, "'It's About Time'"; Giddens, "Miles Wiles," in Kirchner, *A Miles Davis Reader*, 218.

23 Giddens, "Miles Wiles," in Kirchner, *A Miles Davis Reader*, 218.

Boston, 1964.
Photograph by
Lee Tanner.

Miles Davis, until his untimely death on September 28, 1991, was one of the fountainheads of twentieth-century music. A great trumpet player, composer, and bandleader, a restless, controversial, and innovative musician in a career of almost fifty years, Davis crossed geographical, genre, and generational borders and produced a music that blurred and eventually erased musical categories—classical, jazz, rock, rhythm and blues, pop, fusion, funk, world music, hip-hop—with stunning originality. A good way to view Miles today is as a portal, a doorway or entry point to the wide range of African American music.

Miles always searched for new ways to better express what he was feeling at the moment, right up until he suffered the stroke that eventually killed him. He was always headed forward, away from that "blue flame jumping off a gas stove someone lit" that almost burned him. That blue flame was his first conscious memory from early childhood. Listen to the way he recounted the incident in *Miles: The Autobiography*, a book I was privileged and honored to write with him:

I remember being shocked by the whoosh of the blue flame jumping off the burner, the suddenness of it. That's as far back as I can remember; any further back than this is just fog, you know, just mystery. But that stove flame is a clear as music is in my mind. I was three years old.

I saw that flame and felt that hotness of it close to my face. I felt fear, real fear, for the first time in my life. But I remember it also like some kind of adventure, some kind of weird joy, too. I guess that experience took me someplace in my head I hadn't been before. To some frontier, the edge, maybe of everything possible. I don't know; I never tried to analyze it before. The fear I had was almost like an invitation, a challenge to go forward into something I knew nothing about. That's where I think my personal philosophy of life and my commitment to everything I believe in started, with that moment. I don't know, but I think it might be true. Who knows? What the fuck did I know about anything back then? In my mind I have always believed since then that my motion had to be forward, away from the heat of that flame.

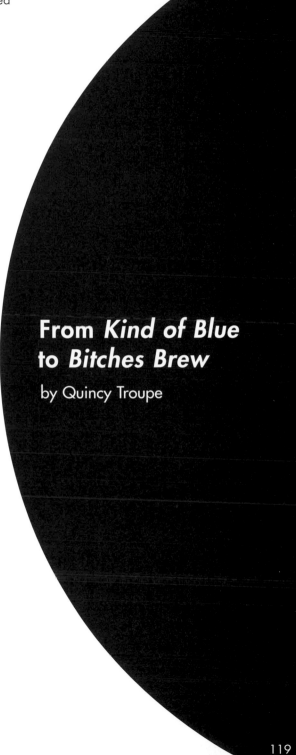

From *Kind of Blue* to *Bitches Brew*

by Quincy Troupe

This moment, "the whoosh of the blue flame jumping off the burner" and almost burning him seems, in Miles's view, to serve literally as inspiration for a life of artistic risk-taking with no looking back. It also works as a metaphor for creativity; a flame can burn, but it also can inspire.

A quick check on the Internet reveals nearly one hundred albums available under Miles Davis's name, and that doesn't count imports, tribute albums, Miles's presence on samplers, and the recordings of his work by other artists. Columbia/Legacy continues its ambitious reissue program of thirty years of Miles Davis on that label, and Fantasy/Prestige and Capitol have followed suit with selected recordings. Miles ran from that flame right into a permanent place in the music marketplace, but amid the flotsam of reissues, repackagings, and rediscoveries, it is easy to lose the thread of development over the course of this career.

As I listen to Miles on record, I continue to be fascinated by a remarkable twelve-year period from 1958 to 1969 in which, record-by-record, his sound changed from the elegant tranquility of *Kind of Blue* to the boiling cauldron of *Bitches Brew*. I'm interested primarily in two groups that Miles led, and I will share my thoughts on some of the music of this period, as well as the new music that followed the breakup of his great quintet in 1968.

Before analyzing some of Miles's music, I have a disclaimer to make. I'm not the most objective person in evaluating Miles Davis. He was so much a part of my formative experiences, and I worked so closely with him later in life in assisting in the telling of his life story, that I confess from the outset that it is sometimes difficult for me to get perspective on the man.

I've told this story before, but it bears repeating because of the impact it had on me and the impact it still has as I think about Miles. The first matter is that I grew up in north St. Louis, so I know Miles's home turf pretty well. I grew up around people who spoke like Miles, had attitudes similar to his, and experienced the same type of humid St. Louis summers as he did. That's the first thing.

The second thing is an incident that occurred when I was fifteen years old and trying to figure out a few things about life, like a lot of fifteen-year-olds do. I don't remember just when it was, but I know it was in 1955 when I went into a fish joint on Fair Avenue to get a jack-salmon sandwich, the same kind of sandwich Miles remembered from growing up in East St. Louis. This nondescript fish joint had a prefab look that later defined fast food "restaurants" all over America. There was nothing "greasy-spoon" about it, which made it a little suspect. As we often said, the joint was "trying to look white."

Here is how I remember it in my memoir, *Miles and Me*:

Once inside, I immediately noticed a booth filled with four black, hip-looking older guys wearing the latest "in" clothes. Smoking cigarettes and wearing shades, their wide-brimmed hats hanging majestically on the prongs of two steel poles, which seemed to grow beside their booth like facing trees.

The men were sitting there talking and eating deep-fried "jack-salmon" sandwiches doused with hot sauce, with sides of potato salad and cole slaw. They were also listening to the juke box that was jamming sounds I had either never heard before or never paid attention to. Whatever it was, it was new to me. . . .

They talked about the sounds they were hearing on the box. One man said the trumpet was played by a "homeboy" from across the river, someone named Miles Davis. Another said the tune was called "Donna." (112–113)

Well, that moment changed my life. These hip older men and these new sounds seemed to be the signal for something different in my life. I've never been the same since. Miles's music later helped me to become a poet, and that's why I'm a music lover rather than a music critic. Miles hated the term jazz, thought it demeaned and pigeonholed what he was trying to accomplish, and he told me on many, many occasions that what he was doing was simply "playing music." Good or bad, it was "all just music" to him. Miles once said to me, "If critics can put us artists in a box it's easier for them to deal with what we do." He thought most critics imposed genre limits on artists because they were "lazy" and didn't want to do the extra work required when an artist changed and went in another direction. Further, he felt that critics dismissed or panned art that they had no references for or didn't understand—especially if the reference point was black.

I have no boxes or categories for Miles.

Nevertheless, here are the thoughts of a "homeboy" on a remarkable period in Miles's music—1958–1969—and on two amazing groups he led and on the extraordinary music he made at the end of the period. My analytical reference point is the one with which I'm most familiar: Miles himself.

The first, the sextet of 1958–60, grew out of his first great working quintet and recorded what is generally acknowledged as perhaps the masterpiece of small group jazz, *Kind of Blue*, in 1959. The members of this group included some of the finest musicians of the century: John Coltrane on tenor saxophone, whose intense, questing music inspired so many in the 1960s; Julian "Cannonball" Adderley on alto, whose popularity in the subgenre of soul jazz nearly rivaled that of Miles in years to come; pianist Bill Evans, whose pristine piano trio work sketched new harmonic possibilities; pianist Wynton Kelley, a master of the blues, swing, and thoughtful accompaniment; bassist Paul Chambers; and drummer Jimmy Cobb, who formed perhaps the finest rhythm section of the era in partnership with Kelley.

The second group is known as the second great quintet, consisting of tenor saxophonist Wayne Shorter, perhaps the most original composer of his generation; pianist Herbie Hancock, the very definition of versatility; prodigal drummer Tony Williams; and steady Ron Carter, one of the most sought-after session musicians of all time. As remarkable as these groups were, by the end of the period under review Miles had left acoustic jazz behind forever. The journey from *Kind of Blue* to *Bitches Brew* is a perfect example of Miles never looking back, but it is also a good example of him looking around along the way and responding to the culture around him.

For me, the journey begins with "Milestones" from the 1958 album of the same name. It ushered in Miles's modal period, a style that influenced and changed the entire musical scene. On this recording Miles really begins, for the first time, to write and play in the modal form, which he explained in our book as "seven notes off each note, a scale off each note, a minor note." He went on to say that he "found out that music played in this way didn't lock the musician or music in, that the music could go on seemingly forever, that musicians didn't have to worry about traditional changes." He added that the challenge for him when he worked in the modal way was to see how inventive he could become melodically.

Again, in our book he said: "It's not like when you base stuff on chords, and you know at the end of thirty-two bars that the chords have run out and there's nothing to do but repeat what you've done with variations. I was moving away from that way of playing," he goes on, "and into more melodic ways of doing things. And in the modal way I saw all kinds of possibilities." On "Milestones," Miles reduced a tune of formerly multiple changes down to a few scales and time signatures and provided a forum for, according to Gary Giddins, his "middle range, measured lyricism, his hot-ice disposition" and style.[1]

Miles had begun thinking modally about music after attending a performance of the Ballet Africaine from Guinea in 1957 with his wife Frances Taylor Davis, who was a great dancer. It was the rhythm of the African dancers and the African finger piano that, according to Miles, "blew his mind." The drummers. The time signatures they played, in the rhythms of 5/4, 6/8, and 4/4, that were always changing and popping and it seemed like they could go on dancing and playing forever, because of the open form. He said he knew he couldn't copy what they were doing because "they were African" and he wasn't. He hadn't lived their interior life experience, but he could do something that would embrace that feeling that he got when he saw them

dance and heard them play, and that "something" would be a concept that he and George Russell, another fine musician and composer, would call the "modal" way, and which Miles continued with his next sextet album, *Kind of Blue.*

"So What" sets the tone on this album of dark, flowing introspection. Miles added a little gospel, bluesy sound and feeling to the music, because he remembered hearing once, back when he was six, the disembodied sound of an old black woman's voice floating through the darkness and quavering like a ripple over the ghost shadows of trees as he walked with his cousin along a very dark road in Arkansas. He assumed that this lonely, plaintive, haunting, but ultimately very human voice was coming from some church hidden somewhere back in the trees and dark woods. He didn't know and he never found out where that voice had come from. But he heard it and it stayed with him all his life and he told me that it was *that* voice that he was always trying to get close to when he played a ballad, or a blues, or a love song.

Now, in 1959, he tried to imbue some of his playing, the sound and feeling of some of the compositions and group sound on Kind of Blue, with what he heard in that old black woman's voice. The combination of that gospel/blues voice with Bill Evans's floating chords is particularly beguiling on "Blue in Green" and "Flamenco Sketches."

Miles told me that when he recorded *Kind of Blue,* and to get closer to a certain way of group playing he felt he needed on the album, he didn't write out the parts for the musicians. But instead, he brought into the New York studio musical sketches of what everyone was supposed to play, because he wanted a lot of spontaneity and improvisation in their playing. He hoped in this way that they might come close to the interplay he remembered seeing and hearing between the dancers and musicians of the Ballet Africaine.

Almost everything on *Kind of Blue* is a first take (there were two complete takes of "Flamenco Sketches"), and this was accomplished without even one rehearsal, because, as Miles has said, "all the musicians were great and that's the only way they knew how to play." Many have called *Kind of Blue* the greatest single jazz recording of all time. It is truly a great album, a seamless, beautiful, and magnificent accomplishment. The album only sells more over time as it is reissued and as contemporary listeners look for something that is classic, accessible, and substantive all at once.

Kind of Blue was released in 1959, just before the beginning of the tumultuous, revolutionary decade of the 1960s. Like that decade, *Kind of Blue* was a radical departure, breaking away from the old ways of doing things, and, as the 1960s forever changed the way Americans viewed each other, the album had a similar impact on American music, influencing the great virtuosos of the new rock music as well as providing a standard of excellence in jazz. It may not have sounded quite as radical as Ornette Coleman's *The Shape of Jazz to Come*, released in the same year, but *Kind of Blue* provided a bridge between the mainstream bop of the 1950s and the free improvisations that followed, all the while grounding the music in African

American traditions. As usual, Miles was ahead, helping to lead the monumental musical changes that were to come.

Miles's second great period of musical invention that I will discuss came when he formed the quintet of Hancock, Shorter, Williams, Carter, and himself. After John Coltrane left during the spring of 1960 to form his own band, Miles's once stable group started on a slow slide toward disintegration. Between 1960 and 1962, Miles tried different combinations of musicians in his working band, all fine musicians and some even great. But soon the band became like a turnstile, with players like Sonny Stitt, Hank Mobley, Sonny Rollins, George Coleman, Frank Strozier, J. J. Johnson, Jimmy Heath, Victor Feldman, Frank Butler, and Harold Mabern moving in and out of it. Then, in 1962, one by one, beginning with Ron Carter, Tony Williams, and Herbie Hancock and ending with the last piece of the "second great quintet," Wayne Shorter, Miles had himself another super band. Soon he was off and running in the fast lane of music once again, but this time he was as much a student of his young players as he was their teacher and leader.

First, allow me a digression to set up my discussion of this seminal band and the new musical trends that influenced and fed into its group sound. By 1960 Miles had totally absorbed the modal way of playing and composing. But beginning in 1961, the Gil Evans collaboration *Sketches of Spain* having been released the year before, he

became restless with the music he was playing and wanted to move on. But where? The entire country was changing. It was the beginning of the radical sixties, and there was an angrier, less melodic, more fragmented mood afoot across the nation. Race relations were deteriorating, fast, as they are now today. Race riots would soon occur, and people in the country would soon be at each other's throats. I remember living through those tense times. And the music composed and played in the avant-garde black jazz community was mirroring this mood. In New York, the discordant and dissonant music of Coleman and his partner Don Cherry, Cecil Taylor, Archie Shepp, Albert Ayler, and Eric Dolphy, to name just a few, were beginning to be recognized by prominent jazz critics.

Miles was at first disdainful of this development. He had no used for what he thought to be a strident, unstructured, unmelodic and fragmented music. But all the members of his new band had been deeply influenced by some of the music, especially that of Ornette Coleman. Up until now, Miles had been the primary composer and arranger for all of the groups he led, but with his new band all that was about to change, and fast. Miles quickly found out that he had fallen behind the cutting-edge trends in progressive music. Suddenly, and to his complete shock, he found himself playing catch-up. He told me once that "music was changing a lot" around this time, and that "a lot of people, who were just fans and listeners, started saying jazz was dead. They blamed the free thing."

Further, he went on to say, "the music people like Archie Shepp, Albert Ayler, Cecil Taylor, and Ornette Coleman were playing didn't have no melodic line, wasn't lyrical and you couldn't hum what they played." But according to Miles, critics pushed the "way-out thing" and all of a sudden people started turning off of jazz in droves. Up until this point, jazz had enjoyed great popularity, and Miles was as popular as any other jazz musician at this time, with a strong international fan base. But soon many people stopped listening to jazz and started really getting into white rock and roll, which had, according to Miles, already

"stolen the music and rhythms" of black popular rock and roll stars like Little Richard, Ike Turner, Fats Domino, Chuck Berry, and the new Motown sound. Jazz clubs began closing across the nation as the sixties went on.

Miles also began losing his popular base around this time. People became indifferent to what he was playing. He believed "the magic was gone" from his working band, because he no longer had a consistent group of great musicians with which to work. "Great musicians love to play with each other," he told me, "and this feeling is picked up by the audiences. If a band isn't great they fall apart and the music gets stale." He thought his working band had been stale since his *Kind of Blue* band had fallen apart.

But now with this new group, he had great musicians and an outstanding band once again. He said in our book: "To have a great band requires sacrifice and compromise from everyone. Without it, nothing happens. I thought my new band could do it and they did. You get the right guys to play the right things at the right time and you got a motherfucker; you got everything you need." He went on to describe the band:

If I was the inspiration and wisdom, Tony was the fire, the creative spark; Wayne was the idea person, the conceptualizer of a whole lot of musical ideas we did; and Ron and Herbie were the anchors. I was just a

leader who put us all together. Those were all young guys and, although they were learning from me, I was learning from them, too, about the new thing, the free thing. Because to be and stay a great musician you've got to always be open to what's new, what's happening at the moment. You have to be able to absorb it if you're going to communicate your music. Creativity and genius in any kind of artistic expression don't know nothing about age; either you got it or you don't and being old is not going to help you get it. I understood that we had to do something different. I knew I was playing with some great young musicians that had their fingers on a different pulse.

To his credit, Miles let them play that "different pulse," and he learned from them and rode their creative energy and musical genius and expression every night they played together, which was close to six years. Miles, influenced by the compositions of Shorter and by the incredible interplay between all the members of the group, soon began playing freer, picked up on Shorter's concept of "experimenting *with* form instead of someone who did it *without* form." He said of Shorter, "That's why I thought he was perfect for where I wanted to see the music go."

The music this group played on the road swirled around the room, flashing colors and incredibly complex time signatures and rhythms. And the music changed every night. Miles, released from his former melodic self, found that his playing now flew into the stratosphere. He played higher and in faster tempos, attacking the trumpet in his approach, splintering off notes and chords as if they were pieces of wood flying through a wood threshing machine. It seemed as though he was almost spitting out notes, exploding them upwards and outwards in bursts that were incredible in their improvisatory heat and verve. All of a sudden, it seemed as if Miles had been reborn, that he had transformed himself from a magnificently lyrical, melodic trumpet player, one with a soft, tender, almost feminine, muted, romantic, brooding attack and approach to the horn, into a power player. The transformation was quite remarkable for those of us who had been listening to him for a long time.

Miles loved this band, as he told me on many occasions. "If we played a song for a whole year and you heard it at the beginning of the year, you wouldn't recognize it at the end of the year," he said in our book as a way of describing how creative the band was. He also told me:

The way I had been playing before these guys came into the band was kind of getting on my nerves. Like a favorite pair of shoes that you wear all the time, after a while you've got to change them. I finally realized that what was good about Ornette Coleman was that his musical ideas and melodies were independent of musical styles, and being independent like that would make a musician, if they played in that way, appear to be creating spontaneously.

I have an almost perfect sense of melodic order, but I discovered after really paying attention to some of the things Ornette was playing and talking about then—especially after Tony came into the band and listening to what he had to say about what Ornette was doing—that when I played one note from my trumpet I was really playing about four and that I was transposing guitar solos to my trumpet voice.

This was a revelation for Miles. A guitar in his trumpet playing? Where had that come from? Then he realized it had come from his deep roots in blues and roadhouse funk music, the guitar- and organ-based music he had grown up with back in East St. Louis and St. Louis. So he went back again, as he did with the old black woman's voice from Arkansas on *Kind of Blue*, and "started putting the back beat in the drums out front and on top of everything, like in African music," the ultimate source of the blues and roadhouse funk, with both depending heavily on the concept of rhythm.

"In Western music," he said in our book, "white people at this time were trying to suppress rhythm because of where it came from—Africa—and its racial overtones. But rhythm is like breathing," he went on, "so that's what I began to learn about rhythm in this group and it just pointed the way forward."

By 1968 his new group had recorded and released a series of stunningly fine studio albums: *E. S. P.* (1965); *Miles Smiles* (1966); *Sorcerer*

1967); *Nefertiti* (1967); *Miles in the Sky* (1968); and *Filles de Kilimanjaro* (1968). The live material is best represented by the box set *The Complete Plugged Nickel,* 1965.

Miles in the Sky and *Filles de Kilimanjaro* represented a moment of change for Miles once again, and by the time the second album was completed, Hancock and Carter had moved on. The last pieces recorded by the quintet, "Petits Machins," "Tout de Suite," and "Filles de Kilimanjaro," were all Davis compositions, and the more insistent rhythm patterns and the use of electric bass and piano signaled a new direction. By 1968 Miles also realized that he had learned and absorbed all he could from his great young players. (Hamiet Bluiett, the great baritone sax player from Brooklyn, Illinois, which is across the Mississippi River from St. Louis, once told me he thought Miles was the "biggest sponge in the world," and that he just "soaked up everything when it came to music.") Now, as was his habit, he was ready to move on to something new. Those East St. Louis/St. Louis musical roots had a powerful pull

on him, but he also had his ears open to the musical world around him.

He wanted less abstraction and more funk, "whatever that was," he once told me. All he knew precisely, is that he had to move on. Some of the music he had been playing was already pointing toward *In a Silent Way* and *Bitches Brew.* If one listens closely to some of the music on *Filles de Kilimanjaro,* it can be heard as a bridge to the more overt statements on the subsequent albums. In particular, the droning sound of the electric piano and the ensemble interplay in a continuous flow of music point the way to Miles's future.

For Miles, there were several musical voices missing on *Filles de Kilimanjaro,* the main one being the guitar, which Miles now heard as an electric guitar, rather than an acoustic one. He had already long been using Herbie Hancock on electric piano, and now Chick Corea took that chair, replacing Herbie, who was ready to lead his own group. On the earlier *Miles in the Sky,* George Benson had sat in on "Paraphernalia," and Miles

had also experimented with guitarist Joe Beck on material that remained unreleased for several years. Benson's contributions on "Paraphernalia" are somewhat muted, but the overall tone of the recording reveals the influence of James Brown and Sly Stone. The guitar comping, and the choppy, stop-and-go rhythms point to Miles's recasting of blues and funk for his own purposes. His ideas would receive fuller expression on *In a Silent Way* and *Bitches Brew,* both recorded in 1969.

Miles also had been listening to the music of Charles Lloyd and two of his musicians: pianist Keith Jarrett and drummer Jack DeJohnette, both of whom he would later hire for his band. Miles loved the way Lloyd fused elements of rock and jazz in his music. But the biggest influence on Miles's music in 1968 was that of guitarist Jimi Hendrix, who had been introduced to Miles by his wife, Betty Mabry (the relationship between Hendrix and Mabry eventually broke the marriage). Miles wanted to incorporate some of Hendrix's incendiary, snarling guitar sound into his band by fusing rock and roll, jazz, rhythm and blues, funk, and blues into his music, a style many would later call "fusion." He had finally caught up with the new musical language and was now ready to begin putting his own stamp on the music that would be played for the next decade, just as he had when he had popularized modal playing.

When *In a Silent Way* was released, it sounded radically new, international, and yet rooted in the music Miles had heard growing up in East St. Louis and St. Louis. On the other hand, the music presented here was far more elastic and freer than that music, because Miles was now attempting to explode and expand the traditional roadhouse funk, rock and blues forms. He was trying to fuse them with elements of American jazz and European classical music to better utilize the formidable composing, arranging and playing talents of Josef Zawinul, who was born and raised in Austria. Guitarist John McLaughlin and bassist Dave Holland were also from Europe, both hailing from England, and this also helped imbue the album with a more European feel and sound. Zawinul wrote the title tune of the album, while Miles wrote the other two tracks: "Shhh/Peaceful" and "It's About That Time." On *In a Silent Way* Miles finally added an organ as an equal voice in the group sound; the guitar, too, worked on a par with the horns and the pianos. The addition of these two instruments locates the music in that roadhouse funk, semi-rock, blues mode, though their roles and voices in the ensemble sound are very different from what they had been in traditional African American music.

From the beginning of "Shhh/Peaceful" at the start of the album, the organ lays down a droning tone that is almost mournful. It moves in and out of the music, embellishing and accenting it here and there, comping like a regular jazz piano. The organ

and piano have interchangeable roles, both weaving in and out, as the guitar wails and punctuates the music, also in a droning style. Shorter's saxophone has the same function, and Miles's trumpet approach retains the general tone.

The ensemble playing on *In a Silent Way* is continuously interactive, with long, snake-like musical lines repeating themselves in an antiphonal call and response manner; the music stretches out and then winds back around itself in such a way that it almost becomes a droning monotone but one that helps to build the song because of the spacing of the solos taken, which help break up the sameness of the sound. Miles plays especially bright and effective solos on this album. Much of the album came

about as a result of postproduction splicing and overdubbing techniques that had grown popular in the recording industry since the Beatles' legendary 1967 *Sgt. Pepper's Lonely Hearts Club Band* and which Miles's producer, Teo Macero, had been developing to better capture Miles's musical vision. This is a mysterious, compelling, intriguing album, one that I didn't like at first but found myself continually drawn back to. It was almost as if some magical and mysterious elements were bubbling just beneath the surface of this music, like an underground river, and I keep waiting for it to totally surface but it never has in all these years.

If *In a Silent Way* was intriguing, *Bitches Brew* was almost like a slap in the face when I first heard it. Nothing in my listening experience had quite prepared me for it. I was living in Athens, Ohio, at the time and teaching at Ohio University. After I had bought the album, which had such a strange, cosmic cover, I went into my front room and put it on the record player and listened to it over and over again until late into the evening. At first, I was repelled by the music, but gradually over time it hypnotized and seduced me, no matter how weird I sometimes found it. But before I went to bed that evening, I found the music truly compelling, and it has demanded my attention ever since.

In my sonic imagination, *Bitches Brew* seems to mimic the urban traffic sounds of great cities like Paris, or New York's Times Square, with car horns honking and people screaming, a hurricane of all kinds of voices which sound like a swirling maelstrom of electrical sounds that pulsate, probe, riff, and suck the listener into a strange, almost violent musical world. But this music came at the end of the 1960s, after the race riots had occurred, after all the chaos. So, in my view, Bitches Brew was a summing up of an era that was going out, with something new on the verge of coming in. What that something was, nobody knew at the time. We just hoped it would be something better.

Miles and Teo Macero just let the recording tape run on *Bitches Brew* with no interruptions. Sometimes Miles would conduct the band, maybe write down new chords and notes while musicians were playing and passed them out. Sometimes he would tell one of the musicians to play something different, and as the music grew over the three days of the recording sessions, things began to come together and a shape started to emerge in the music. "It was loose and tight at the same time," Miles recalled. "It was casual but alert to different possibilities that were coming up in the music. While the music was developing," he went on, "I would hear something that I thought should be extended or cut back. So that recording was a development of the creative process, a living composition. It was like a fugue, or motif, that we all bounced off of. . . . That was a great recording session."

On the album Miles uses three electric pianists, three percussionists, acoustic and electric basses, a soprano saxophone, and a bass clarinet. He had never used this combination of instruments before (had anyone?), and he grew to love the combinations and group sound. He would later add sitars and tablas to subsequent albums, including *Live-Evil*, recorded in 1970. After *Bitches Brew* Miles's music would seldom return to the old melodic, lyrical style so many who loved him had become accustomed to. It would also be the beginning of the savage critical assault on his music by those who never would accept his new style.

Between 1958 and 1970, Miles produced as remarkable a body of recorded work as one can find anywhere. The recordings still sound fresh today, thirty and forty years after their release. During this period Miles, along with Coltrane, Jimi Hendrix, the Beatles, James Brown, Sly and the Family Stone, Bob Dylan, and the music of the Motown artists influenced entire generations of musicians and music lovers, and their impact is still felt today. I have a feeling, though, that Miles's music will outlast them all.

Beyond all that, I simply miss him, his presence in the world, his unique talent, personhood, and vision. Happy seventy-fifth, Miles, wherever you are. Thank you for coming this—and my—way.

Some material for this essay was adapted from:
Miles Davis with Quincy Troupe, *Miles: The Autobiography* (New York: Simon and Schuster, 1990).
Quincy Troupe, "Overview: *Bitches Brew*." Liner notes for Miles Davis, *The Complete Bitches Brew Sessions* (Columbia/Legacy, 1998).
Quincy Troupe, *Miles and Me* (Berkeley: University of California Press, 2000).

1. Gary Giddins. "Miles Davis (Kinds of Blues)" in *Visions of Jazz: The First Hundred Years* (New York: Oxford University Press, 1998).

At home in New York,
1971.
Photograph by
Anthony Barboza.

Miles Davis in life, and now in the ten years after his death, has been a central figure in debates over the meaning of jazz in American culture. His long career and participation in several major shifts in modern jazz—bebop, cool, modal, and fusion—have made him a symbol for jazz history in the post–World War II era. With this has come great controversy and contradictory value judgments on the musician and his art, assessments that are products of shifting historical contexts, the cloak of ideological noise that has always surrounded jazz, and Davis's own music, actions, and commentary. Perhaps the most controversial time of Davis's career is his electric period. At the end of the 1960s Davis changed his sound and precipitated one of the great debates in jazz history. As Quincy Troupe remembers, *Bitches Brew* generally "polarized his audience into two distinct and separate groups; those who avidly listened to and loved his music before *Bitches Brew*, and those who loved and got into his music after."[2] Although this phase of Davis's musical life has recently been celebrated through a series of CD re-releases and tribute albums, musicians, fans, and critics still argue about it thirty years later.

Unlike some who have commented on the electric period, I am not invested in condemning it; and though I am a fan of this music I am not seeking to rescue it from its detractors. Rather, I am interested in understanding some of these recent evaluations of the electric period by other African American intellectuals—namely those of Amiri Baraka, Stanley Crouch, and Greg Tate—as part of an eighty-year struggle to define a healthy and potentially liberating black musical aesthetic through jazz. Guiding such discussions have been a complex of ideas about race, masculinity, class, genius, cultural authenticity, artistic integrity, commercialism, the relative values of musical styles, the idea of "America" as both physical space and ideological construct, and the responsibilities that black artists and intellectuals have to their communities. I am further fascinated by the ways assessments of Davis's electric music written in the 1980s and 1990s stand as commentaries on the legacy of Black Power–era cultural politics, their relative merits and failures, and their relevance for the present. In the end, these interpretations also testify to the extraordinary power and influence Davis has wielded as a musician and icon over the past half century.

"It's About That Time":

The Response to Miles Davis's Electric Turn[1]

by Eric Porter

For much of the 1960s Davis generally adhered to the mainstream of modern jazz established in the 1950s. Although he expressed some interest in the innovations of the avant-garde, he did not embrace them outright. The quintet Davis worked with for much of the 1960s—with band members Ron Carter, Herbie Hancock, Wayne Shorter and Tony Williams—occasionally experimented with free improvisation, but the group generally stuck to melodic ballads, spare modal pieces, and swinging, boppish numbers. Yet, toward the end of the decade, Davis began to change his sound. He developed an affinity for the music of James Brown, and thanks to his wife Betty Mabry, Jimi Hendrix and Sly Stone, whom she introduced him to both musically and personally.[3] Over the next several years, until his temporary retirement in 1975, Davis fused avant-garde jazz and the blues with elements from rock, funk, and soul, as well as African and Afro-Brazilian rhythms, South Asian instruments, and the ideas of composers Paul Buckmaster and Karlheinz Stockhausen.

Davis long had been interested in an array of musical expressions, and at a certain level his integration of multiple elements was not inconsistent with an aesthetic he had adhered to on recordings such as *The Birth of the Cool* or *Sketches of Spain*. However, the use of electric and electronic instruments and his emphasis on rhythm as an organizing principle marked a distinct change nonetheless. On the 1968 album *Miles in the Sky* Davis experimented selectively with electric piano, electric guitar, and R&B rhythms. On *Filles de Kilimanjaro*, recorded later that year, he used electric piano throughout and, on two cuts, replaced keyboardist Herbie Hancock and bassist Ron Carter with future band members Chick Corea and Dave Holland.[4]

These changes were portents for the more radical shift Davis articulated on his 1969 album *In a Silent Way*. Davis employed a larger rhythm section, electric guitar, and multiple electric keyboards. Rather than harmonic complexity or the subtle interplay between soloist and rhythm section, this music showcased multilayered textures generated by the simultaneous improvisations of horn players and members of the rhythm section alike. Davis charted his electric turn more spectacularly with *Bitches Brew,* an album recorded later in 1969 and released in 1970. Here he added an extra bass player and multiple percussionists, creating an even denser rhythmic texture that would define much of his music of the early 1970s. The album showcased funk and rock rhythms and electric guitar work, as well as free, open-ended improvisations. Davis continued to explore multiple cultural and musical referents on a series of albums recorded in the first half of the 1970s. On the 1972 album *On the Corner*, for example, one can hear funk rhythms in the vein of James Brown, Hendrix-inspired guitar licks, sitar and tablas, free improvisations, and open-ended musical structures—the latter apparently inspired by the ideas of Stockhausen. And on *Pangea* and *Agharta*, recorded at a Tokyo Concert in 1975, African polyrhythms and funk guitar work take center stage as Davis moved, in his own words, even "further into the idea of performance as process." Davis facilitated his multicultural experiments by his use of interracial, as well as international, ensembles, which he described, in sometimes racially essentialist terms, as products of his desire to combine the relative skills of white and black musicians to chart a new course for his music.[5]

Davis's electric music is also notable because at least some of it sold well. Although Davis was among a handful of African American jazz musicians who made a good living from recordings and performances during the 1960s, his record sales fell at the end of the decade. That changed with *Bitches Brew*, which thanks in part to a heavy marketing campaign by Columbia Records sold more than 400,000 copies

its first year, reached number 35 on the *Billboard* chart, and won a Grammy for best jazz album. Many have condemned Davis for "selling out" and purportedly acquiescing to Columbia's demand that he make a popular record, but *Bitches Brew* is hardly crossover music. Although it is worth noting here that Columbia's marketing strategy emphasized that this music was beyond category, and as with Davis's previous two albums, there was no mention of the word *jazz* on the jacket.[6]

Whatever financial aspirations may have compelled Davis or Columbia to move beyond the boundaries of jazz were accompanied by Davis's stated beliefs that jazz was an increasingly moribund art form and that artists had a duty to make their music relevant to young people. During the 1960s, education networks in black communities were disintegrating and performance opportunities in urban areas became scarce, as nascent de-industrialization, urban renewal programs, discriminatory housing loan policies, highway construction, and other factors led to the degeneration of urban infrastructures and encouraged middle-class flight to the suburbs. To make matters worse, after postwar jazz reached an apex of popularity and profitability circa 1960, competition from other music and media ushered in a period of decline in the jazz business, during which the music industry increasingly directed its resources to rock & roll and soul music. Davis was one of many African

American musicians who during the late 1960s and early 1970s sought to revitalize jazz and reach a younger audience by incorporating aspects from contemporary popular music.

So how do we understand this controversy, and particularly the assessments of the music by African American cultural critics? Gary Tomlinson brings us part of the way there in his essay "Cultural Dialogics and Jazz." Beginning his analysis of Davis's music and responses to it by quoting Amiri Baraka, Stanley Crouch, John Litweiler, and Martin Williams, who evaluated the electric period during the last years of Davis's life, Tomlinson identifies two rhetorical tropes—absence and transgression—used to pass judgment on the musician. Davis's music was flawed, some argued, because it lacked certain elements found in previous jazz styles. And Davis transgressed because he engaged in reprehensible personal behavior, sold out the artistic integrity of jazz in pursuit of pop commercial success, and stopped playing authentically black music. Tomlinson refutes these critiques, arguing that they fail to take into account the ways that Davis's personal behavior was probably no better during his proclaimed artistic heyday in the 1950s and that the production of jazz always has been impacted by market values and developments in popular music. Drawing on the work of Greg Tate, as well as a more favorable account of the music by Baraka, Tomlinson rejects charges of "inauthenticity" by describing the electric period as an extension of Davis's lifelong, "dialogical" project of embracing difference, synthesizing diverse musical and cultural elements, and engaging in an interethnic exchange that remained consistent with an expansively defined jazz tradition.[7]

While I welcome Tomlinson's effort to rescue this music from its detractors and his insistence that we forego narrow litmus tests of musical and ethnic/racial authenticity when analyzing jazz, or any form of music for that matter, I want to rethink some of these assessments of Davis's electric music. For understanding the controversy over this period of Davis's career demands that we situate it in its historical context. If Davis's detractors at times presented contradictory analyses, it was not merely because they failed to understand the inherent musical and cultural hybridity of jazz. They also were immersed in a conversation where questions of musical value intertwined with a host of long-standing economic, political, social, aesthetic, and ethical questions, which resonated in particular ways at different periods of time.

The response to Davis's electric music by Baraka, Crouch, and Tate should be understood as part of a dialogue about the merits of black music and its potential role in social change that dates back to the antebellum period. Since W. E. B. Du Bois's *The Souls of Black Folk*, black music has served, as Paul Gilroy notes, as a primary marker of African American "double-consciousness," a "central sign of black cultural value, integrity, and autonomy," and a potential vehicle for the reconciliation of diverse black communities.[8] During the 1920s New Negro musicians and other intellectuals turned their attention to jazz and sought to make sense of its symbolic and functional role, as they struggled to define its relationship to a diasporic cultural community and a North American body politic. But from the beginning, this struggle to locate black meanings in jazz has been complicated by the reality of a multiracial jazz community and audience in America and abroad, the multiple cultural referents from which its practitioners have drawn, the music's position as a culture industry commodity, and the diverse musical tastes of members of the black community. And African American musicians and cultural critics have viewed jazz simultaneously as a symbol of black success and limitation because of its denigration by various cultural gatekeepers and the often oppressive economic relationships that have structured the music industry. The history of jazz has also involved a struggle between musicians, the jazz industry, and various commentators over who has the right to define this music. But despite these complicating factors, jazz has retained great power as a symbol for African American creativity and genius.

At the moment Davis began his electric turn, this conversation about jazz resonated with the conflicts, demands, and rhetoric of the Black Power movement, which gave the discussion of "black cultural value, integrity, and autonomy" a particular resonance. Activist musicians and other intellectuals revisited the New Negro conversation about the spiritual and political possibilities of black music as they adhered to a Black Arts Movement imperative, which Larry Neal described as a duty to "speak to the spiritual and cultural needs of black people." During the 1960s and 1970s African American jazz players, like writers and other artists, were in various ways trying to connect with their audience and fulfill what they viewed as their communal responsibilities. Some retained rather grandiose ideas that sonic production could usher in sweeping social transformations. Others pursued modest goals, viewing music as a vehicle for promoting individualized, personal growth.

A major dilemma facing activist musicians in the 1960s, however, was that the jazz business was declining in general and losing a good deal of its African American audience due to the rising popularity of soul and funk music and the social transformations sketched out above. A frequent topic of discussion was the question of how one might make his or her music relevant and meaningful to a mass and youthful black audience. Members of the jazz community were aware of the declining African American audience for jazz, and some looked to the recuperation of this audience as a means of financial and political fulfillment.

Tempering any impulse to change one's musical style, however, was the common belief that jazz—and especially free jazz—held the key to psychic, spiritual, and physical liberation of black communities precisely because its

practitioners refused to compromise their creative visions. But some musicians recognized that they might have to change their style to cultivate a mutually beneficial relationship with a black audience. In a 1965 conversation with Larry Neal in *Liberator*, Archie Shepp admitted the difficulty of reaching African American working people through avant-garde music. "I think it would be very difficult for Cecil or Ornette or myself to just go up to Harlem and expect to be accepted right away— as good as our intentions may be." Like other musicians, Shepp believed that the separation of the "Black artist" from the "Black community" stemmed from "economic reasons." He made an oblique reference to the economic restructuring that moved entertainment venues out of black communities and compelled artists to follow them. Though sanguine about the ultimate impact music could have on society, Shepp said he was willing to do what it took to reach black people through music. "Even if the artist has to forsake some of his most cherished things—then he must forsake them. If I have to get into rock and roll,

somehow, I've got to slide into that, and refer to the people so that they'll know what I mean."[9]

Although Davis appears not to have gone as far as some of his colleagues in arguing that music could be a force for social change, he does seem to have responded to the Black Power movement by trying to make his music relevant. As he recalled in his autobiography:

It was with *On the Corner* and *Big Fun* that I really made an effort to get my music over to young black people. They are the ones who buy records and come to concerts, and I had started thinking about building a new audience for the future. I had gotten a lot of young white people coming to my concerts after *Bitches Brew* and so I thought it would be good if I could get all these young people together listening to my music and digging the groove.[10]

It should be noted that Davis's music, like Shepp's, probably did not have the broad impact on a mass black audience that he desired. As Davis himself suggested, many of the 400,000 copies of *Bitches Brew* were sold to rock fans, whose appetite for this music had been whetted by Hendrix, Stone, Blood, Sweat and Tears, and other musical fusions. As Gerald Early points out, neither *Bitches Brew* nor the self-consciously, black youth-oriented *On the Corner* were as popular in African American communities during the 1970s as Donald

Byrd's funk/jazz fusion album *Blackbyrd* or Davis alumni Herbie Hancock's *Headhunters*. And *Kind of Blue* was probably more popular among black college students in the early 1970s than *Bitches Brew*.[11]

But regardless of his ability to reach black youth, Davis's challenge of generic and cultural boundaries, his multiracial ensembles, and his attempt to reach a larger audience both threatened and vindicated activist musicians working within the paradigms of Black Power–era cultural politics. Throughout the 1960s Davis publicly defended his right to hire white band members, even if he sometimes bought into racially essentialist ideas about creativity while doing so. Speaking of the possibilities of rock and roll fusion in 1969, Davis said:

There's two kinds, white and black, and those bourgeois spades are trying to sing white and the whites are trying to sound colored. It's embarrassing. . . . But Jimi Hendrix can take two white guys and make them play their asses off. You got to have a mixed group—one has one thing and the other has another. For me, a group has to be mixed. To get swing, you have to have some black guys in there.[12]

And through his musical bricolage, Davis challenged prescriptive black aesthetics, whether rooted in straight-ahead or avant-garde formulations. As Waldo Martin demonstrates, Davis's

dissatisfaction with certain directions where the black musical avant-garde headed in the 1960s went hand-in-hand with a rejection of "a separatist and chauvinistic black politics." Still, Martin continues, Davis did want to be musically relevant, and his gradual adaptation of elements of free jazz, rock, soul, and funk paralleled a growing political commitment on his part during the Black Power era.[13]

Public responses to Davis's electric music at the time of its creation resonate with the politics of the era, and they anticipate more recent interpretations of this period of his career. Many criticized Davis for selling out the jazz tradition and turning his back on an African American cultural tradition. Yet this critique sometimes hinged on assumptions about what he, as a leading black musician, owed to his community. Saxophonist Eddie Harris, for example, who in 1966 had himself begun experimenting with electric saxophone and various kinds of amplifiers and signal processors, had no problem with Davis's music, but he did object to his interracial bands. At a 1970 press conference Harris expressed resentment toward Davis because he believed that a job with his band was a well-paying gig that should go to another African American.[14]

Writing at the end of the 1970s, multi-instrumentalist and composer Anthony Braxton discussed Davis's electric music in his aesthetic manifesto, *Triaxium Writings*.[15] Braxton had theorized the centrality of African

American improvised music—which he called "creative music"—in collective consciousness raising and global social transformations. Although he embraced multiple cultural referents, including European concert music, and rejected the narrow aesthetic prescriptions of cultural nationalists and Eurocentric critics alike, he maintained a Black Arts Movement belief that black music's power to create social change lay in its spiritual purpose and opposition to Western values and aesthetics.

Braxton discussed Davis's central role in the development of "jazz-rock" and saw in this music the potential for financial, aesthetic, and political vindication. On one level, this music "solved the dilemma of the creative improvising musician" who wanted "to continue to work in the area of improvised music and enjoy audience support." Braxton believed that this music had the potential to fulfill the artist creatively while appealing to and perhaps inspiring a black audience's will to social equality. He saw the potential in jazz-rock of establishing the "vibrational balance," as he termed it, found in Duke

Ellington's swing, but which largely had disappeared once bebop helped established jazz as an art music. Beyond that, he saw this music as a challenge to cultural boundaries, and in its complexity a distinct refutation of the stigma that commentators had placed on popular black music.[16]

Yet Braxton also saw problems with immersing oneself in the popular. Although he refused to make any judgments about fusion musicians' skills or integrity, he thought that regardless of musicians' own motivations, fusion signaled greater interference on the part of record companies. He thought that the music industry devoted an inordinate amount of resources to white jazz-rock artists, and that participation in the genre ultimately placed restrictions on musicians creativity. Braxton believed that the creative musician needed a kind of "separate vibrational identity" to fulfill his or her function as an agent of social transformation. In other words, black musicians needed a degree of creative autonomy, free from the dictates of the market, to raise consciousness and transmit cultural values.[17]

Another assessment that made sense of Davis's electric music was critic Ron Welburn's 1970 essay "Miles Davis and Black Music in the Seventies." Welburn thought the music on *Bitches Brew* lived up to standards Davis long had established. "Miles is still Miles," he asserted, and this "music is magical, episodic, cosmic, tenacious and brilliant." Yet it was precisely Davis's status and power as a cultural icon that gave Welburn pause. "Miles Davis the creative musical genius is without parallel as a cultural phenomenon, and in this cultural context we should not overlook the historical ramifications as they relate to the critical state of Black music culture today."[18]

With centrality to the history of black cultural production came responsibility. Welburn believed that Davis's *The Birth of the Cool* unwittingly spawned the West Coast jazz phenomenon of the 1950s, the marketing of which tended to benefit white musicians to the detriment of African Americans. He feared that *Bitches Brew* might be ushering in a similar situation. "Because the music is heavily amplified, he has again,

inadvertently perhaps in view of musical license, prefigured a focus on a particular articulation of what is another mode that white (specifically Rock) musicians can relate to with ease as a cultural grouping." As with Braxton, the issue was not Davis's own musical integrity but the impact that his electric turn might have on the community of black musicians and the broader African American society. Believing that music "holds the key to the prognosis and outcome of race relations," Welburn called on other musicians to make a defiantly black counter-statement to Davis's as a means of creating "another 'resurgence' having more emphasis on Afro-rhythms and new unamplified instruments."[19]

Davis may not have created the most successful or popular musical fusions of the era, but as Welburn's essay makes clear, the attention his electric turn received resulted in part from his status as a cultural icon. As mentioned above, Davis's participation in several major musical shifts in modern jazz had made him almost synonymous with innovation in the idiom, and he had a particular caché in black intellectual circles as a "central sign of black cultural value, integrity, and autonomy." By the 1960s, African American intellectuals long had linked jazz genius to standards of personal behavior and certain codes of cultural or racial legitimacy, the latter being defined by musicians' adherence to or rejection of certain formalistic or generic boundaries, their ability to maintain their creative vision in the face of racial discrimination and market forces, and their ability to speak to a black audience.

Jazz genius, of course, usually has been a gendered category, and one of the striking things about Davis's legacy is how he came to represent black male genius.[20] Davis's iconic status as a black musical genius resulted not only from his long and successful career and his ability to maintain an innovative creative vision while negotiating a racist music industry; it also had much to do with his persona. Davis's musical accomplishments dovetailed with his cool on-stage demeanor, his sense of sartorial style, his well-publicized boxing hobby, and his penchant for driving fast European sports cars. His biting social commentary and his refuse-to-put-up-with-any-mess persona made him a model of masculine assertiveness as well. As he told the *Saturday Review* in 1971, "I am not a Black Panther or nothing like that, . . . I don't need to be, but I was raised to think like they do and people sometimes think I'm difficult because I always say what's on my mind, and they can't always see what I see."[21]

This persona is well described in recent writings by black, male intellectuals who discuss how Davis provided them with a model for personal deportment as African American men coming of age during the 1950s and 1960s. Gerald Early recalls being drawn to Davis at about age twelve in the early 1960s: "What instantly struck me about Miles Davis one day . . . was that what made Miles Davis special was that he was a man who was not afraid to be himself."[22] Quincy Troupe describes how it was:

Miles Davis, the man, his no-nonsense, take-no-prisoner attitude that would force me to look at myself as an African American male living perilously in the United States. I also learned a lot from him through his great sense of personal style, the impeccable clothes he always wore and his sense of himself in them. All these things helped change me, the way I began to view myself in the world.

And in his recent memoir of his relationship with the musician, Troupe speaks fondly of Davis as an "unreconstructed black man" who refused to compromise his ideals.[23]

In addition to identifying the powerful gendered symbolism of Davis's musical genius in the 1960s, these considerations of Davis also illustrate how assessments of his music, and particularly his electric period, often still hinge on whether he lived up to his potential as a musical genius. For Troupe, Davis's electric turn was consistent with a lifelong refusal of musical category and a sensible attempt "to further advance his art, his music, and his own playing."[24] Early also celebrates Davis's ability to incorporate a variety of musical elements without losing track of his musical vision, and he recognizes that his electric turn was consistent with the synthesis he strove for in earlier years. But Davis's aesthetic vision failed him after 1969, not because the elements he brought together were any "better or worse" than those he used before, but because he could not adequately control them. Thus, "the power of his style was merely consumed by the loudness of the music." Still, whatever its failings, this music remained an expression of his arrogance and his genius, his need "to conquer a frontier as he simultaneously created it."[25]

The question of whether Davis lived up to his potential as black musical genius has resonated in particular ways with feminist critics, especially in light of the tales of spousal abuse and misogynistic comments in his 1989 autobiography. Notable here is Pearl Cleage's 1990 performance piece "Mad at Miles," where she describes Davis's music as "perfect," ponders the important function Davis's music played in the construction of her identity as a black woman, and asks whether "we continue to celebrate the genius in the face of the monster" who emerges on the pages of the autobiography. As she explores the contradictory meanings of Davis, her refrain is that he "was guilty of self-confessed crimes against women such that we ought to break his records, burn his tapes and scratch up his CD's until he acknowledges and apologizes and agrees to rethink his position on The Woman Question." Hazel Carby's answer

to this dilemma in her book *Race Men* is that Davis's ideas about his own genius, in fact, were inextricably bound to the portrayal of women in his autobiography and emblematic of the way jazz genius often has been constructed in juxtaposition to the materiality of women's bodies.[26]

Turning finally to Baraka, Crouch, and Tate's evaluations of Davis's electric music in the 1980s and 1990s, we find value judgments expressed through the tropes of absence and transgression situated in anxieties over the survival of black musical genius, a legacy of Black Power–era cultural politics, and the needs of a postindustrial, postnationalist African American community. Linking these critical perspectives with a Black Arts imperative are explicit or implicit engagements with Baraka's concept of "unity music," which he defined in his 1966 essay, "The Changing Same: R&B and the New Black Music." The resonance of the concept of "unity music" in these critics' assessments of Davis's electric music helps explain how Davis is made to answer for the legacy of Black Power–era cultural politics.

Baraka defined "unity music" as a fusion of "jazz and blues, religious and secular" music, and the "New Thing [i.e., avant-garde jazz] and Rhythm and Blues." He predicted that the emergence of this music would in turn herald "the emergence . . . of the new people, the Black people conscious of all their strength, in a unified portrait of strength, beauty and contemplation."[27] Baraka's formulation is a notable statement of

cultural nationalist aesthetics. Like other Black Power–era activists he believed that music could be a vehicle for social change. Rejecting the idea that music could create personal or social transformations through polemics, he considered its role constitutive of a defiantly black identity, a transmitter of cultural values, a therapeutic device, and a tool in collective-consciousness-raising. Yet his desire to forge a new musical synthesis also speaks of the anxieties avant-garde writers and musicians alike experienced over their ability to reach a mass black audience. Avant-garde jazz held a special place in black aesthetics because of the spiritual approach taken by some of its practitioners toward their art, its imagined distance from Western values and aesthetics, and its supposed autonomy from music industry interference. Yet, this music simply did not have a widespread impact on a mass black audience. R&B, on the other hand, did have mass appeal, but its commercial status seemed to make it more susceptible to appropriation, and its practitioners were thought to lack the social consciousness of jazz players.

Baraka sought the reconciliation of diverse black communities. He explained the fragmentation of black musical styles as a result of the marketing practices of the music industry as well as class divisions in the African American community. Unity music, then, was a means of rectifying social divisions. Baraka theorized a cultural expression that maintained its cultural legitimacy through the artistic integrity of jazz and the mass appeal of R&B, and he called on African American musicians to create a populist music that would appeal to a wide spectrum of black America and perhaps lessen the social divisions that threatened the utopian vision of a unified racial and cultural community.

As one might imagine, the responsibility for creating unity music sat primarily with male musicians. Like many Black Power–era aesthetic statements, "The Changing Same" assumed a masculinist stance. Baraka juxtaposed the accomplishments of male R&B musicians with female crossover star Leslie Uggams and the Beatles, whom he described as "myddle-class white boys who need a haircut and male hormones."[28] As one might also expect, Baraka adhered to certain aspects of cultural and racial essentialism as well. He imagined core characteristics of a distinct black spirit, consciousness, and racial body and identified a hermetic boundary between black ways and white ways of living. Yet by embracing a musical "changing same," Baraka refuted the idea of a fixed, black cultural

essence and recognized that black music was a product of historical contingencies.[29] He emphasized the fluidity of generic boundaries and acknowledged the multiple cultural referents that could be incorporated into culturally relevant music.

Ultimately, the concept of unity music linked value both to the form and function of the music and identified a communal duty to which black musicians—and especially black male musicians—were expected to adhere. It marked an aesthetic simultaneously prescriptive in its allegiance to racial thinking yet expansive in its consideration of genre. Unity music looked forward both to mass appeal and artistic autonomy, and it gave special power to music as a means of forging a politics of reconciliation not reliant upon polemics. Davis's musical synthesis during his electric period and his commitment to reaching a wider audience made his vision in some ways consistent with the concept of unity music, while his refusal of racial separatism and the belief that he unduly was influenced by record company marketing decisions seem at odds with it.

I now want to turn to the assessments of Davis's electric turn by Baraka, Tate, and Crouch, whose writings were anticipated by musicians' comments and actions a decade or two earlier. But here an attention to the commercial viability or "selling out" shifts from a concern for musicians' livelihoods and creative autonomy to an assessment

of a broader culture industry and the marketing of black music in the 1980s and 1990s. Moreover, unity music and its echoes exist not as a utopian, forward-looking black aesthetic but as a commentary on the legacy of a failed Black Power–era politics, fused with the belief that music still holds some power to impact the position of black people in American society. And just as Baraka figured the production of unity music as a masculinist enterprise, the invocation of this concept speaks of the continued responsibilities of black male artists.

In 1985, Baraka, writing at the time as a Marxist, contributed a piece on Davis to the New York Times. Based in part on interviews with Davis and other musicians, it charts the trumpeter's musical history. Baraka linked Davis's musical transformations to shifts in African American political consciousness, intellectual life, and a collective sense of cultural identity.[30] Beyond that, Davis's music helped shape the contours of American culture as a whole. Baraka's tone was generally celebratory, and he opened the article by describing Davis in gendered terms as both cultural hero and artistic "genius." Yet, he still posed the "fundamental question" that lay behind all the others he wanted to ask Davis: "How did you get from there to here?" Or in other words, how did Davis move from the bebop of his youth to the heavy mix of rock, funk, and jazz that defined his music in the 1970s and then somewhat differently in the 1980s. Baraka hoped that he "could say something useful about Miles's journey and perhaps we could all learn something."[31]

The answer to Baraka's question is that Davis's embrace of "black populism" parallels his own rejection of cultural nationalism. Baraka argued that saxophonists John Coltrane and Cannonball Adderley, who performed with Davis's sextet during the 1950s, represented "philosophical" as well as "musical" orientations. Adderley's soul and gospel leanings represented a populist and "American" vision, while Coltrane symbolized an emergent jazz avant-garde and an "African American" approach to music. Coltrane's music was revolutionary, Baraka argued, but it potentially led to "a kind of black cultural nationalism, atavism, mysticism," which would not do for Davis, just as it "could not to the majority of political forces of the black movement." Therefore, rather than following the lead of Coltrane, who according to Baraka, was philosophically closer to Malcolm X and the Nation of Islam, Davis adhered to Adderley's vision as he made his electric turn. In Baraka's words, "Miles's new changes placed him much closer to the Black Panther Party, in terms of a social metaphor his new aesthetic reveals." Even the inclusion of white musicians on these albums "was akin to the coalition politics of the Panthers rather than the isolating nationalism of the cultural nationalists."[32]

Challenging those who passed judgment on Davis for selling out, Baraka argued that Davis remained true to the blues (the standard litmus test for black musical legitimacy) as he sought to construct a musical vision that was not isolationist but that still actively sought out a mass African American audience. The populist impulse that Baraka championed was consistent with his earlier formulation of unity music in its commitment to a black audience, but it differed in its rejection of black separatism. Written in Reagan-era America, Baraka's assessment of Davis's music marked his shift from cultural nationalism to Marxism, yet still spoke of a continuing belief that black musicians could play an important social role by maintaining connections with a black audience. Baraka believed Davis's music from this period, as well as the music he recorded in the early 1980s, challenged directly the "compartmentalization" of black music into genres—a product of both corporate marketing strategies and the deepening class divisions in black America during the 1970s and 1980s—and perhaps maintained an ability to speak to African Americans across class lines.[33]

As one might expect, we get a very different assessment of Davis in the works of Stanley Crouch. Once a cultural, nationalist poet heavily influenced by Baraka and an avant-garde drummer, Crouch more recently has made a name for himself as a critic of black nationalism and champion of jazz traditionalism. Those familiar with

Crouch's work know that he has seen black nationalism as a profound moral and intellectual failure on the part of African American intellectuals and activists and, ultimately, American society as a whole. Building instead upon the work of Ralph Ellison and Albert Murray, he has for the past twenty years or so emphasized the heroic and "Omni-American" aspects of an African American culture—most notably expressed, the blues—that simultaneously speak of African American distinction and place black people at the center of American political, spiritual, and cultural life.

Like Baraka, Crouch, too, has used Davis to chart his rejection of black nationalism. In the late 1970s, even after he had rejected aspects of this political ideology and began to distance himself from the jazz avant-garde, Crouch still saw possibilities in jazz-fusion and pondered what might be salvaged from a Black Arts Movement vision. In a 1979 Village Voice piece entitled "Bringing Atlantis to the Top," Crouch criticized the jazz avant-garde, whose shortcomings symbolized recent failings of black political and intellectual life. He equated the avant-garde with "simplistic and ludicrous ancestor worship, intellectual irresponsibility, primitive mask-wearing, and counterfeit militancy that frequently had more to do with renegade dilettante romance than more fascinating combinations of notes, sounds, colors, and rhythms." Yet Crouch affirmed Baraka's call for "unity

music" and remained hopeful that jazz musicians could play an important role in African American communities. Though not particularly fond of Davis's electric music, he still was interested in the "jazz-funk language" Davis created for electric instruments. And he looked forward to a new synthesis of jazz and rhythm and blues that would infuse new life into both idioms.[34]

But Crouch's embrace of this populist vision did not last. More recently, Crouch has located the possibilities of social change not in an interclass collaboration of unity music but in talented-tenth fashion in the refinement, heroism, and democratic values embedded in the blues and articulated most eloquently by Louis Armstrong, Duke Ellington, and currently Wynton Marsalis. In his 1990 essay "Play the Right Thing," Crouch waxed eloquently about Davis's accomplishments at different moments of his career, but his tone changed dramatically when he described Davis's "fall from grace," beginning with *In a Silent Way*. Now Davis represented the failings of Black Power–era cultural politics. As Crouch put it:

As usual, where Davis led, many followed. His pernicious effect on the music scene since he went rapaciously commercial reveals a great deal about the perdurability of Zip Coon and Jasper Jack in the worlds of jazz and rock, in the worlds of jazz and rock criticism, in Afro-American culture itself. The cult of ethnic authenticity often mistakes the lowest common denominator for an ideal. . . . Davis's corruption occurred at about the time that the "Oreo" innuendo became an instrument with which formerly rejected street Negroes and thugs began to intimidate, and often manipulate, middle-class Afro-

Americans in search of their roots, and of a "real" black culture. In this climate, obnoxious, vulgar, and antisocial behavior has been confused with black authenticity. This has led to blaxploitation in politics, in higher education, in art . . .

Like Baraka, Crouch saw similarities between Davis's music and the politics of the Black Panthers, although there was nothing to celebrate here. In Crouch's view, both represented the failings of black society in the 1960s and early 1970s that continued to impact the present.[35]

In a Silent Way, in Crouch's view, marked the moment when Davis sold out, but Davis's transgression did not merely involve pursuing a more commercially viable music or straying from the harmonic, rhythmic, or acoustical basis of the jazz tradition. Davis, precisely in his attempt to create a commercially viable and socially relevant music, replicated the problems with the cultural wing of the Black Power movement. By infusing his records with rock and funk rhythms and instrumentation Davis

symbolized the ways African American artists, intellectuals, and the black middle class in general rejected bourgeois convention, embraced cultural and moral relativism, and bought into stereotypical images that the culture industry used to sell black America to itself. Davis represented an unmitigated failure of black male genius. Not only did he engage in the antisocial and misogynistic behavior represented in his autobiography, he turned his back on the inherent heroism of the jazz tradition and neglected his duty as role model and agent in social uplift by letting popular tastes dictate his aesthetic and social vision and presentation of self.

Greg Tate, a cultural critic influenced by both Baraka and Crouch, put a somewhat different spin on these issues in a two-part 1983 *Down Beat* article on Davis's electric turn and in a couple of posthumous accounts of Davis's life. In the *Down Beat* piece, Tate celebrated Davis's music from this period precisely because of its "revolutionary aesthetics" and his self-conscious attempt to forge a socially relevant "unity music" that still remained rooted in the blues. Davis in part succeeded by participating in a patrilineal act of succession, wherein he heard in the music of Brown, Hendrix, and Stone "the blues impulse transferred, masked, and retooled for the Space Age" and saw in these personae models of masculine behavior. "Like James Brown he was a consummate bandleader who knew his way around a boxing ring, like Sly he was a bourgeois

boy who opted to become a street fighting man, and like Jimi he was a musician whose physical grace seemed to declare itself in every bent note and sensual slur."[36]

Several years later, in a 1991 *Village Voice* memorial, Tate presented Davis as the embodiment of black genius, in part because of his socially attuned, expansive aesthetic vision. Speaking of Davis's electric period, Tate wrote:

The funny thing is that as disorienting as this period was for his old fans, Miles stepped into the era of black power politics and hippie rebellion like he'd had a hand in creating it all along. He never seemed like the old jazz hand who was trying to get hip to the Youth and Soul movements of the day. Homeboy came off like he was redefining cool for that generation too.

He compared Davis to Nat Turner, "proud without being loud because it was about plotting insurrection. In this sense Miles never changed. His agenda remained the same from day one: stay ahead." But Davis's masculine genius also was flawed. Referring to the dissonance between the beauty of Davis's music and his misogynist posturing in the autobiography, Tate concluded by saying, "Miles may have swung like a champion but on that score he went out like a roach." Still, at a conference presentation on Davis a few months later, Tate recuperated Davis as a cultural hero to the extent that his music and persona provide a model of artistic, if not personal, integrity. Davis was a "a holdover from a time when Black intellectual and artistic achievement was a major currency through which racial progress could be bought and symbolically sold—on a rarefied, individual basis—a time distinct from the postnationalist present where Black representation is a market force capable of raking in corporate profits without being allied to our agendas of social advancement and reform." Thus Davis again represented the possibility of a communally and socially oriented music, resonating with the goals of Black Power–era cultural politics and providing a lesson for our times.[37]

So how do we make sense of this? Although they come to different conclusions about whether Davis's electric turn was transgressive, Baraka, Crouch, and Tate are linked by their commentary on the communal responsibilities of black male artists and their participation in a long-running debate over the value of black music in its political context. For much of this century jazz has played an important role in these conversations, but as the comments of musicians and aestheticians in the 1960s and 1970s make clear, this conversation has been complicated by the political demands of the moment, the precarious status of jazz as an art form within and without black communities, the marketing of this music, and other factors.

These recent treatments of Davis's electric period also are expressions of a contemporary cultural politics, which as George Lipsitz reminds us, "[have] become a kind of referendum on the cultural politics of the 1960s."[38] The 1980s and 1990s witnessed, among other things, a backlash against the civil rights movement, the acceleration of de-industrialization, deepening class divisions in African American society and U.S. society as a whole, a perceived failure of black leadership, a widespread fear of black youth, and a proliferation of contradictory media representations that celebrate black accomplishments on the one hand and mark black people as deviant on the other. Such factors have shaped a growing anxiety among African American intellectuals that the black cultural community is in crisis. In this context, the cultural and social movements of the 1960s (and 1970s) continually are revisited as a source of both the cause and solutions of the problems of the present.

Davis has been a threat and inspiration, not merely because his music challenged racial, cultural, or aesthetic boundaries, but because these challenges have come to represent the political, social, and cultural ruptures of the 1960s and 1970s read from the perspective of the present. All of these writers suggest that Davis's electric music has something to teach us in the present because of its musical synthesis, racial politics, and populist commitment.

For Baraka and Tate, Davis's electric music, with its wide-ranging appeal, performance by multiracial groups, and multiple cultural referents, challenges a prescriptive cultural nationalism. Although the antiwhite rhetoric and separatist posturing of cultural nationalism may be gone, what remains is the possibility that music can be a vehicle for social change. Davis's music represents the possibilities of black musical integrity surviving not only in the culture industry of the 1980s and 1990s, but as expressed in a hybrid, popular form, serving a social purpose by appealing across race and class lines and mending the "cultural fractures" of postindustrial society.[39] Thus, it affirms a movement-era belief that music can articulate black desires, transmit cultural values, and uplift a cultural community. Davis's electric music speaks of the possibility of combining two standards of legitimacy that make for a socially relevant music: artistic integrity and popular appeal, the latter perhaps consistent with but not necessarily the same as the desires of the marketplace. Davis also represents for both the survival of male genius, a significant reality now when the breakdown of male cultural authority frequently is seen as a fundamental problem facing black America.

Crouch, too, looks to jazz as a source of cultural and artistic integrity, but he champions the work of others. He sees almost nothing to redeem in Davis's electric music and, by extension, black nationalism; both represent a breakdown of social vision and a failure of black male cultural authority. Davis's embrace of funk and rock and roll signifies a commercial, rather than an aesthetic, construction of black authenticity and a retreat from the heroic artistic vision established by musicians Armstrong and Ellington and passed along in patrilineal succession to Wynton Marsalis and other jazz traditionalists. Yet even Crouch, precisely in his condemnation of Davis, maintains a belief in the functional role of black music and sees it as a crucial vehicle for the articulation of African American values and the improvement of black society. This critique remains linked to a Black Power–era evaluation of jazz and jazz musicians through their transmission of cultural values and their

ability to mend class divisions in black society in healthy ways.

In the end, Davis remains a contradictory and influential figure, as he has been for much of his career. He is a symbol of jazz orthodoxy and anti-traditionalism, black aesthetics and universalism, masculine accomplishment and misogyny, and venal commercialism and artistic integrity. In the present, his electric period carries particular weight because of the way it links the moment of its inception with the present and because of the staying power of Davis as a symbol, warts and all, of black male genius. Davis's electric turn, then, both heralds and provides a sounding board for the contentious debates about the contradictory side of contemporary black popular culture.

1   The author wishes to thank Catherine Ramírez for her careful readings of several drafts of this essay and Gerald Early, Darlene Clark Hine, and participants in the University of New Mexico Cultural Studies Colloquium for their comments on presentation versions of it.

2   Miles Davis with Quincy Troupe, *Miles: The Autobiography* (New York: Simon and Schuster, 1989), 288; Troupe, liner notes, Miles Davis, *The Complete Bitches Brew Sessions*, 92.

3   Troupe, liner notes, *The Complete Bitches Brew Sessions*, 66.

4   Harvey Pekar, "Miles Davis: 1964–69 Recordings," in Bill Kirchner, ed., *A Miles Davis Reader* (Washington: Smithsonian Institution Press, 1997), 174–77.

5   Pekar, "Miles Davis," 177–78; Gary Tomlinson, "Miles Davis: Musical Dialogician," in Kirchner, *A Miles Davis Reader*, 242–43, 246; Quincy Troupe, liner notes, *The Complete Bitches Brew Sessions*, 45, 62–79; Stuart Nicholson, *Jazz Rock: A History* (New York: Schirmer Books, 1998), 113, 117–24; Greg Tate, *Flyboy in the Buttermilk* (New York: Simon and Schuster, 1992), 77–80. Davis quoted in Kevin Whitehead, liner notes, *Pangea*. For a detailed description of the relationship between Davis's and Stockhausen's music and ideas, see Barry Bergstein, "Miles Davis and Karlheinz Stockhausen: A Reciprocal Relationship," *Musical Quarterly* 76 (winter 1992): 502–25.

6   Columbia's advertising copy read, "*Bitches Brew* is an incredible journey of pain, joy, sorrow, hate, passion, and love. *Bitches Brew* is a new direction in music by Miles Davis. *Bitches Brew* is a novel without words." Quoted in Nicholson, *Jazz Rock*, 114.

7   Gary Tomlinson, "Cultural Dialogics and Jazz," *Black Music Research Journal* 11, no. 2 (fall 1991): 249–64. Excerpted as "Miles Davis, Musical Dialogician," in Kirchner, *A Miles Davis Reader*, 234–49.

8   Paul Gilroy, *The Black Atlantic: Modernity and Double Consciousness* (Cambridge, Mass.: Harvard, 1993), 90–91.

9   Lawrence P. Neal, "A Conversation with Archie Shepp," *Liberator* (November 1965): 24–25.

10 *Miles: The Autobiography*, 324.

11 Early made this comment in his response to a presentation of this paper at the Organization of American Historians meeting, April 2, 2000

Just for the record, I came to this music as a teenager in the late 1970s, discovering Davis's electric albums in the bargain bins of record stores on Telegraph Avenue in Berkeley. I knew who Davis was but was unfamiliar with this music. I was initially drawn to *Bitches Brew* by Abdul Mati's cover art, but I quickly found out that I dug the music, too. Of course I had already been pre-conditioned to appreciate it by my interest in "fusion" groups like Earth, Wind and Fire, Funkadelic, Slave, Jimi Hendrix, and Weather Report.

12 Don DeMichael, portrait, *Rolling Stone* (December 13, 1969): 23.

13 Waldo Martin, "Miles Davis and the 1960s Avant-garde," unpublished manuscript in the author's possession.

14 Leonard Feather, "The Name of the Game," *Down Beat* (October 15, 1970): 11.

15 Although Braxton's volumes were not published until the 1980s, there are several references in this discussion on jazz rock indicating that he wrote at least part of this chapter during the 1970s.

16 Anthony Braxton, *Triaxium Writings*, vol. 2, 375–77, 385–88, 394–98, 403, 417. Braxton sees the roots of jazz rock in the music of Horace Silver and Bobby Timmons in the 1950s, which he thought eloquently balanced the blues and bebop.

17 Ibid., 380–81, 397–98, 409, 412, 419–20.

18 Ron Welburn, "Miles Davis and Black Music in the Seventies," *Liberator* (October 1970): 21.

19 Ibid., 21, 23.

20 For a discussion of masculinity in the jazz community in the postwar era, see "Re-Masculating Jazz: Ornette Coleman, 'Lonely Woman,' and the New York Jazz Scene in the Late 1950s," *American Music* 16, no. 1 (Spring 1998): 25–44.

21 Chris Albertson, "The Unmasking of Miles Davis," *Saturday Review* (September 1971): 68.

22 Gerald Early, "Miles Davis as Ahab and the Whale," 31–32.

23 Troupe, liner notes, *The Complete Bitches Brew Sessions*, 41; Quincy Troupe, *Miles and Me* (Berkeley: University of California Press, 2000), 117, 166–67.

24 Troupe, liner notes, Miles Davis, *The Complete Bitches Brew Sessions*, 37, 94.

25 Early, "Miles Davis as Ahab and the Whale," 31–32.

26 Pearl Cleage, "Mad at Miles," in *Mad at Miles: A Blackwoman's Guide to Truth* (Southfield, Mich.: The Cleage Group, Inc., 1990), 13–21. Hazel Carby, *Race Men* (Cambridge, Mass.: Harvard University Press, 1998), 135–65. Carby juxtaposes the misogyny and sexism in Davis's narrative with what she considers a healthier performance of masculinity in black gay science fiction writer Samuel Delany's autobiography. Carby attempts to redeem Davis somewhat in the second half of the piece, where she argues that certain musical performances exemplify a healthier, more democratic sense of masculinity than that which Davis portrays in the autobiography.

27 LeRoi Jones [Amiri Baraka], "The Changing Same (R&B and New Black Music)," *Black Music* (New York: William Morrow, 1967), 192, 210.

28 Ibid., 205.

29 Paul Gilroy embraces this essay for just this reason. See Gilroy, *The Black Atlantic*, 101. Speaking of the need to move beyond fixed essences, Gilroy writes, "Today, this involves the difficult task of striving to comprehend the reproduction of cultural traditions not in the unproblematic transmission of a fixed essence through time but in the breaks and interruptions which suggest that the invocation of tradition may itself be distinct, though covert, response to the destabilising flux of the post-

contemporary world."

30 Amiri Baraka, "Miles Davis: 'One of the Great Motherfuckers,'" *The Music: Reflections on Jazz and Blues* (New York: Morrow, 1987), 286–316. This was originally published in a somewhat different form as "Miles Davis," *New York Times*, June 16, 1985. Baraka argues, for example, that Davis's move from bebop and cool jazz to hard bop paralleled a collective shift from the hipster cool of the late 1940s to the defiant militancy of the late 1950s to early 1960s.

31 Ibid., 286.

32 Ibid., 286, 301–2, 309–14.

33 Ibid., 310–14.

34 Stanley Crouch, "Bringing Atlantis to the Top," *Village Voice* (April 16, 1979).

35 Stanley Crouch, *The All-American Skin Game, or, The Decoy of Race: The Long and the Short of It, 1990–1994* (New York: Pantheon Books, 1995), 180, 185. "Play the Right Thing" originally appeared in *The New Republic* 202, no. 7 (February 12, 1990). The essay is titled "On the Corner: The Sellout of Miles Davis" in Crouch's book.

36 Tate, *Flyboy in the Buttermilk*, 73.

37 Ibid., 88–89; Greg Tate, "Preface to a One-Hundred-and-Eighty Volume Patricide Note: Yet Another Few Thousand Words on the Death of Miles Davis and the Problem of the Black Male Genius," in Gina Dent, ed., *Black Popular Culture* (Seattle: Bay Press, 1992), 243–48.

38 George Lipsitz, "Who'll Stop the Rain? Youth Culture, Rock 'n' Roll, and Social Crises," in David Farber, ed., *The Sixties: From Memory to History* (Chapel Hill: The University of North Carolina Press, 1994), 228. Lipsitz says that it is a 1990s cultural politics that serves as a referendum for the 1960s, but I argue that the same holds true for the 1980s.

39 Writing about hip-hop culture, Tricia Rose situates its emergence in postindustrial urban America: "It is the tension between the cultural fractures produced by postindustrial oppression and the binding ties of black cultural expression that sets the critical frame for the development of hip hop." Tricia Rose, *Black Noise: Rap Music and Black Culture in Contemporary America* (Middletown, Conn.: Wesleyan University Press; Hanover, N.H.: University Press of New England, 1994), 21.

Aura sessions,
Copenhagen,
1984.
Photograph by
Jan Persson.

The moment a Negro writer takes up his pen or sits down to his typewriter he is immediately called upon to solve, consciously or unconsciously, this problem of the double audience. To whom shall he address himself, to his own black group or to white America? Many a Negro writer has fallen down, as it were, between these two stools.

—James Weldon Johnson (1928)

Miles Davis was only two years old when James Weldon Johnson published his essay "The Dilemma of the Negro Author." Yet the problem named by Johnson did not disappear during Davis's lifetime. Indeed, Davis spent most of his career impaled on the horns of a similar if not identical dilemma: that of the black musician who commands the loyalty of both black and white audiences, but who harbors very different feelings toward each.

That Davis distrusted whites is clear from the countless cuts and slashes left by his razor tongue—injuries sufficiently numerous and at times unfair to make it fashionable in some circles to call him a racist. Davis was not a "racist" (unless by overuse the word is stripped of all meaning); he was a proud, prickly character, or if you prefer an arrogant cuss. He was self-consciously the son of a "race man" who (to quote one of his favorite expressions) "didn't take no shit off nobody."[1] And he was a consummate artist who strove to overcome his own biases and fathom why whites as well as blacks loved his music. To say that he communicated with two audiences is not to disparage him. As Amiri Baraka writes, "Miles's special capacity and ability is to hold up and balance two musical (social) conceptions and express them as (two parts of) a single aesthetic."[2] For the vitality of any art, it may well be that two audiences are better than one.

A previous draft of this essay focused exclusively on Davis's later career, his attention-getting forays into various genres of popular music from rock, soul, and funk in the late 1960s to contemporary rhythm and blues and hip-hop in the 1980s. In its present form it takes a longer view, roughly chronological, because I have come to believe that Davis's fusion and postfusion

Miles Davis and the Double Audience

by Martha Bayles

music is best understood in the context of his lifelong struggle with the unforgiving conditions faced by the great black jazz musicians of the 1940s and 1950s. In Gerald Early's formulation, these gifted men and women were "neglected by the white Western world because they were black" and "ignored by an essentially grasping, wealth-obsessed society because they were artists."[3] Now that their names are world famous, it's easy to forget the bitter adversity under which they first cultivated their gifts. That adversity is also easy to sentimentalize. I hope to do neither.

Johnson's "problem of the double audience" dovetails with the current academic interest in the contextual dimension of art. At the boundary between musicology and ethnomusicology many scholars now aspire to take music out of the deep freeze of purely formal analysis and hold it up as a warm-blooded process whose full meaning derives from the specific circumstances of its production and reception. This contextual approach seems especially fruitful with jazz, which despite its enshrinement as "America's classical music" remains vitally connected with roots that reach into every nook and cranny of American life.

Yet the contextual approach is controversial. The defenders of traditional formal analysis protest that it neglects the art object. To study context, they argue, is to place every musical work on the same level and to say nothing about the unique qualities that elevate some works above others. Not long ago it was acceptable in academia to dismiss such concerns as reactionary, on the grounds that aesthetic value is but a smokescreen covering the injustices of the political and social status quo. But how does that apply to jazz? To elevate Duke Ellington above Guy Lombardo is not to reinforce the racial caste system they both lived under but to cut against it. Similarly, Ellington's superiority is based on artistry, not color.

My gripe with the contextual approach is that along with neglecting the object it often neglects the *context*. I agree with Robert Walser that it is worthwhile to analyze musical performances not as isolated objects but as activities "grounded in a web of social practices, histories, and desires."[4] But it is also difficult. Ideally the scholar would be a participant-observer at the performance, ears and eyes open to every nuance. Most of us, however, must work with remnants: what is known about a performance space; recollections of those who were present; the odd photograph or film; perhaps a recording's ambient sound. Unable to transport ourselves back to the Fillmore East in 1970, much less to Minton's Playhouse in 1949, we gather what evidence we can and venture our best guess. Yet this, too, is difficult. We must scrutinize the time and place, the setting and the characters, as painstakingly as an archivist scrutinizes a score, and use what imagination we possess to decipher the meaning. Among contextualists there is also the danger of basing one's interpretations on simplistic notions of "dialogue" and "contestation" that pre-empt genuine insight.

In the case of Davis, whose career crossed many genres and market niches, to analyze context is a tall order.[5] Like the cat with nine lives, Davis had a flair for landing on his feet after brushes with oblivion. Some of these brushes occurred with literal death: a police beating, sickle cell anemia, a sniper bullet, heroin, cocaine, a totaled Lamborghini. Others were with the figurative death of being out of step, a moldy fig, passe. The last thing Davis wanted to do was "sit down in some rocking chair and stop thinking."[6] But that is why we find him so beguiling: we ponder his self-transformations as we would a Rorschach, hoping to discern in their cloudy depths, lyric lines, and spectacular disruptions some revelation about life and art in the twentieth century.

About Davis's later music in particular, opinion remains sharply divided. So protean was he, even when frail and ill, that the world was stunned in 1991 when he finally ran out of lives. Friends and foes came together to pay tribute, but then the battle resumed between the Miles worshipers who genuflect before every clam and wah-wah, and the jazz curators who dismiss every note after 1969 as rank opportunism. Skeptics call this battle silly. Music is music, they say. Either listen to it or don't, but what's the point of labeling and judging it? Davis himself said this, especially within earshot of critics he scorned. But it would be a mistake to say that he had no use for criticism. Read his "Blindfold Tests" with Leonard Feather, and you will see that Davis bristled with critical opinions.[7] And so did the musicians he respected; his musical colleagues were never yes men. Davis's problem with critics was not that they had opinions but rather that their opinions were sometimes self-indulgent and ill-informed.

Still, the skeptics have a point. What *are* musical judgments based on? The question has driven European and American modernism for the past century and applies with special force to jazz, a music grossly misjudged by the "serious" musical establishment. And it was perpetually on Davis's mind. This essay also will seek to identify some of the yardsticks used to judge Davis's later music and, by sketching where those yardsticks came from, weigh their appropriateness. My perspective is not that of a musicologist but that of a critic who has wrestled with the good, the bad, and the ugly in popular music and does not apologize for using such terms.

To begin with a remnant: It is widely reported that in July 1944 Billy Eckstine's band used the front door (as opposed to the rear "colored entrance") of the aptly named Plantation Club in St. Louis, and for this effrontery were promptly fired. Never one to miss a beat, Eckstine went across town to the Riviera Club, a Negro establishment described by Clark Terry as "a big, plush sort of place."[8] There, that amazing band, which included Charlie Parker, John Birks "Dizzy" Gillespie, and Art Blakey, performed with fiery beauty before an enthusiastic black audience—and hurled a lightning bolt of inspiration at an eighteen-year-old trumpeter named Miles Dewey Davis, III, who many years later would confess that he had tried in vain all his life to recapture that moment: "I've come close to matching the feeling of that night in 1944 in music, when I first heard Diz and Bird, but I've never quite got there. I've gotten close, but not all the way there. I'm always looking for it, listening and feeling for it, though, trying to always feel it in and through the music I play every day."[9]

Why in vain? In a career full of musical refulgence, why does Davis insist that this particular lightning struck only once? What made that night unique?

The usual answer is that Davis was witnessing a moment of "pure" artistic genius. The purity of art versus the corruption of commerce was a major theme with the critics who first championed bebop. They saw bebop as art for art's sake, a principled protest against the money-grubbing priorities of the swing era. To Ross Russell, the new music was a "revolt against big bands, arrangers, vertical harmonies, soggy rhythms, non-playing orchestra leaders, Tin Pan Alley—against commercialized music in general."[10] Because of bebop's highbrow origins this way of praising bebop quickly was espoused as the conventional wisdom. But in 1964 Ralph Ellison dissented, writing that "the creators of the [bebop] style were seeking . . . a fresh form of entertainment which would allow them their fair share of the entertainment market, which had been dominated by whites during the swing era."[11]

Scott DeVeaux develops this point: "The insistence that bebop is anti-commercial may well continue to suit the needs of contemporary jazz discourse. . . . But it is a singularly poor basis for historical research."[12] DeVeaux argues further that the "progressive" musicians of the swing era, notably Coleman Hawkins, understood "progress" in terms of "the rhetoric of black self-help . . . internalized by hundreds of thousands of African American households eager to escape the cycle of poverty and despair."[13] The swing musician, with his polished appearance and aura of worldly success, was less a bohemian artiste in the European mold than a figure very much in the American mold—a *professional.*

It's easy to see how this image resonated with Davis, the son of a dentist who was "one of the pillars of the black community in East St. Louis."[14] But like so much else in jazz, color complicated the professional aspirations of Davis and his peers. As Ellison says, "the entertainment market . . . *had been dominated by whites*" (emphasis added). So, to return to that magical night at the Riviera Club, it also mattered to young Davis that the audience cheering for Bird and Diz were black. In the prologue of

his autobiography he stresses that "black people in St. Louis love their music, but they want their music right. So you *know* what they were doing at the Riviera."[15]

These same themes, polished professionalism and the discriminating taste of the black audience, intertwine in Davis's account of the famous cutting sessions at Minton's Playhouse on 118th Street in Harlem:

People who came to Minton's wore suits and ties because they were copying the way people like Duke Ellington or Jimmie Lunceford dressed. Man, they was cleaner than a motherfucker. But to get into Minton's didn't cost anything. It cost something like two dollars if you sat at one of the tables, which had white linen tablecloths on them and flowers in little glass vases. It was a nice place—much nicer than the clubs on Fifty-second Street.[16]

In sharp contrast to his warm memory of Minton's is Davis's chilly recollection of the jazz clubs on Fifty-second Street. "There were *some* good white people who were brave enough to come up to Minton's," he concedes, but "you went to Fifty-second Street to make money and be seen by white music critics and white people." Not only that, but "no matter how good the music sounded down on Fifty-second Street, it wasn't as hot or as innovative as it was uptown at Minton's." As for the white critics who "tried to act like they discovered" bebop

on Fifty-second Street, "that kind of dishonest shit makes me sick to my stomach. . . . The musicians and the people who really loved and respected bebop and the truth know that the *real* thing happened up in Harlem."[18]

Davis also paints Fifty-second Street as a magnet for white adventurers for whom bebop meant not the high life but the low. Ellison had these people in mind when he compared Louis Armstrong's "*make-believe* role of clown" with Parker's public persona as "a sacrificial figure whose struggles against personal chaos, onstage and off, served as entertainment for a ravenous, sensation-starved, culturally disoriented public." Ellison clarifies which public he means: "Race is an active factor here, though not in the usual sense. When the jazz drummer Art Blakey was asked about Parker's meaning for Negroes, he replied, 'They never heard of him.' Parker's artistic success and highly publicized death have changed all that today, but interestingly enough, Bird was indeed a 'white' hero."[19] Whites loved Parker's music, but some of them were also the voyeurs of his self-immolation.

During the Harlem Renaissance, when Johnson wrote about the "double audience problem," the whites he had in mind were genteel, puritanical—and inclined to "stencil" the Negro as either "a simple, indolent, docile, improvident peasant" or "an impulsive, irrational, passionate savage."[20] Two decades later, the white cult of Bird was *anti*-genteel, *anti*-puritanical—and inclined to stencil the Negro as a role model for would-be hipsters, as described most candidly by Norman Mailer: "The Negro (all exceptions admitted) could rarely afford the sophisticated inhibitions of civilization, and so he kept for his survival the art of the primitive . . . relinquishing the pleasures of the mind for the more obligatory pleasures of the body. . . . For jazz is orgasm."[21]

Having suggested that two audiences are better than one, I now offer in evidence those European and American modernists who, during jazz's lifetime, came to believe that one audience was too many. This introverted tendency first appeared in 1918, when Arnold Schoenberg and Alban Berg founded the Society for Private Musical Performances in Vienna, which sponsored concerts by invitation only and allowed no press. By 1958 it reached the point where Milton Babbitt could title a famous essay "Who Cares If You Listen?" For Babbitt the progress of music was similar to that of science, "the result of a half-century of revolution in musical thought . . . whose nature and consequences can be compared only with, and in many

respects are closely analogous to, those of the mid-nineteenth-century revolution in mathematics and the twentieth-century revolution in theoretical physics."[22]

Jazz musicians, too, believed in progress. Remarked Hawkins in 1946: "Look at what medicine and science have accomplished in the last twenty or thirty years. That's the way it should be in music."[23] But consider the difference: Babbitt, who worked in the academy, compares music with theoretical physics, an abstract realm remote from most people's lives; Hawkins, who worked in show business, compares it with medicine.

The idea of a "pure" art uncontaminated by contact with the popular audience—or the profit motive—

is a modernist shibboleth. Just as it does not describe bebop, it does not describe the greatest composers. Observes Henry Pleasants: "Both Bach and Beethoven knew perfectly well how to address themselves to a large lay public, and both of them did it, repeatedly and successfully."[24] Nor is this of merely pragmatic concern. High art arises from popular art and must sustain a connection to it or else lose all vitality. This is what happened to total serialism, the method of composition practiced by Babbitt, as well as to the other branches of modernism that pursued noise, aleatory experiments, and the holy grail of total freedom. These composers didn't care if the audience listened, and the audience returned the compliment.

I am not forgetting that Davis (following Parker) turned his back on the audience—isn't that a bandstand version of Babbitt? But here again, jazz is different, and part of the difference has to do with the double audience. By all accounts Davis saved his coldest contempt for ignorant white fans (and for "no-playing" black pretenders). Further, Davis's contempt, unlike Babbitt's, was directed at an audience who *did* listen. The problem, for black jazz musicians, was that listening often led to larceny. Amiri Baraka calls it "the Great Music Robbery": the seemingly inexorable process by which successive styles of African American music have been most profitably exploited not by the artists who created them but by white imitators working in a white-controlled industry.[25] To Baraka this dynamic suggests that the capitalist system is inherently racist. Some beboppers gave lip service to this idea, as did many jazz musicians in the 1960s. But as Ellison saw, the beboppers were not anticommercial. They struggled not for socialist revolution but for their rightful piece of the capitalist pie.

This view casts fresh light on Davis's back-turning. Like the posturing of many of today's "political" entertainers, back-turning was both an outlet for resentment and a clever marketing device. As Davis reportedly quipped after rebuffing a white female fan: "When you have stock in Con Edison and make all the money I make, you have to act the way people expect you to act—they want me to be their evil nigger, and that's what I'm ready to be."[26]

But posturing is not art. Beyond commercial success, a musician of Davis's caliber aspires to the social esteem due any serious artist. DeVeaux notes that during the swing era a version of this esteem existed "within the black community" toward the bandleaders and musicians who "had proved their worth in open competition with their white counterparts."[27] These people had *cultural authority*—something taken for granted by the composer-theoreticians of European modernism but less common on an American bandstand. With acuity DeVeaux describes bebop as the offspring of this cultural authority, born in the narrow but fertile space between the familiar material the public wants and the innovative material it is willing to handle. When the black popular audience called for the blues, the Eckstine band "reacted by adding an ironic layer of complexity that (not incidentally) flaunted their special skills. . . . Yet it worked. Instead of parody, black audiences around the country heard a sophisticated updating of the old blues sound, and they clamored for more."[28]

A glorious moment, but short lived. "People still talk about that legendary Billy Eckstine band," Eckstine said later. "Man! The legendary Billy Eckstine was about to starve with that motherfucker."[29] As bebop grew more dense and virtuosic, the black popular audience turned toward the more accessible pleasures of rhythm and blues, leaving a core of loyal fans but no reliable market niche. The ravages of heroin, Parker's death, and the condescension of the mainstream media only made matters worse. For Davis as for many others, the sweet taste of success in Europe was made bitter by the fact that "whatever we played over there, right or wrong, was cheered . . . and when we came back over here . . . [we] couldn't even get no work."[30] In the early 1950s he succumbed to heroin, and his successful debut came close to being a mere footnote in the history of jazz.

Then the cat landed on his feet, with a vengeance. Critics still debate the merits of Davis's *The Birth of the Cool* recordings. To Andre Hodeir they represented "a new classicism," taking the necessary next step beyond the "spectacular effects" of bebop.[31] To Max Harrison their "muted colors" and "lucid proportions" were nothing new, these "'cool' possibilities" having always been present in jazz.[32] To Stanley Crouch *The Birth of the Cool* represented merely "another failed attempt to marry jazz to European devices," and Davis's subsequent collaborations with Gil Evans—*Miles Ahead, Porgy and Bess,* and *Sketches of Spain*—mere "pastel versions of European colors."[33] Nevertheless, all parties agree that the new style was popular with whites—as was *Kind of Blue*, described by Gary Giddins as "so accessible few people recognized the album for the insurrection it was."[34] This "insurrection" remains the only jazz album that many whites own.

When Gerry Mulligan moved to California in the early 1950s, the cool sound became the immensely popular West Coast sound as developed by Dave Brubeck, Paul Desmond, Jimmy Guiffre, Chet Baker, and others. Because its leading figures were white, the media and recording industry played up the West Coast style, and in those racially tense times a reaction was bound to set

in: it was called hard bop. By 1970 Ron Wellburn, an ardent proponent of the "black aesthetic," would describe hard bop in these terms:

Percussionist Art Blakey has made several trips to Africa since the mid-forties. When he returned in 1955, he literally brought in a drum fever, which served as the primary impetus to the black musician's reaction to the West Coast "cool," a predominantly white jazz musicians' thing that had sucked its blood from Lester Young and Miles Davis back in 1949.[35]

Why does Wellburn condemn cool but not Davis? The answer is simple: Davis also helped to create hard bop. Giddins puts it in a nutshell: "The warring subcultures, West Coast jazz (cool) and East Coast jazz (hard bop) had the same midwestern parent: one Miles Dewey Davis."[36] To the *yang* of hard bop Davis brought stillness, melodic beauty, and understatement; to the *yin* of cool he brought rich sonority, blues feeling, and an enriched rhythmic capacity that moved beyond swing to funk. By refusing to color-code either his music or his audience, Davis rose at the end of the 1950s to the summit of artistic excellence.

Then the ground shifted. During the 1960s American music underwent drastic change that would confound even Davis. Legend has it that jazz was born in a brothel. If so, then perhaps it can be compared with the brothel-born infant

brought before King Solomon, and black and white America with the two harlots who claimed to be its mother. Solomon said, "Bring me a sword. Divide the living child in two, and give half to the one, and half to the other." Everyone knows what happened next. The first woman cried, "Oh, my lord, give her the living child, and by no means slay it." The second woman said, "It shall be neither mine nor yours; divide it." And wise Solomon gave the infant to the first, declaring, "She is its true mother."[37]

Yet here the analogy breaks down, because jazz did not remain whole. Davis was well positioned to play Solomon, being intimately familiar with every part of the child: rhythm, shapely melody, and sophisticated harmony. And for a while he exerted his best musical wisdom. But the case was too complicated, involving not only the racial parentage of jazz but also the following three changes: first, the transformation of jazz into a high-minded yet esoteric art music; second, the emergence of a large, enthusiastic, racially mixed audience for popular music; and third, a sea change in Western music-making that would pervasively alter the relationship between aural and visual media. Each of these three changes had an impact on Miles Davis.

Consider first the transformation of jazz. Long before the 1960s, jazz had been borrowing musical ideas from European and American modernism. Indeed, it now is widely acknowledged that jazz made better use of modernism than vice versa. Throughout the early decades of the twentieth century, jazz musicians exploited with stunning speed and originality such modernist ideas as chromatic harmony, modal scales, electronic instruments, and electronically altered sound. It is tricky to take a balanced view of this process, because while many in the "serious" music establishment dismiss jazz as a Johnny-come-lately rummaging in modernism's cast-offs, many in the jazz establishment belittle or deny the role of European ideas.[38]

This impasse intensified during the 1960s, when the leaders of the "new thing"—Ornette Coleman, John Coltrane, and Cecil Taylor—expanded the sound vocabulary of traditional instruments; eliminated cadential harmony and the modal system; explored polytonality and atonality; adopted irregular meter; and then, increasingly, abolished metric time. The goal, imperfectly achieved, was total improvisatory freedom. Viewed through a European lens, this was a case of artists undertaking the quintessentially modernist project of dissecting the fundamentals of their art. Viewed through the lens of

black nationalism, however, it was a case of *African American* artists purging jazz of a despised European ancestry. In a typical 1968 effusion, Baraka (then LeRoi Jones) declared that "colored peoples' music demands, at least, that many many [sic] half, quarter, etc. tones be sounded, implied, hummed, slurred, that the whole sound of a life get in," while "the 'precision' that Europeans claim with their 'reasonable' scale" produces "only the sounds of an order and reason that patently deny most colored peoples the right to exist."[39]

The black innovators of the "new thing" did not embrace all of modernism. For example, they ignored the rigorously mathematical techniques of serialism—perhaps because they were less willing than academic composers to purchase intellectual rigor at the price of musical rigor mortis. They also made scant use of the random or "aleatory" experiments of John Cage. Some scholars equate the concept of free jazz with aleatory music, but the two are not equivalent.[40] As African Americans living through the civil rights and Black Power movements, the "new thing" musicians were preoccupied with their own capacity to utilize freedom, not with the role of chance and indeterminacy in the universe. Even when most "out there," they understood their music to be expressing human (and God-given) creative powers. Indeed, they would have agreed with Yehudi Menuhin that "improvisation is not the expression of accident but rather of the

accumulated yearnings, dreams and wisdom of our very soul."[41]

Baraka insists rightly that black jazz musicians never borrow a European idea without giving it a powerful idiomatic twist. In the "new thing" the borrowings from modernism are often coupled with (or duplicated by) importations from African, Indian, and other non-Western traditions. This can make tracing the influences on "new thing" musicians a bit like retrieving eggs from an omelette. As Giddins writes about Cecil Taylor, "people tend to hear in his music echoes of what they already know. Some find traces of Ellington, Powell, Monk, Silver, or Brubeck; for others, it's Brahms, Stravinsky, Cowell, Messiaen, or Boulez; for still others, it's Africa, the pentatonic scale, and microtones."[42]

A less sanguine perspective on the "new thing" was that of the jazz elders, who instead of savoring the rewards of maturity in the 1960s felt themselves tossed into the dustbin of history. Not surprisingly, they were quick to warn that the heady concept of free expression opens the door to fakes and charlatans. "They're playing 'Freedom' and they're playing 'Extensions,' whatever those things are," growled Hawkins in 1964. "Man, I don't know what they are. These guys are looking for a gimmick, a short cut. There is no short cut."[43]

To some extent, Davis was one of these elders, commenting to Feather that Taylor's "Lena" was "some sad shit, man. . . . Is that what the critics are digging? Them critics better stop having coffee."[44] But here again, Davis landed on his feet. He sought out four ferociously talented young men—Ron Carter, Herbie Hancock, Wayne Shorter, and Tony Williams—and set off a controlled explosion that equaled the excitement of the "new thing" but through a disciplined route that tolerated no short cuts. It would have been the perfect solution, had jazz not plunged to its nadir in the 1960s. Viewed from the twenty-first century, this Davis quintet made the kind of music, like Bach's Goldberg Variations or Beethoven's late quartets, that occupies an elite niche within a vibrant, broad-based tradition. But this niche did not seem very desirable at the time; according to the catchword, "jazz was dead."[45]

Oddly, Davis blamed whites for promoting the "new thing". He even remarks that "pushing the free thing among a lot of the white music critics was intentional, because a lot of them thought that people like me were just getting too popular and too powerful."[46] Giddins faults this "incoherent" remark, noting that Davis "forgets LeRoi Jones."[47] But beneath the incoherence, not to mention the egotism and paranoia, lurks a valid perception: despite the urging of Baraka and others, the "new thing" never became the voice of the black masses. Coltrane was the only figure to command a large black following, and that had more to do with his earlier music (including his association with Davis) and his impressive spirituality than with his post-1965, avant-garde sound. Today, when hindsight reveals a more durable commitment to the "new thing" among intellectually inclined Europeans than among everyday black Americans, Davis's odd attitude makes intuitive sense.

An introverted modernist like Babbitt—or Taylor, for that matter—tends to cultivate his art and neglect his audience. Not Davis. "I never was one of those people," he writes in his autobiography, "who thought . . . the fewer hear you, the better you are, because what you're doing is just too complex for a lot of people to understand."[48] Creatively if not psychologically, Davis was an extrovert who cultivated *both* his art *and* his audience and refused to neglect either. This is not a flaw. On the contrary, it

may be a necessary qualification for greatness. Davis's audience-seeking antennae were long and sensitive, and in the mid-1960s they picked up the unwelcome but unavoidable fact that popular music was eclipsing jazz in every way that mattered.[49] What he did next was what came naturally: he gravitated toward the action.

Musically speaking, the 1960s were the best of times—and the worst. To the extent that authentic black gospel flowed into the secular market as "soul," and the musical and lyrical talents honed in the folk movement shaped rock and roll into sophisticated rock, the period was incredibly fruitful. But to the extent that self-indulgent theatrics supplanted musical sound, the 1960s laid the groundwork for the deterioration of the 1970s. The seemingly miraculous spectacle of the double audience blending into one attracted Davis. In the mid-1960s the crossover appeal of both white and black performers, often playing together in the same bands, was so great, *Billboard* suspended its policy of running color-coded charts. In this spirit Davis noted Coltrane's role as "a guiding light" not only for young blacks but also "for many intellectual and revolutionary whites and Asians."[50] Also catching his eye was the Charles Lloyd Quartet, whose 1966 appearance at the Fillmore West led to sudden success with the huge racially mixed youth audience.[51]

The new woman in Davis's life, the singer Betty Mabry, was his bellwether. She and countless other young people saw in performers like Sly Stone and Jimi Hendrix a power beyond the usual categories of entertainment or even art. It was erotic, to be sure (her marriage with Davis ended when she hooked up with Hendrix). But it was also spiritual. Here is a parallel between the lightning that struck Davis at the Riviera Club and the fireworks generated by Stone and especially by Hendrix at the top of their form. Both recall the history of African American music as ritual, and the musician as priest or shaman. This is true of gospel, obviously, but also of jazz (think of Bird, or especially Monk) and of the blues; as Albert Murray reminds us, the blues is secular, but as traditionally performed it is "a ritual of purification and affirmation nonetheless."[52] Before the 1960s counterculture succumbed to drugs, political fanaticism, and mindless hedonism, its better instincts were buoyed up by a mode of music-making whose aim was spiritual ecstasy.

Davis was not cut out to play shaman. Unlike Sly Stone, he did not come from the Pentecostal church, and he was not about to start leaping about the stage in an effort to take his audience higher. But as the Summer of Love gave way to Woodstock, and Woodstock to Altamont, Davis found the perfect niche. Rather than ride the jubilant crest of the counterculture (which by 1968 already had past), he made music that spoke to its undertow.

To be sure, it was not Davis but the Rolling Stones who strutted their stuff in a blood-red spotlight at Altamont, belting out "Sympathy for the Devil," "Brown Sugar," and "Under My Thumb" while the Hell's Angels hacked and stomped a black fan named Meredith Hunter to death. But listen to those classic Stones numbers today, and you will feel like tapping your toe and grinning. Listen to Bitches Brew, and you will feel like burning the house down. I mean this as a compliment. With its bottomless, shifting rhythmic ostinatos, its eddying scraps of guitar and snarling bass clarinet; its dissonant chords in unmentionable keys; and the recurring pitchfork thrust of Davis's horn, Bitches Brew stretched the imaginations of both black and white listeners at a time when rock was ossifying into hard rock and soul was losing its (gospel) soul.

Part of Bitches Brew's success was that it departed from the high-mindedness of jazz. Like the nationalist movements in nineteenth- and twentieth-century European music, 1960s jazz involved an extra-musical search for heroes, symbols, myths of the people. From Sonny Rollins's Freedom Suite to Coltrane's Ascension, Archie Shepp's abstract blues to Sun Ra's far-out fringe, this music expresses lofty emotions: anger, sorrow, righteousness, spirituality. By 1969, however, the black revolution was mired in violence and backlash, and the love-and-peace counterculture ran low on love and peace. Bitches Brew captured this moment both musically and extra-musically. And it did so for both audiences: in the cover painting by Mati Klarwein a pensive African-looking face, beaded with moisture, is depicted in both ebony and pink—a detail that, along with the photograph of Davis with Teo Macero, reassured whites that this music belonged to them, too.

Yet Bitches Brew is not rock. When late-1960s rock tried to conjure darkness and danger, it did so by cranking up the volume, setting off smoke bombs, applying too much eye makeup, and making the music cruder as well as louder. The general tone is suggested by the British reviewer who described the hard rock band Black Sabbath as offering "anguished screeching about war pigs, rat salads, iron men and similar gloomy topics set to an endlessly repeated two-chord riff."[53] This kind of hard rock was a hit with the junior testosterone crowd, and in the 1970s its monstrous offspring, heavy metal, became one of the most durable genres in the history of popular music. But none of this has anything to do with Davis's direction at the time.

In the controversy over Davis's fusion, the most puzzling factor is the third transformation mentioned above: the sea change in Western music-making that also occurred during the 1960s. Both the champions and the critics of Davis's later career tend to hold him responsible for this transformation and to assign praise or blame accordingly. But this is a mistake. Davis absorbed the sea change and adapted his remarkable talents to it in ways both creative and calculating. But he did not cause it.

The sea change is part of a massive cultural shift away from the ear and toward the eye. Literary people complain about the conquest of print by images; a profounder complaint could be made by musicians. It is beyond the scope of this essay to pin down all the forces at work in this shift. But there is no doubt about its impact. At all levels, from the Broadway stage to the latest youth craze, listening is now distinctly subordinate to looking. In the visual feast of a culture dominated by photography, film, video, computer graphics, and high-tech stagecraft, music is rarely more than aural sauce.

Ironically, the musicians who contributed most to this change had the exact opposite intention. In 1965 Philip Glass was inspired by Indian raga to try a new compositional approach where the Western tendency to "take time and divide it" would be replaced with the Eastern one to "take very small units and add them together." So he took brief, simple melodic-harmonic motives and repeated them over and over, along with "cycles of different beats, wheels within wheels, everything going at the same time and always changing."[54] Similar ideas occurred to the jazz avant-gardist La Monte Young, and to composer-engineers such as Terry Riley, Steve Reich, and Mike Oldfield. Dubbed "minimalism," the music that emerged from these efforts was conceived emphatically not to serve as mere background. To Reich the goal was to "facilitate closely detailed listening."[55] To Glass it was to supplant the narrative mode of listening associated with "story symphonies and story concertos" with a timeless immersion where "neither memory nor anticipation" would have "a place in sustaining the texture, quality, or reality of the musical experience."[56]

It's important to note that minimalism did not arise from *musical* modernism. On the contrary, Glass consciously rejected his modernist training when he espoused the Indian idea of music as "a meditational mode of perception" that "shares attributes with trance states, religious ecstasy, and drug experiences without being synonymous with them." At the same time, the musical modernists rejected Glass. As John Rockwell explains, Glass's "refusal to come to terms with either conventional tonality or its serial extension . . . enraged the contemporary musical establishment, accustomed as it was to equating technical complexity with artistic worth."[57] Today Glass, Reich, and others are feted in concert halls around the world, and composers from John Adams in America to Henryk Gorecki in Poland have combined minimalism's clear pulse and looping repetition with romanticism's high emotion.[58] But significantly, the first modernists to embrace minimalism were not in music but in the visual arts. "I gravitated toward artists because they were always more open than musicians," admits Glass.[59]

In the popular realm minimalism was an instant hit. Rock fans bought Riley's *A Rainbow in the Curved Air* (1968) and Oldfield's *Tubular Bells* (1973). Today, critics blame minimalism for New Age, the easy-listening mood music they disparaged as "aural wallpaper" or "sonic laxative."[60] Add a shot of computerized rhythm, and you have contemporary dance and techno. But here, too, minimalism keeps company with the visual. Beginning with the passages from *Tubular Bells* used in *The Exorcist* (1973) and continuing through Glass's stunning scores for *Koyaanisqatsi* (1983) and *Hamburger Hill* (1987), minimalism's slowly shifting repetitiveness—its "wallpaper" quality, if

you will—largely has conquered the silver screen. Indeed, minimalist soundtracks often work better than the traditional orchestral kind. What this means, however, is that the high ambition of minimalism's creators—that pulsing, trance-like sound would foster a new, quasispiritual listening—is not fulfilled. Outside the concert hall, in the casual, secular, technologically driven settings where most people now listen to music, minimalist-derived forms succeed precisely because they do not demand the concentrated attention once routinely paid to shaped melodic structures from the symphony to the sonata, the popular song to the jazz solo.

A similar pattern appears in rock. Ask any young fan of today's

"alternative rock" which 1960s band he or she admires the most, and the answer will likely be the Velvet Underground, the obscure New York band that became famous in 1966, when Andy Warhol hired them to accompany his "happening," the *Exploding Plastic Inevitable*. The Velvet Underground had direct ties to minimalism. Along with songwriter Lou Reed, the band's co-founder was John Cale, a violist who had worked with La Monte Young. Reed and Cale claimed to be inspired by 1950s rock and roll: the steady backbeat, the basic chord changes, the simple melodies. Yet as Rockwell notes, "this fascination with the basics was merely a rock extension of the whole lower-Manhattan art world's devotion to minimalism."[61] The Velvet Underground did not sound like 1950s rock and roll—or like 1960s rock, for that matter. Rather than embellish their simple songs with rhythmic counterpoint and blues expression, Reed and Cale added the ingredients of minimalism: the drone, the unaccented 4/4 pulse, the melody shards set against dissonant chords. Writes Charlie Gillett, this "deliberately primitive musical accompaniment seemed to have filtered all the black influences out of rock and roll, leaving an amateurish, clumsy, but undeniably atmospheric background."[62] This atmospheric minimalism did not top the charts at the time, but with the rise of MTV and the music video over the next twenty years, it became one of the most important influences on rock.[63]

Against this background, it is hard to know what "jazz-rock fusion" means. The label is highly misleading in the case of Davis's experimental 1970s albums, *Dark Magus* (1974), *Agharta*, and *Pangaea* (both 1975), which take very little from jazz, apart from what Davis had resisted a decade earlier—free improvisation—and very little from rock, apart from a fascination with volume and electronic instruments. The label is more accurate in the case of Hancock, Chick Corea, Wayne Shorter, Joe Zawinul, and John McLaughlin, whose fusion combines jazz improvisation with the volume, electronic instrumentation, and strong rhythms of popular music. Yet these former Davis sidemen drew not just on rock but on soul and funk, which are not the same thing. To call Aretha Franklin a rock musician, for example, ignores the difference between the Chicago blues—the basis of 1960s rock—and black gospel—the basis of soul. And to lump James Brown's music with rock ignores the difference between rock and funk, the African-inspired "drum fever" that entered popular music by way of hard bop. Moreover, the label "jazz-rock fusion" obscures the impact of minimalism on rock and on what Davis and others did in fusion.

A label can also imply a judgment. Many jazz people consider anything connected with rock as "dollar-sign music" and condemn fusion accordingly.[64] For such people the yardstick is anticommercialism. But if fusion was a sell-out, it fell a bit short on

buyers. After the success of *Bitches Brew*, which (as I say) hit the 1969 Zeitgeist on the head, Davis's 1970s records fulfilled no one's gold or platinum hopes. Weather Report, the band led by Shorter and Zawinul, was more commercially successful. But even their best-selling *Heavy Weather* (1976) climbed no higher than number 30 on the album chart.

Meanwhile, the "fusion" part of the label appeals to critics steeped in postmodernism. To Gary Tomlinson, Davis deserves credit for having broken new ground as a musician. The music incorporates "unflinching confrontation" with "dialogical extremes." Not only did Davis spearhead "a departure from the canonized and thereby musically segregated jazz tradition," he also created "an ever-changing melange of ingredients from his (our) fragmented and dizzying varied musical environment." He ventured into "the structural indeterminacy sometimes explored by Karlheinz Stockhausen" while at the same time "coming to grips with the bitch within himself" and recognizing "his own mysterious

otherness, and his desire to enter into a meaningful, non-demeaning colloquy with it."[65]

After reading such a compendium of virtues, it is tempting to add that fusion also sweetens the breath and keeps the trousers from bagging at the knees. *But is the music any good?* For answer I suggest a simpler standard than either anticommercialism or dialogical theory, namely the one customarily used to judge popular music. Here, too, judgment is more problematic than before. But one can still state in general terms the virtues of popular music, as Tomlinson does when he defends "the vitality, subtlety, and expressiveness of the pop traditions that inspired Davis."[66] Vitality, subtlety, expressiveness—not a bad list. Davis himself also favored the other musical qualities. He disliked over-intellectualized music, complaining that Coleman did not "play in rhythm" and that Shepp, Albert Ayler, and Taylor played music that had "no melodic line, wasn't lyrical, you couldn't hum it."[67] With the popular audience Davis shared an appreciation for the primary capacities of music: the power of rhythm to move the body (dance) and the power of melody to move the emotions (song). Perhaps fusion should be judged by these standards.

The question "Can you dance to it?" is philistine only if danceability depends on something as mindless as a heavily accented back beat. Some people require such a beat in order to dance at all and lose their bearings when music shows too much rhythmic life. But danceability cannot be measured properly by these people. The true yardstick is not strict tempo but swing, funk, groove—whatever name is given to that elusive quality that moves the muscles and lifts the spirits of the true dancers among us. By the time fusion came along, jazz had parted company with this quality. It is often said in bebop's defense that people danced to it. So they did, until it grew too complex and they defected to rhythm and blues. With the "new thing", not to mention with Davis's 1960s quintet, percussion became a boiling cauldron that impressed the intellect but defeated the feet.

Was fusion a corrective? Yes and no. Hancock's *Head Hunters* (1973) proved that jazz musicians could match Sly and the Family Stone in making people "dance to the music." But therein lay the problem, because jazz is expected to do more than match popular music. It's expected to aim higher. In the context of funk fusion, this often meant thickening the "bottom" to the point where no danceable rhythm could possibly surface. In Davis's capacious fusion bands of the early 1970s, each player, as Tomlinson notes, had "an extraordinary freedom of colloquy within the ensemble." But at the same time these ensembles had enough instrumental paraphernalia to support three or four funk bands. "The Brazilian and African percussionists and the Indian musicians," writes Tomlinson, "contribute not so much full-fledged styles as raw sound materials. More flavors for the

"mix."[68] O.K., but as any good cook knows, too many flavors can turn melange into mess.

I hate to sound square, but the trumpet is primarily a melody instrument. And while Davis was a fine bandleader, he was primarily a trumpeter who reminded a world dazzled by bebop virtuosity that sometimes less is more. Critics dispute his technique and how well he played in the higher registers. But no one disputes that his horn spoke to people on the lower frequencies of emotion, through melody. Because of its deceptive simplicity, melody is one of the hardest elements in music to explain or evaluate. Writes Aaron Copland: "Why a good melody should have the power to move us has thus far defied all analysis. We cannot even say, with any degree of surety, what constitutes a good melody."[69]

As a melodist Davis has always had a "penchant for minimalism" that, according to Baraka, goes "back to his earliest music. It is the 'fill-in' quality we remember with Bird." Obsessed with "what can be cut out," Davis always preferred sketched understatement to

embellished overstatement.[70] Like a drawing by Matisse, where a single line can suggest a full three-dimensional volume, a melodic sketch by Davis has the power to evoke larger forms. He was proud of this ability, as shown by his storied comment when Coltrane complained about not being able to stop playing: "Try taking the saxophone out of your mouth."

Davis's way with melody also involved repetition, though not in the minimalist sense. In his best music, notes Wynton Marsalis, Davis repeats a "sweet" melodic motive only as long as it takes to squeeze the sweetness out, then drops it and hunts for another.[71] In his pre-fusion music this development of the motive related closely to Davis's awareness of harmonic structure, even within the loose boundaries of modal improvisation. In his autobiography he alludes to this awareness with typical bluntness: "We ain't in Africa, and we don't play just chants. There's some theory under what we do."[72] Not until fusion do Davis's melodies quit suggesting larger forms and become "just chants." And only at the end of his career did he become a minimalist in the sense of recycling a single melodic fragment throughout an entire performance.[73]

The antimelodic tendency within fusion is defended in some quarters as yet another liberation from the hegemony of European music. If liberation means converting from a music based on shapely melody and sophisticated harmony to one based on mere squiggles (or as record producers call them, "melody hooks"), then not just fusion but the great bulk of popular music has now been liberated. I will leave aside the question of whether the emotional power of melody is a tool of "order and reason" (philosophers from Plato to Rousseau thought otherwise). The more relevant point is that only in an atmosphere of mindless racial polarization could melody be rejected on the preposterous grounds that it is of interest only to whites. To the extent that Davis bought into this polarization, he sold out his rarest gift.

Like the child brought before Solomon, African American music is a living whole, where every dance, even the liveliest, partakes of melody; and every song, even the tenderest, partakes of rhythm. Popular music still possessed this wholeness in the 1960s, but clearly by 1975, for lack of a Solomon, the child was being dismembered. It was probably no coincidence that Davis quit music that year. The rift between black and white audiences that had opened after the assassination of Martin Luther King, Jr.,

reached the breaking point. *Billboard* had restored its color-coded charts, and while the disco craze still was integrated, the white fans of heavy metal began to wage their antiblack (and antigay) "disco sucks" campaign.[74] Other whites, including many southern musicians who had performed on soul records, retreated to country rock. Soul began to lose touch with its gospel roots, as Isaac Hayes led Barry White into the swamp of self-indulgent "fuck music." And the New York audience was split between the white downtown clubs that spawned punk and the black uptown clubs that nurtured hip-hop. Popular music was being cut into pieces, with rhythm claimed by the black folks, melody left to the whites, and harmony abandoned to foster care.[75]

Amid this deterioration Davis's final gambit was to market himself as a black youth idol. This is no surprise, since he had always favored the young, stylish, and black audience. But the more he tried to update his image, dressing in Hendrixian glad rags and adorning the cover of *On the Corner* (1972) with blaxploitation cartoons, the more his targets recoiled. Unlike the white

audience, the black audience was not divided by age in the 1970s. Black youth did not flock to Davis's music, but neither did they scorn it the way white youth did the music beloved by their parents. Black youth respected Davis, so when he started posing as a superannuated super-fly, it was a bit like seeing Ella Fitzgerald in a go-go dancer cage. In the wry observation of the writer David Nicholson, "Fusion Miles always seemed like one of my uncles in bell bottoms."

The irony is that by quitting music and attempting to lead a totally hedonistic lifestyle, Davis *did* stay in touch with the times. What is left to say about the late 1970s? To make one tiny detail stand for the whole, I offer the following passage from a 1980 handbook for would-be disco proprietors. After touting mainstream discos as places where people "can abandon themselves to the tidal wave of raw animal emotions that engulfs them," the chapter entitled "Club Safety" notes "the growing problem of damage to noses caused by excessive use of cocaine."[76] Noses were the least of it, as countless addicts can attest. It was during those years of seclusion that Davis came closest to destroying himself.

But then the cat pulled off another landing. Paradoxically, many people who had stopped listening to popular music in the 1970s started again in the 1980s. The 1980s saw the emergence of MTV, clearly the triumph of sight over sound. But it was also a time of renewal. On the white side of the fence, the so-called New Wave rejected the anticommercial, antimusical philosophy of punk and (in Bill Flanagan's words) "decided they were not going to limit themselves or pretend that playing every night does not make you a better musician."[77] Whatever else might be said about videogenic acts such as Elvis Costello, Tom Petty and the Heartbreakers, Blondie, the Pretenders, Dire Straits, the Eurythmics, the Police, or the Talking Heads, their music refreshed some weary ears. The same could be said of the black performers who appealed to Rip Van Davis when he awoke from his six-year sleep: Michael Jackson and, especially, Prince.

For his comeback Davis needed the right musical vehicle, and jazz was not it. Some blame physical frailty. But his chops improved over time, and besides, chops matter less than musicianship. More significant, he dreaded becoming a legend. In the early 1980s the cultural position of jazz was ambiguous: neither moribund nor cutting edge, it was becoming classicized, which is sort of like becoming canonized, only the requirements are different (you don't have to be a saint). Toward this process Davis was of two minds—but only one gut. In his autobiography he says of the great jazz figures, "shit, *their* music is classical." But in the same breath he knocks Wynton Marsalis for playing "old dead European music" and compares the "tired-ass shit" played by many whites with the dynamism of black music, which he extols for not being "the same on Friday and Saturday night."[78]

This need for reinvention ran deep in Davis—both mind and gut are talking here. But can it run too deep? Early suggests that the "keen and bitter" demands made by black audiences on black artists would be "more bearable if blacks were not so quick to condemn their artists for being out of style, so easily able to disengage themselves from engagements of awesome worth."[79] Davis's pet insults—"stale," "tired," "old," "dead"—must have cut close to the bone in the 1980s. Desperate to avoid the taint of age and weakness, he scorned as reactionary the efforts of Marsalis and others to transmit jazz as a living tradition. If Early is right, and such efforts, common to most cultures, meet uncommon resistance among African Americans, the explanation is simple. In Davis's mind, the "sorry-assed imitation" who wins a Grammy for "copying black people's shit" is invariably white. And so is the moldy fig who turns jazz into "something dead that you put under a glass in the museum."[80] If being a legend meant being the object of white nostalgia or a specimen for white collectors, Davis wanted no part of it.

A sizable black audience, of course, did stay loyal to Davis throughout his retirement, and this audience mattered to him as much or more than ever, to judge by this uncharacteristically heart-tugging account of his first live performance after six years:

One night, there was this little crippled black guy who had cerebral palsy sitting down front in a wheelchair. . . . I was playing this blues, and he was sitting right in front of the stage. I played it to him because I knew that he knew what the blues were. Halfway through my solo, I looked into this guy's eyes, and he was crying. He reached up his withered arm, which was trembling, and with his shaking hand he touched my trumpet as though he were blessing it—and me. Man, I almost lost it right then and there.[81]

Such a moment of quasireligious communion would feel distinctly out of place in a Wynton Marsalis concert. It depends on the venue, of course, but, like Billy Taylor, Marsalis is a natural educator who rarely performs without also endeavoring to correct in some small way the public's incomprehension of jazz. Davis did not care to do this. Consider, for example, the evening he spent watching Ray Charles accept a Lifetime Achievement Award at the Kennedy Center. The year was 1987, and Davis also attended a dinner at the Reagan White House, where he was seated next to the (white) wife of a politician. Whether the questions she asked about jazz were as silly as he recalls ("Are we supporting this art form just because it's from here in this country, and it is art in its truest form[?]"), they were doubtless silly enough to irk the average fan, never mind Davis.[82] Such questions would have irked Marsalis, too. But being a politician himself, and I do not mean this as an insult, Marsalis would have sucked it up and delivered a charming and informative reply.

After forty years of celebrity Davis had a celebrity's ego. So his saltiness that evening may also be explained by the fact that *he* wasn't getting the award, which brings us to the main reason for his dread of becoming a legend: his need to command the *whole* landscape, not just a corner of it. While he hated being stifled by fools, celebrity was his oxygen. "That's one of the reasons I have to make money," he explains, "so I can keep my life private. You have to pay for fame—mentally, spiritually, and in *real* money."[83] The burden of the celebrity artist is the need to feel both pursued by one's admirers and protected from them. Like all true celebrity artists, Davis took mischievous pleasure in the game, as when he quipped while showing an interviewer one of his amateur paintings, "Maybe it's not so good, but it's got my name on it, hee-hee."[84]

Thus did Davis make his comeback with the double audience firmly in mind. Playing to the mass audience, he traded on his celebrity, granting puff-piece interviews, making a music video that prominently featured his work,[85] and eventually allowing himself to be feted as a lifetime achiever still busy achieving. Playing to black youth, he mixed it up with the chart-topping genres of "contemporary rhythm and blues" and hip-hop. Again, the most appropriate yardsticks used to evaluate this last phase of his music are the perennial ones of dance and song.

Dance was alive in the 1980s but not well. Many of the lesser talents who cashed in on the disco craze had done so by exploiting various short cuts. James Brown sums up their efforts in this deathless remark about disco: "I taught 'em everything *they* know but not everything *I* know."[86] The most maligned short cut was the "drum machine," or computer-generated rhythm track. One of the first hit singles to use this device was "Family Affair" by Sly and the Family Stone, a record that has never been accused of sounding mechanical. Yet mechanical rhythm soon followed, as the least creative forces in the industry began to grind out disco literally by the pre-measured unit, introducing a new labeling system, "bpm" (for beats per minute), to help rhythmically challenged disc jockeys segue from one record to the next. Nelson George blames this mechanization on "Eurodisco," the imported high-tech dance music whose "metronomelike beat" was "perfect for folks with no sense of rhythm."[87] But in fact many young blacks gravitated toward Eurodisco—and toward Kraftwerk, the West German band whose popularization of Stockhausen had influenced it heavily.[88]

Because computers are easier to control, and to record, than live musicians, many producers, black and white, came to swear by them and to deny that anything was lost in the translation.[89] Sometimes a producer would concede that technology stifled spontaneity, as when Nile Rodgers admitted missing those times when "somebody in the back makes a mistake and you go, 'Wait a minute, what was that again?'"[90] But as suggested by Rodgers's choice of the word "mistake," it was widely assumed that the only thing live musicians added to the mix was *error*. This assumption comes not from African American music, where the performer's role is vital, but from electronic modernism, where the composer-engineer is king. As randomness or accident, error can be programmed into a computer— indeed, such devices are called "humanizers." But no amount of randomness could humanize the "dance music" genres of the 1980s. The chart

headings—"urban contemporary" and "rhythm and blues"—left the disco era behind. But the music did not.

This is not a Luddite tirade. Popular music long has been at home in the electronic media, and people inevitably would explore the new technology. But in terms of what matters, and has always mattered, in music, new toys do not always mean progress. Listening to the best singers of the time, people like Anita Baker and Luther Vandross, perform against the snap-crackle-pop of precision-tooled rhythm tracks is like watching a tennis pro take the court against a ball-serving machine. No matter how skillfully the pro returns the serve, the interaction never develops into a volley. The reason is simple: one of the players is not a player. The essence of swing (or funk or groove) is intuitive, interactive, elastic—like human creativity. The cliché of the 1980s was that computers are better than bad musicians. Maybe so. But what about *good* musicians?

Musicians can be self-indulgent, of course. But so can producers, especially when they have at their disposal all the

goodies in the studio. What changes is the nature of the goodies. In the 1950s the most dreadful mainstream pop came from producers who behaved like little boys in a candy store, dripping syrupy strings and gooey choral voices over already-sugary material. In the 1980s the most dreadful black pop was dominated by producers who acted like little girls in a boutique, dressing up immature material with every kind of synthesizer frippery. Against these sterile and unresponsive backdrops, even the best voices embark on a quest for feeling that quickly dead-ends in empty virtuosity. The results may saturate the ear, but they do not satisfy the soul.

This is the problem faced by Davis on his first two Warner Brothers albums, *Tutu* (1986) and *Amandla* (1989). Never one for virtuosity, empty or otherwise, he picks his cautious way through the state-of-the-art sonic landscapes prepared for him by Tommy LiPuma and Marcus Miller. But he clearly was ambivalent: "Some people say they miss that spontaneity and spark that comes out of recording with a band right there in the studio. Maybe that's true; I don't know." Then he lets down his guard: "I like raw shit, live, raunchy, get down, get back in the alley shit." Davis respected the people who worked on these albums, especially Miller. But to him the process compromised the music: "Rather than get myself, the working band, and Tommy into all kinds of hassles by trying to bring my working band into the studio to record music that

I might like, but Tommy doesn't, we do it this way, laying down tracks on tape."[91] Of all the musicians on earth, surely Davis is the last who should be "phoning in" his part.[92]

The 1980s were not just a sojourn in the studio, however. By mid-decade Davis's antennae were fully extended, and they told him where the good music was. With a new band including alto saxophonist Kenny Garrett, bass guitarist Foley, keyboardist Adam Holzman, and drummer Ricky Wellman, he began to tour, playing tight, powerful pieces that knit together the unraveled strands of fusion.[93] The full impact of this band was not felt until 1996, when Holzman and Gordon Meltzer assembled eleven of the best (unedited) tracks for *Live Around the World*, an impressive album that has caused many nay-sayers to look again at Davis's later career.[94] People who hate the sound of fusion will not be won over. But those who like fusion's sound, but dislike its radical unmooring from dance or song, will be intrigued. Not only do many of these tracks meet the test of variety, subtlety, and expressiveness, they also

meet Davis's own test, which is whether anyone else could have made music that sounded this way at any other time. The answer is no.

From the standpoint of dance, Davis was wise to hire Wellman, previously the drummer for the go-go band Chuck Brown & the Soul Searchers. Regrettably, the best go-go bands never found a significant audience outside the music's home base of Washington, D.C., because unlike disco, go-go *did* know everything the Godfather of Soul knew.[95] Another James Brown apprentice singled out by Davis was Prince Rogers Nelson, a figure both more famous and (to Davis's critics) more controversial than any of his other 1980s collaborators. For Crouch the sight of Davis praising this "Minneapolis vulgarian and borderline drag queen" proves that he had "become the most remarkable licker of moneyed boots in the music business."[96] Crouch is right about the lightweight raunchiness of his extra-musical persona, but Prince the musician had a traditionalist ear, even when brandishing the latest technology. Perhaps not "the next Duke Ellington"—

the comment by Davis that most rankled Crouch—Prince did make some extraordinary music in the 1980s, which Davis hardly can be faulted for noticing. It is too bad for Prince that he did not collaborate with Davis, because the experience might have helped to mitigate his two most glaring faults. Davis could (or would) not have wasted his time correcting the first fault, a sexual narcissism more forgivable in a twelve-year-old than in a mature artist. But Prince's second fault, a vocal style like the bleating of a priapic baby goat, is something that Davis could have corrected, if only by filling the void with his own incomparable sound.

The dismembered state of music, especially song, ultimately hindered Davis's 1980s comeback. Again, it was not his fault that the ability to write, play, *or listen to* melodies longer than two bars seemed as forgotten as the art of the fugue. The sea change had come, and all he only could recognize it. "A lot of people ask me where music is going today," he says at the conclusion of his autobiography. "I think it's going in short phrases. If you listen, anybody with an ear can hear that."[97]

So is that all? Did Davis simply go with the flow, chasing those short phrases down the musical drain? Or can we distinguish between short phrases that work and those that do not? I say we can but hasten to add that this distinction is as elusive as the one between good and bad melody on a larger scale. Both depend on what

Copland calls "the power to move us." Even the briefest motif can have this power, as Davis knows better than most. Who can explain the appeal of the short phrases that open and close a track like "Miles"?[98] They are, to borrow the lowbrow term, *catchy*, meaning we cannot get enough of them even while listening to them. Davis understood catchiness, which explains why he covered hit songs such as Cyndi Lauper's "Time After Time" and Michael Jackson's "Human Nature." *Live Around the World* features both, and when Davis says (amid wild applause following an electrifying performance of "Human Nature") "That ain't nothing, I do that every night," the pride in his scratchy voice is real.

So is the joy, which raises a question. Did Davis finally retrieve the lightning, that original thunderbolt that struck him back in 1944? If so, here's another question. *Live Around the World* traces a global itinerary: New York, Los Angeles, Graz, Montpelier (France), Rome, Montreux, Osaka, Chicago. Most of these places are long way from the Riviera Club in East St. Louis. During his final years, while reveling in the applause of a global audience, did Davis forget about the (black) folks back home?

I don't think so, though his final attempt to connect with the African-American audience was less than well received. In 1989 Quincy Jones made *Back on the Block*, an eclectic album that enlisted hip-hop and contemporary rhythm and blues to introduce young listeners to jazz. At the time, *Parade* quoted him as saying, "Black people, we have no sense of our musical history. And that's a shame, man. I just hope, before I get out of this world, that I can do something about it."[99] This effort may have spurred Davis toward *Doo-Bop*, the collaboration with rapper Easy Mo Bee that he worked on before he died.

About *Doo-Bop* the obvious comment is one that I have already made: when the melody shrinks, so does Davis's room to maneuver. The lack of melody in hip-hop is not a crime against music, as some would have it. It simply reflects hip-hop's origins in an oral tradition stretching back through Jamaican "toasting" and Trinidadian calypso to the griots or bards of West Africa. Hip-hop came from immigrants, specifically West Indian immigrants to New York, such as Joseph "Grandmaster Flash" Saddler, the second-generation Barbadian whose celebrated club act, featuring improvised patter and the skilled manipulation of two turntables ("wheels of steel"), was a Bronx update of the traveling "sound system" shows that dominate popular music in the islands. From these low-tech roots hip-hop quickly evolved into a high-tech operation. The basic formula is a sound collage that combines programmed, sampled, or performed rhythms with rhymed wordplay. But hip-hop soon came to include a universe of other sounds producers-creators cared to add, as well as the visual components of dance, fashion, graffiti, and eventually video and film. Given this rich mixture, hip-hop has tremendous potential as an art form. So it would be foolish to wish it away or to condemn it just because certain popular strains of it have worked hard at being offensive.[100]

Nor is hip-hop hostile to melody. The so-called East Coast school long has sampled melodic lines from soul records, and it is now customary for rappers, even gangsta rappers, to sing or to use backup singers. The melodies involved being very simple, this does not exactly make hip-hop a natural showcase for the talents of a Miles Davis.

Nevertheless, it is hard to fault Davis for taking an interest in hip-hop. And to his credit, he did not repeat the mistake—made with *On the Corner*—of playing to the mainstream's cartoon images of black people. Today, when the rivalry between East and West Coast hip-hop makes the exploitative gangsta style a topic of debate, it is cliché to say that ghetto youth have enough problems without being made to represent "the collective unconscious garbage heap of neuroses for whites."[101] But it was not cliché in 1990, when Davis decided to make *Doo-Bop*. Back then gangsta rap was the cutting edge hip-hop style that grabbed all the headlines. And yet Davis the alleged trend-chaser refused to touch it. His critics may call him a "licker of moneyed boots," but he did not lick those of Dr. Dre.

Judged as a tribute to Davis, *Doo-Bop* wins points for sincerity, if not eloquence. Judged as a hip hop album, it is middling. Judged as an album worthy of Davis's talents, it cannot be said to light the way to future collaborations between jazz masters and their hip-hop admirers. But by attempting to convey to young listeners a little memory, a little taste of what music once meant to someone like Miles

Davis, it is, in the context of cultural politics writ large, a worthy finale.

Most jazz people prefer to remember a different Davis finale: the concert of classic Gil Evans arrangements that he played with Quincy Jones at the twenty-fifth anniversary of Montreux Jazz Festival. Jack Chambers offers this moving account of the occasion, as captured on video:

Visually, Miles Davis is the focus. The camera cannot stay off him for long. He was dying, we now know, but he is there in his plumage. He snarls once and smiles more often than you would expect. He looks and acts very tired. He takes his solo turns gamely, ponderously; his tone is as fragile as an icicle. [Wallace] Roney sits beside him, always alert, ready to go forward in his place on short notice. . . . Roney's love for the weary old trumpeter, so plainly caught by the camera, beams out the gratitude of a couple of generations of jazz musicians. It turns what might have been an anti-climax into a shining finale.[102]

Why not accept both finales? Combined, they reveal that Davis was up to his old tricks, having it both ways: in the spotlight as presiding jazz elder *and* with a hip-hop CD in the works. For this I can only admire him, as I admire his courage and agility in eluding most,

though not all, of the dangers in his path, the many shapes of figurative death that stalked his musical generation. His long struggle to stay on top was messy and unseemly at times, and some have argued that by his refusal to "age gracefully" he contributed to the decline of American music. But that decline would have happened anyway, and I for one lack the presumptuousness to blame a man for not walking in a straight line across a minefield.

I also think that Davis made it across the minefield. By staying on top throughout all the vicissitudes of America's postwar musical culture, he helped to keep alive the lightning—the living memory of his musical generation, one of the most brilliant that ever lived. He did not do this in the mode of a curator, preservationist, or classicist; but in his cranky, egotistical way he was an educator. Countless young people who hear of him through hip-hop or catch his image in an advertisement will seek out his later music then work their way back to the rest. This happens all the time. Unlike Davis, I have no gripe against jazz repertory groups and university jazz programs; it does my heart good to see jazz at Lincoln Center and on PBS. But this is America the unpredictable, where culture and tradition get handed down in funny ways, some straightforward, some backhanded. And for many audiences, from the two discussed here to innumerable others around the globe, the backhanded way may be the best.

1 Miles Davis and Quincy Troupe, *Miles: The Autobiography* (New York: Simon & Schuster, 1989), 23.

2 Quoted in Gary Tomlinson, "Miles Davis, Musical Dialogician," in Bill Kirchner, ed., *A Miles Davis Reader* (Washington: Smithsonian, 1997), 240.

3 Gerald Early, *Tuxedo Junction: Essays on American Culture* (New York: Ecco, 1989), 315.

4 Robert Walser, "Out of Notes: Signification, Interpretation, and the Problem of Miles Davis," *Musical Quarterly* 77, no. 2 (1993): 360.

5 The point is illustrated by Walser's essay on Davis's 1964 performance of "My Funny Valentine," which begins with a spirited defense of the contextual approach but then fails to practice what it preaches. Not discussed in Walser's text are the following facts: Davis was playing not in a club but in New York's Philharmonic Hall (mentioned in an endnote); playing with him were George Coleman, Herbie Hancock, Ron Carter, and Tony Williams (the full roster recited by every jazz radio announcer); the band had never

played Philharmonic Hall before; the concert was a benefit for the voter registration efforts of the NAACP, CORE, and SNCC; some band members were disgruntled at not getting paid; and Hancock thought afterward that the rhythm section had sounded bad but changed his mind when he heard the tapes. For this "thick description" I resort not to some obscure monograph but to Davis's autobiography and to a conversation with Bill Kirchner (*Miles: The Autobiography*, 265–66).

6 *Miles: The Autobiography*, 329.

7 Leonard Feather, "The Blindfold Tests," in Kirchner, 123–39.

8 Quoted in Jack Chambers, *Milestones: The Music and Times of Miles Davis* (New York: Da Capo, 1998), 20.

9 *Miles: The Autobiography*, 10.

10 Quoted in Scott DeVeaux, *The Birth of Bebop: A Social and Musical History* (Berkeley: California University Press, 1997), 14.

11 Ralph Ellison, *The Collected Essays of Ralph Ellison* (New York: Modern Library, 1995), 283.

12 DeVeaux, 16.

13 DeVeaux, 45.

14 *Miles: The Autobiography*, 24.

15 *Miles: The Autobiography*, 9.

16 *Miles: The Autobiography*, 53.

17 *Miles: The Autobiography*, 54.

18 *Miles: The Autobiography*, 55.

19 Ellison, 261–62.

20 James Weldon Johnson, "The Dilemma of the Negro Author," *The American Mercury* 15, no. 57 (1928): 478.

21 Norman Mailer, *The White Negro* (New York: City Lights, 1957), 4.

22 Milton Babbitt, "Who Cares If You Listen?" ("The Composer as Specialist"), in Bryan R. Simms, ed., *Composers in Modern Musical Culture* (New York: Schirmer, 1999), 154.

23 Quoted in DeVeaux, 42.

24 Henry Pleasants, *Serious Music—and All That Jazz!* (New York: Simon & Schuster, 1969), 143.

25 Quoted in DeVeaux, 19.

26 Quoted in Stanley Crouch, "Play the Right Thing," *New Republic* (February 12, 1990), 33.

27 DeVeaux, 27.

28 DeVeaux, 340–41.

29 Quoted in DeVeaux, 339.

30 *Miles: The Autobiography*, 129.

31 Andre Hodeir, "Miles Davis and the Cool Tendency," in Kirchner, 22–37.

32 Max Harrison, "Collector's Items," in Kirchner, 46–51.

33 Crouch, 39.

34 Gary Giddins, *Visions of Jazz: The First Century* (New York: Oxford University Press, 1998), 349.

35 Ron Wellburn, "The Black Aesthetic Imperative" in Addison Gayle, Jr., ed., *The Black Aesthetic* (New York: Anchor, 1972), 130.

36 Giddins, *Visions*, 341.

37 1 Kings 3:16–28, *The New Oxford Annotated Bible* (New York: Oxford University Press, 1973), 418.

38 Modernism came later to music than to the other European arts. Literature and painting, for example, became modernist during the late nineteenth century. Music held out until World War I (perhaps because it was more deeply imbued with romanticism). Because modernism came of age with jazz, modernists from Milhaud to Copland understandably tried to include "jazz effects" in their work. The ungainliness of these efforts, typically executed (in both senses) by nonjazz musicians, convinced a generation of critics that jazz could not rise to the level of "serious" music—while ironically, the more vital borrowing was on the jazz side.

39 LeRoi Jones, "The Changing Same (R&B and New Black Music)," in Gayle, 124–25.

40 Michael J. Budds, *Jazz in the Sixties* (Iowa City: Iowa University Press, 1990), 80.

41 Quoted in Ian Crofton and Donald Fraser, *A Dictionary of Musical Quotations* (New York: Schirmer, 1985), 78.

42 Giddins, *Visions*, 457.

43 Quoted in DeVeaux, 449.

44 Quoted in Feather, 132.

45 Jack Chambers, *Milestones: The Music and Times of Miles Davis* (New York: Da Capo, 1998), 79.

46 *Miles: The Autobiography*, 271.

47 Gary Giddins, *Faces in the Crowd: Players and Writers* (New York: Oxford University Press, 1992), 162.

48 *Miles: The Autobiography*, 205.

49 Chambers, 80–81.

50 *Miles: The Autobiography*, 286.

51 Chambers, 136–39.

52 Albert Murray, *Stomping the Blues* (New York: McGraw-Hill, 1976), 38–42.

53 Irwin Stambler, *The Encyclopedia of Pop, Rock, and Soul* (New York: St. Martin's, 1977), 57.

54 Quoted in Donald Clarke, ed., *The Penguin Encyclopedia of Popular Music* (New York: Viking, 1989), 467.

55 Quoted in Andy Mackay, *Electronic Music: The Instruments, The Music & The Musicians* (Minneapolis: Control Data, 1981), 107.

56 Quoted in Don Michael Randel, *The Harvard Biographical Dictionary of Music* (Cambridge, Mass.: Harvard University Press, 1996), 313.

57 John Rockwell, *All American Music: Composition in the Late Twentieth Century* (New York: Knopf, 1983), 113-114.

58 Bryan R. Simms, *The Art of Music* (New York: HarperCollins, 1993), 422–23.

59 Quoted in Rockwell, 116.

60 Clarke, 850–51.

61 Rockwell, 235.

62 Charlie Gillett, *The Sound of the City: The Rise of Rock'n' Roll* (New York: Pantheon, 1983), 309.

63 Just to cite one example, the Irish band U2 rose to prominence in the 1980s on a rich enveloping sound developed not from the blues but from the basic formula used by the Velvet Underground. To quote Bono, the band's lead vocalist, "U2 grew up saying 'Fuck off' to the blues" (quoted in Bill Flanagan, "The Age of Excess," *Musician*

November 1989, 450). Other influences on today's "alternative rock," such as feedback noise and the frantic beat known as "thrash," come from punk, which also began in the lower-Manhattan art world then exploded across Britain in the late 1970s. But punk, too, filters out all the "black influences." To hear the extent of this change, compare punk's taste for feedback as chaotic noise with Hendrix's masterful blues-based control of it.

64 Amiri Baraka, quoted in Tomlinson, 237.

65 Tomlinson, 236-247.

66 Tomlinson, 237-238.

67 *Miles: The Autobiography*, 250, 271.

68 Tomlinson, 246.

69 Aaron Copland, *What to Listen for in Music* (New York: McGraw-Hill, 1957), 49–51.

70 Baraka, 72.

71 "Miles Davis" (segment 20), in Murray Horwitz and Wynton Marsalis, prods., *Making the Music*, National Public Radio.

72 *Miles: The Autobiography*, 400.

73 Harrison, 226.

74 Steve Perry, "Ain't No Mountain High Enough: The Politics of Crossover," in Simon Frith, ed., *Facing the Music: A Pantheon Guide to Popular Music* (New York: Pantheon, 1988), 53.

75 To be sure, Davis bought into the dismemberment of music less by rejecting melody than by embracing rhythm as his racial birthright. See, for example, his comment that during the 1960s "white people were trying to suppress rhythm because of where it comes from—Africa" (*Miles: The Autobiography*, 277).

76 Joe A. Radcliffe, *The Business of Disco* (New York: Billboard Books, 1980), 185.

77 Flanagan, 32ff.

78 *Miles: The Autobiography*, 360–61.

79 Early, 270–71.

80 *Miles: The Autobiography*, 325, 272.

81 *Miles: The Autobiography*, 347.

82 *Miles: The Autobiography*, 380.

83 *Miles: The Autobiography*, 409.

84 "Retirement and Rebirth: The 70s and 80s" (fifth segment), in Steve Rowland and Quincy Troupe, prods., *The Miles Davis Radio Project*, National Public Radio.

85 According to Georgia Bergman, who produced Davis's first video for Warner Brothers,

Davis was won over by the suggestion that the video might serve as a showcase for his paintings.

86 James Brown and Bruce Tucker, *James Brown: The Godfather of Soul* (New York: MacMillan, 1986), 242–43.

87 Nelson George, *The Death of Rhythm & Blues* (New York: Pantheon, 1988), 154.

88 Stambler, 397.

89 I leave aside for the moment the practice of sampling, which in the hip-hop era has transformed the way rhythm tracks are programmed.

90 Quoted in Ted Fox, *In the Groove: The Stories Behind the Great Recordings, The People Behind the Music* (New York: St. Martin's, 1986), 334.

91 *Miles: The Autobiography*, 371.

92 To illustrate the point: compare the studio-assembled version of "Full Nelson" on *Tutu* and the live performance taped at Montreux in 1990 (on *Live Around the World* 1996).

93 *Miles: The Autobiography*, 384.

94 I am indebted to Bill Kirchner for bringing *Live Around the World* to my attention.

95 By a cruel irony of timing, go-go failed to make it big because of a film, *Good to Go*, which connected the music with D.C.'s burgeoning crack wars. That was in 1986, just three years before Ice-T, NWA, and countless other gangsta rappers would get rich exploiting the same connection.

96 Crouch, 30.

97 *Miles: The Autobiography*, 393.

98 On *Milestones* (1958).

99 Quincy Jones, interview in *Parade* (November 18, 1990), 26ff.

100 I am on record as a critic of gangsta rap, the commercially successful brand of hip-hop that since 1987 has made the image of the promiscuous bloodthirsty black a staple of youth entertainment worldwide. But this latter-day minstrelsy is by no means the whole picture.

101 Early, 296.

102 Chambers, introduction, xvii.

Arhus, Denmark, 1987.
Photograph by
Jan Persson.

Born in 1971, Philadelphia's Joey DeFrancesco has played the Hammond B-3 organ since the age of four. Growing up with an organ-playing father in the city where the organ sound in jazz began, DeFrancesco's own prodigal abilities ensured that music would be his future. That future came remarkably fast; by age ten he was performing in Philadelphia with former Davis sidemen Philly Joe Jones and Hank Mobley. He entered Philadelphia's Settlement Music School in 1981; at seventeen in 1988 he was playing keyboards for Miles Davis himself. Striking out soon after to lead his own band, he recorded a series of albums on Columbia that sparked a revival of organ jazz in the 1990s, bringing new attention to older masters and inspiring a younger generation to examine the instrument's possibilities in a variety of musical contexts.

DeFrancesco has managed to maintain his basic trio—with guitarist Paul Bollenback and drummer Byron Landham—for more than ten years, a remarkable exception to the pattern in jazz. All the while, DeFrancesco has remained true to the classic Hammond B-3 sound. "Philly for years was an organ mecca," says DeFrancesco. "All the great jazz organists have come from there, starting with Wild Bill Davis." He also names Jimmy Smith, Jimmy McGriff, Groove Holmes, and Shirley Scott as major influences, and he recently completed a collaboration with Smith called *Incredible*. "I feel that I'm carrying on the tradition of the instrument," DeFrancesco says, "and also stretching it, taking it some different directions." He's also well aware of Miles Davis's connection to his hometown. "Miles had the whole band, practically, from Philly, man. Red Garland, Philly Joe, John Coltrane, Jimmy Heath. And I played with Philly Joe and Hank Mobley. I was too young to really realize the greatness of that, and had no idea that later on I would be playing with Miles."

BC: At age seventeen you played with Miles Davis. How did that gig happen?

JDF: The way I met Miles was on a television show in Philadelphia called *Time Out*, and they were gonna have Miles on the show as a guest, like, to interview him. So they wanted to have music for this particular show that day. So they got the all-city of Philadelphia jazz trio, and I was in that trio, of course. And then they had four young trumpet players that they wanted to have play for Miles and have him critique them, and that was a disaster.

"Here's God Walking Around":
Joey DeFrancesco

interview by Benjamin Cawthra

BC: What happened?

JDF: Miles told the truth, you know? [in Miles's whisper] "The way you sound, you need to practice." So on one of the tunes I took a solo, and Miles heard me, and he said, "What's your organ player's name?" "The organ player?" Threw the host all off because he was talking about something else with Miles. And then Miles told me, "You can play, motherfucker," as he would say. I was like "Oh my God." I was sixteen at that time, and he took my phone number. A year later he called. And I didn't believe it was him; I thought maybe it was one of my friends or something. And he said, "What are you doing tomorrow or the next day? Come on up to New York." So I went up to New York and there he was, and he asked me to join the band. And I said, "Of course." I played with him for about four months, and then my first record came out with Columbia. The record company made me leave Miles to pursue my own career. But Miles understood. But we remained real close. I have mouthpieces of his and everything. I started playing trumpet from that whole thing.

BC: I didn't know if you had played trumpet before or what.

JDF: No, I started playing it right after I got off the road with Miles. And pretty much started playing it just like him. I mean, I heard it every night, and I knew that's just what I wanted to play. And he heard me about a year later. I told Miles I'd been playing some trumpet, and he handed me his trumpet. So I ripped off one of his licks or something, and he turned around and said, "What? You sound just like me." That's what he said. I don't tell too many people that, you know, but it's the truth. In fact, Denzel Washington was there that night too, because he was doing that movie 'Mo Better Blues, and he was asking Miles questions. We were both blowing Miles's horn and stuff. And after that, next time I saw him, he always would want me to play for him and would always tell people, "Listen to that." And he gave me a couple of mouthpieces of his. He was just a great guy, man.

BC: Miles was fierce, gentle, mischievous. . . . What kind of person was he?

JDF: One of the nicest, warmest people I ever met, you know. He treated me . . . I mean, I was so much younger than him. I think it was almost like a son thing, you know. But at the same time he taught me about all kinds of stuff. We talked about music. I think I was probably refreshing to him too, because I was a bebopper when I joined his band. I didn't play that style of music they were playing at all, and he didn't care. He heard what I played and liked it. And I'm taking solos, like block chords, and all that stuff, and I'm playing all my jazz, bebop stuff. And he dug it. All he ever talked about with me was the old stuff, and I knew how much. . . . You know, he used to put people on with, "That's old, that shit is boring" and all that. But he loved it. That's really what he loved. But Miles was the kind of guy that, the reason he wouldn't play something like that is because he loved it too much, and he felt if he played something he loved too much, he wasn't moving on and progressing, and Miles was very innovative and liked different directions. That was him. "Directions in Music by Miles Davis," you know?

BC: He's perhaps the greatest small bandleader in jazz history. Did you see him as a great bandleader?

JDF: Well, by the time I got there Miles . . . he said a few things here and there, he made some rehearsals with us, but mostly he wasn't real heavy duty, like telling the band what to do. Because most of that music was the stuff from the studio, and then we would learn it off the records. It was a different thing. But to me, everything he did is great. Every time he put the horn to his lips it was great. But the stuff that we all loved, from the fifties, the sixties, the seventies, I think that was more a time when he was really into directing the band, you know.

BC: By the time you were born, he had already released *Bitches Brew, Jack Johnson,* and *Live-Evil.* By the time you're ten, he's making his comeback.

JDF: That's right.

BC: So you grew up with the Miles Davis of the eighties. You didn't have that reference point with him; I mean, you had the records. But he never played "So What" in your lifetime.

JDF: Right, but like to be able to go see that, or something, it wasn't happening.

BC: Does that put you outside of that whole controversy about what Miles was doing in the eighties?

JDF: Well, when he first came out, like *We Want Miles,* man, he was playing his ass off. Those records, to me they sounded like sixties Miles, what he was doing. Then he had some stuff that had some straight-ahead rhythms on it. But the direction of the music? I'm not sure how to answer that. I mean, even though I grew up in the eighties, and he was playing and made his comeback with *The Man With the Horn,* those kind of records, I didn't particularly listen to that stuff or really care for it, because at that time I was so hardcore, straight-ahead jazz, as a young kid. To me, Miles Davis was the records *Cookin'* and *Relaxin'.* I wasn't even advanced enough to like the stuff he did with Tony Williams and Wayne Shorter. I was very swing-oriented. I can remember when, I think, I was thirteen, we went to go see Miles. And I really wasn't even aware of what he was doing. I thought I was going to go hear "Tune Up," you know, and he came out there and they played some wild shit, man. But I liked it, you know. I was just mesmerized, just watching him. So then I started checking out more of what he was doing, and eventually I became a fanatic. All the stuff. Now, right with me now, I've got the Plugged Nickel sessions. Which may not be his best performances—he was very ill when they did that stuff—but those ballads and stuff he plays on there just kill me. You know, I hear all these comments all the time about Miles. "Miles didn't have that great a technique," or, "Miles couldn't play this," or high notes. I don't know what these people are listening to, because I hear all of that. I mean he could play fast . . . to me he was the greatest trumpet player, and he had the greatest tone of anybody. The open sound, the best.

BC: When you played with him, he was in his sixties already. What did you notice about his performance and his technique then?

JDF: By the time when I was playing with him, he was only alive another year and a half after that. Well, no, about two years. And he was getting real frail, you know. He had that sugar diabetes, and that was taking its toll on him. So he didn't have the strength, I don't think, to really do everything he wanted to. But there were nights where he came in there and sounded like 1965, you know what I mean? And I was just on the edge of my seat, man. So it was there, just depending on how he felt, you know. I remember the last gig I did with him in Europe, of the first tour I did with him. He played so incredible that night. I got a tape of that, and he was killin'. And that night he got so sick, we had to cancel the rest of the tour. So it's a funny thing. First of all, the trumpet, man. The instrument itself decides how you're going to play. You don't decide.

BC: You also played on *Amandla*. What did you do on that record?
JDF: I did a little something. The record was done. I think Miles, just 'cause he liked me and wanted to make sure that I had something on the record for my own career, just something for a feather in my cap, said [in Miles's whisper], "I want Joey on there." So I went in there and played about six notes on something.

BC: You took a lot of solos live. Here's Miles Davis, and here's this seventeen-year-old. He's recognized your talent, but more than that, he gives you all of this room to show what you can do.
JDF: It meant so much to me, because at that time, with his bands, he wasn't featuring soloists to that point. Guys were taking solos, but it wasn't like the bebop or hard bop era, play as long as you want kind of stuff. You know, there was a certain set amount of time. And it also started trouble in the band, too. Because until that point, keyboard players didn't take solos in the band. Because he didn't like the way they soloed, or he had just heard enough keyboard solos through his life. Then he hires this little kid in here, and I'm soloing on almost every tune. And long solos. I just thought, "Wow, this is unbelievable, man. A man like this

likes what I'm doing so much. Miles Davis, man, here's God walking around."

BC: Did you feel like he was hearing more in you than you knew you had?
JDF: Yeah, definitely. I mean, I knew I sounded okay, and I knew I could play, but I think he probably heard more. I still tend to get excited and play a lot, you know. But at that time I probably wasn't as selective and as mature. I mean, Trane always played a lot of notes, but it was mature. That's the misconception about some artists, "there's too many notes." Play those notes, and if they've got feeling, it all fits.

BC: You're probably the youngest living musician who can say he played with Miles Davis.
JDF: Yeah. Yeah, I am.

BC: What did you learn?
JDF: Oh, all kinds of stuff. I learned to take chances, not try to be so careful. You know, go for it. If you're going for it, you're going to make some mistakes, but that's cool, because the instrument, man, it's your voice. It's an extension of what you're doing. And about harmony, and how to take one note, man, and make it sound like everything everybody else did was nothing. He was the master of that. And I learned how beautiful it was to play ballads and stuff and how great a ballad can be, because

when you're younger you don't want to play that stuff. I learned a lot of things.

BC: During your time with him, "Time After Time" seemed to be a ballad he kept coming back to. A lot of jazz critics didn't like that because it was a simple pop song.

JDF: I thought it was great, man. He loved ballads, I mean, that's obvious. Miles was just an excellent ballad player. So he just found a couple of tunes that were similar, with a pretty melody. That and "Human Nature." But man, live, that wasn't a ballad. That turned into. . . . He played everything faster live than he did on record. He had this philosophy: the more familiar a tune, the faster it should be played live.

BC: You certainly hear that on the sixties records.

JDF: Sure. On *"Four" and More* and all that stuff. I asked him one time, I said "Miles, why do you play everything so fast?" He said, "'Cause the white people won't feel it the same way if it's too slow." [laughs] Oh, he's funny. And then he'd laugh, you know. That's just how it is. I play everything faster, too. It's the adrenaline, it's the rush, you know.

BC: How do you think that keyboard role in the band changed over the years?

JDF: Well, it became more like an orchestral thing. He was trying to get a Gil Evans sound cheap, is how he would put it. A cheap Gil Evans sound. Because he loved Gil Evans and the way he arranged and made things. So basically, that's why he had two keyboardists. That was what the approach was to the keyboards. They both played different things, to get that full sound.

BC: Miles dabbled in the organ, especially in the 1970s. Did you ever give him a tip?

JDF: Yeah, don't play it! [laughs] Miles was funny. He knew that I was an organ player. Of course, when I was with him I'm playing keyboards and stuff. And so he used to mess with me all the time. [in Miles's whisper] "I play the organ," you know, all that kind of stuff. But, not really. He had some junk, some Yamaha cheesy-sounding. . . . Yeah, I never did dig that so much [laughs]. I did like it when he would play the trumpet and the keyboard at the same time. That was just a great sound. That was awesome.

BC: Thinking back over all those great pianists and the guys who played electric piano, it's almost like an all-star list of keyboard players who played for Miles. Which ones stand out for you? What did they contribute?

JDF: Well, Red Garland. He liked Red because Red reminded him of Ahmad Jamal, and he loved Ahmad Jamal. And Red had those block chords, and I think that made Miles hear things differently. He loved the way Red played block chords. And Wynton Kelley, who put a heavy swing element in the rhythm section. His phrasing was real dance-like. And then Herbie, man, what could you say? He took all that, you know, he took Red Garland, Wynton Kelley, Bill Evans, and dumped it all into a funnel. And then added tenfold more stuff, and he just played so great harmonically, and intricate stuff, and no matter how out and intricate it was it still swung, and had some grit in it. And then Keith Jarrett and Chick [Corea], man. And you could tell that those cats all influenced what he was doing, too, because the music would change with the keyboard players. Because Chick was out there. At that time when he was with Miles, he was really out there. If you listen to a lot of this bootleg stuff that's coming out, they were still playing a lot of the straight-ahead tunes, and basically when Miles would solo they'd keep it pretty in, and with Wayne, it would start getting outside. . . . By the time it got to Chick, man, it was full-on avant-garde. But great stuff. And then there was Adam Holzman, and Bobby Irving, and myself. And there was a couple others, Kei Akagi, and after me, the last guy [Deron Johnson].

BC: When you were seventeen and playing, did you have that sense of "Red Garland, Bill Evans . . ."
JDF: Definitely.

BC: . . . and here you are.
JDF: I definitely felt that. I mean, I felt that, being in that chair, you know. I didn't think that the music was the caliber that it was when those guys were playing with him at that time, but I just didn't understand it. It was, but it took me time to understand it. There was some great stuff that we were doing there, too. Just different.

BC: You signed with Columbia, started your own career, put your own trio together. And a couple of years later Miles died. Do you remember what you were doing?
JDF: I remember exactly where I was. I was Orlando, Disney World, playing. We were on tour with the Manhattan Transfer, two bands on a tour together. And I had talked to his sister two weeks before he died, just asking how he was doing, and she said, "He's not doing too good," you

know. And we did a sound check, and we got off the stage. And the keyboard player from the other band said, "Did you hear about Miles?" and I said, "What?" and he said, "He died." Man, it just tore me up. I just didn't think . . . I just knew he would pull out of it. He always did. But he just couldn't, I guess. It was very terrible news. But, I mean, the thing is, he'll live on forever, you know. And I'm glad that a couple of months before he died I spent some nice time with him. We hung out. I was grateful that I got to do that. I was there in Montraux when he did the Gil Evans stuff. I was upstairs playing, and he was downstairs playing, and I got to see him on the breaks. I was at the rehearsals. If you see that video, when he walks into rehearsal I'm right next to him. I went with him. He's still alive to me.

BC: Speaking of Montraux, here's a moment where we don't know it's the end of his life, but for once, he stops and says, "I'm going to go back and play this."
JDF: Then he dies, right?

BC: What do you think it meant for him to do that?
JDF: Well, I know that he was terrified. I remember going to the hotel with him. Meeting him at his hotel, because we were in town on tour in Switzerland too, and I called. I knew where he was. "Come on over." So I came

over, and I said, "Hey Miles, what's happening." And he was a wreck, man. He had music all over the place. He said, "I gotta go play this, I haven't played this music in thirty something years, man, but I gotta do it." And he did it, and I think he did a great job, man. He must have known that it wasn't going to be long. I think he wanted to do it one more time. It had to be. It couldn't be that much of a coincidence. And he was sick, too. At that time he just didn't look right to me.

BC: And then six weeks later he's gone. What was the feeling among other musicians when that news came down?

JDF: Oh, everybody was very. . . . Anybody I was around, it was a very upsetting thing, you know. It was just so hard to believe. It still is for me.

BC: Ten years later?

JDF: Yeah, he would have been seventy-five. Yeah, I just can't believe it. I can't believe that ten years have gone by already, too.

BC: What do you think Miles Davis meant or continues to mean to musicians?

JDF: Probably everything. I mean, he changed the music three or four times, and he was just one of the great pioneers of how to play this music. You learn so much from one of his records, one of his solos. You hear him play a ballad. He represented the greatest things in music, in all aspects.

Newport Jazz Festival, 1990.
Photograph by
Herb Snitzer.

There's something in his [Miles's] sound that is so strong, so masculine. But at the same time there's another thing so intimate it seems almost feminine. He covers everything. His music speaks to all of us on a very real level. His artistry is something we should all value. I know I do.

—Cassandra Wilson

I also remember how the music used to sound down there in Arkansas, when I was visiting my grandfather, especially at the Saturday night church. Man that shit was a motherfucker. I guess I was about six or seven. We'd be walking on these dark country roads at night and all of a sudden this music would seem to come out of nowhere, out of them spooky-looking trees that everybody said ghosts lived in. . . . I remember a man and a woman singing and talking about getting down. Shit, that music was something, especially that woman singing.

—Miles Davis[1]

Ladies Sing Miles

by Farah Jasmine Griffin

While walking along a country road, a boy named Miles was moved by a black woman's singing. Her voice, an indelible part of the southern night, floating like ghosts through the trees, would haunt his own playing throughout his life. Like Jean Toomer before him, Miles Davis recalled the impact of that voice on his own artistic sensibility. While Toomer tried to render it in his writing, Davis carried her melody in his horn. Davis's biographer Quincy Troupe writes that Davis heard that "voice of an old black churchwoman singing plaintively" and, knowing it was special, filed it away and returned to it in his own "lonely trumpet sound."[2] Perhaps this is what women, particularly black American women, especially creative black American women, hear in Davis's horn. Perhaps we hear something akin to our own voices.

For some Miles Davis's music seems to provide a safe aural space where we can be emotionally vulnerable. His horn is seductive not because it is harshly masculine but because it is not. In the sounds that emanate from Miles there is space for a woman's tears, vulnerability, anger, love, sexuality, creativity: a space simply to be. Perhaps this is why many felt so betrayed by his admission of emotional, verbal, and physical violence against women. His music seemed to provide such a safe space, a space that allowed for personal, creative and spiritual growth, that we experienced these admissions as brutal slaps to our collective brown faces.

How do we come to terms with the violation? Writers and critics Pearl Cleage and Hazel Carby have devoted their efforts to eloquent and sophisticated critiques of him. Cleage sounds the much-needed alarm, calling our attention to the horror hidden beneath that beautiful sound. Carby theorizes the disjuncture between his behavior toward women and the possibilities for more progressive gender relations found in his music. Musician vocalists Shirley Horn and Cassandra Wilson have devoted entire albums in seeming defense of him. Horn and Wilson call us to remember the beauty with which he left us, to recall why we fell in love with him in the first place. Horn gives us a Miles she knew: a man who was different from the abuser of women who emerges from his autobiography or the pens of Cleage and Carby. Wilson manages both to celebrate and criticize him. In so doing she transports Miles to a place where she can express her own creative ambition through, over, and at times, against him.

Even Pearl Cleage and Hazel Carby acknowledge the power of Davis's music, especially the classic album *Kind of Blue*. This album has served as an introduction to jazz or to Miles for many listeners; a starting point. It serves this purpose for Cleage and Carby, introducing the first to the trumpet as a jazz instrument and providing the latter entrée into the male dominated field of jazz criticism. In both instances the album offers path into a new personal or intellectual direction.

In her now classic essay "Mad at Miles" Pearl Cleage writes that Miles Davis served as an escort to a deeper dimension of womanhood. "I spent the night curled up . . . listening to Miles Davis play me into the next phase of my life . . . The Bohemian Woman Phase . . . now I'm thirty phase . . . The need of a current vision of who and what and why I am phase. The cool me out quick cause I'm hanging by a thread phase." This is a testimony to the spiritual power Cleage grants Davis's music. Here is an intimacy beyond that of the seduction ritual she describes later on and for which Miles provides the soundtrack. This relationship between listener and musician allows her to become the woman she wants to be, the woman who by playing Miles will "give the gentleman caller an immediate understanding" that she was "a woman with the possibility of an interesting past, and the probability of an interesting future."

What is it about Davis's music that grants him such entry into a woman's life? I think his music promises a feather bed upon which to fall while taking the risks required of a multidimensional womanhood. That sometimes lonely, always lyrical horn seems to promise "Go on, I will bear you aloft, allow you to fly, and I will provide a soundscape for your landing." Who wouldn't fall in love with such a man? We forget that the music, not the man, made this promise. Is it possible to separate the two? Cleage poses this question when she asks, "Can we continue to celebrate the genius in the face of the monster?" Later she asks, "How can they hit us and still be our heroes? How can they hit us and still be our leaders? Our husbands? Our geniuses? Our friends?" Then she answers her own question: "They can't. Can they?"[3]

I want to suggest that these men should not be our heroes and they ought not to be our leaders. We need to reserve those roles for those who provide protection for our needs, interests, and physical selves. But unfortunately, they are often our friends, brothers, fathers and yes, they are our geniuses. Because genius is quirky like that—it can appear in the oddest places.

If we lend Charles Mingus's autobiography the credence we lend Davis's, then certainly he was as misogynist and abusive. Davis's bandmate Coltrane seems to have been far more progressive in his relations with women than either Miles or Mingus. He suffered harsh criticism for putting his gifted second wife, Alice, in his band, not as vocalist but as pianist, replacing the revered McCoy Tyner. He believed her capable of providing the sound he needed for the music he wanted to create. Coltrane scholar Salim Washington notes, "Classic recordings of this band [including Alice Coltrane], such as *Live in Japan*, or *Live at the Village Vanguard* are evidence that . . . Alice found a way to support his direction with a piano style that was devoid of bebop clichés or conventions."[4]

Nonetheless, Mingus doesn't receive our scorn in the way that Miles does and while we love him, sisters don't seem to be invested in Coltrane in the same kind of way (though perhaps we should be). Again, I think it is because of the promise of safety and understanding offered by Davis's horn—the safety of the black woman's voice within a black man who, for all we knew, appeared to like black women.

His symbolic gestures serve as an example of this sensibility. While he was personally involved with women across the color line, during much of his career Davis refused to allow record labels to put white women on his album covers. Instead he often insisted that his ladies of the moment, his black ladies, serve as cover models. His wife Frances appears on more than one cover, as do his two later wives, Cicely Tyson and Bettye Mabry. On one hand, someone could interpret this as one-dimensional objectification of women; on the other hand, in the context of white supremacist standards of beauty and what some black women view as a fetish for white women on the part of some black jazz musicians, it is in no way insignificant that Davis insisted black women grace his album covers.

Suppose we think of Davis as some think of Thomas Jefferson. Architect and theorist of democracy, Jefferson was a slaveholder, and if we believe *Notes on the State of Virginia*, also a white supremacist. We must be harshly critical of his white supremacy and challenge those who offer excuses for it. Yet, we also must recognize the value of his contributions that allow us as a people and as a nation to move beyond his own limitations. From the beginning, struggles for black American freedom have been built upon the tenets of freedom and equality for all espoused in Jefferson's Declaration of Independence. Much of that struggle has focused on pointing out the failure of the nation to live up to its promise of democracy, insisting upon the hypocrisy of a government that claims to be founded upon such principles and yet denies them to a significant portion of its population. The contradictions of the nation are the flaws at the core of its being; bringing attention to these flaws and working to address them makes for a better nation in the long run.

I think a similar reading of Miles does the same thing for his music and for jazz as well. This reading comes to terms with the human capacity for contradiction, an understanding that recognizes Davis as both Prince of Darkness and Bearer of Light.

Hazel Carby's controversial rendering of Miles Davis in her book on black masculinity, *Race Men*, attempts to do just this. Carby is critical of the sexist man, makes the connection between the sexism in the life and its embodiment in a misogynistic, socially homogenous musical arena, and argues nonetheless that the music offers new possibilities for gender relations.

Carby writes, "I think it's very important to challenge the apparent distance between Davis's violence against women and the genius of his music as if they were enacted on different planes of existence." According to Carby, Davis's disdain for women resulted in his need to create a distance between them and a homogenous realm of male creativity where his music was born. The absence of women from this space grows from a contempt for them— a sense that their presence is antithetical to the atmosphere where the music can happen. She argues this is a false division because in many instances the world of women's labor enable the conditions that create this male creative realm. Significantly, Carby finds that a male-only environment offers alternative, nonhierarchical versions of masculinity even as it banishes women. She turns to

Kind of Blue to reveal a level of "intimacy and interdependence" between musicians that create "an unconventional, gendered vulnerability."

For Carby, Miles's legendary distance from the audience allowed him to protect his world from the "world of women perceived as the threatening realm of bitches."[5] I have learned a great deal from Carby's eloquent and sophisticated analysis of Davis's music. However, I differ with her on this point. It was not necessarily the world of women that Davis feared in guarding his creative space. The audience comprises men and women. Perhaps a division emerges between those part of the music-making and those not. What happens when women are part of the creative

space as creative contributors to it? Before moving on let me say that I am not defending Davis or providing an excuse for his aborrhant abuse of woman. However, I am curious about the women in his musical space—his interaction with them and the possibilities offered by his music for female artists.

Miles Davis, as discussed, often physically and emotionally abused the women in his life. According to some reports, so was Billie Holiday, who although beaten by men, reportedly beat women as well. She certainly referred to them as bitches on occasion. Incidentally, Holiday is one woman whom Davis respected a great deal professionally. He even cites her influence on his own playing. Furthermore, as a young musician he worked with her. In his autobiography he notes, "I loved playing with Coleman Hawkins and behind Billie when I got a chance. They were both great musicians, really creative and shit." Later he notes, "Whenever I'd go to see her, I always asked Billie to sing 'I Loves You, Porgy,' because when she sang 'don't let him touch me with his hot hands,' you could almost feel that shit she was feeling. It was beautiful and sad the way she sang that. Everybody loved Billie."[6]

He later recorded his own version of the song. If Davis looked up to Holiday, he served as a mentor to another female vocalist, Shirley Horn.

The phrase, "Honey from a horn so sweet," sung at the end of her version of "Blue in Green," characterizes Shirley Horn's depiction of her friend and mentor. Horn, already an accomplished pianist, came to Davis's attention following her first recording, *Ashes and Embers*. After hearing the album, he invited her to come to New York so that he could hear her play in person. Shortly thereafter Davis insisted that the young pianist and vocalist open for him at the Village Vanguard. As a result, Horn got greater exposure and went on to sign a Mercury Records recording contract with Quincy Jones.

Even before meeting Miles Davis, Shirley had been identified as a gifted artist. She started playing the piano at four; she began studying composition at twelve and always has led her own trio. According to Horn, her relationship with Davis was familial: "He was like an uncle to me." While at the Vanguard she often sat in with Davis though she didn't record with him until 1991 on her album *You Won't Forget Me*; he is guest soloist on the title tune. In 1998 she recorded her tribute to him, *I Remember Miles*. In addition to her performance, Horn also arranged all the songs and co-produced the album.

I Remember Miles is a memorial, testimony, and a celebration. A reproduction of a Miles Davis sketch graces the cover of the album. A gift from Davis to Horn, the sketch depicts a man and a woman wrapped in an embrace; they appear to be kissing, though it is unclear whether they kiss as lovers or as friends. It is signed with x's (kisses) and "Miles." The ambivalence of the cover sketch characterizes the entire album—both the images and the music. A sepia photo on the inside cover shows a young Horn dressed elegantly in an off-the-shoulder cocktail dress, holding a martini and looking off into the room. Davis sits next to her, looking in her direction, pensively listening. He may be looking at her chest; he may be looking beyond her. Again the viewer is not certain. Clearly, the two people are very close, yet the nature of their relationship remains unknown. In the accompanying booklet appears a photo of an older Davis and Horn taken in 1990 at the recording session for *You Won't Forget Me*. The photo reveals a couple that shares a deep affection. They look at each other, he listening attentively and lovingly like an older brother or a man still in love.

With the exception of one tune, all of the songs on *I Remember Miles* are associated with early Miles (1956–1963). Most of them are ballads; Horn recalls, "He liked for me to sing ballads." He renders each song with such care, tenderness, and beauty that it rises above the trite sentimentality often associated with love songs. Horn's musicianship— her singing, piano-playing, and arranging—create an intimate space where the work remembered happens with dignity and grace.

Horn's spare, haunting way with lyrics, the space where a note lingers, and the way she drives a dramatic tension between voice and piano all help us hear Miles Davis's horn as a female voice. On the one hand, his influence on her seems clear; on the other hand, perhaps he heard his voice in the way she handled a lyric and in her phrasing. After all, Davis recorded three of the songs here, "Baby Won't You Please Come Home," "I Fall in Love Too Easily," and "Basin Street Blues" on *Seven Steps to Heaven* after hearing Horn do them at the Vanguard.

On *I Remember Miles* the brilliant Roy Hargrove often accompanies Horn. Their encounter on "I Got Plenty of Nothing" recalls that between Sarah Vaughn and Clifford Brown on "September Song." Behind her, Miles is playful, flirtatious, now urging, now echoing. In his solos he takes off on exuberant flights. Horn is the grounded one, her voice swinging him back to earth. "My Man's Gone Now" is an extended drama, not unlike Davis's recording of it on his *Porgy and Bess* album. But it is on the final song, an instrumental version of "Blue and Green," that one hears the impact of her loss. Her piano, so much like the spare, space-filled playing that Davis liked in his own pianists, seems to leave open space for him to enter. Yet, no friend responds to her call; no one fills the void. Instead comes Horn's voice, "Honey from a horn so sweet." While she is talking about the lost voice of Miles, the listener hears that honey in this Horn:

> traveling miles
> crossing time
> shifting style
> traveling miles . . . and miles
>
> you can hear him humming
> on a country road
> as the shadows grow to night
> swinging through seventh avenue
> underneath the city lights

In 1997, Cassandra Wilson became one of the few women to receive a commission by Jazz at Lincoln Center. She used the opportunity to explore the work of Miles Davis. Wynton Marsalis, Director of Jazz at Lincoln Center, had been one of the most vocal critics of Davis's experimentation with hip-hop, rock, fusion, and smooth jazz; Wilson chose to present Davis's music in the house that Wynton built. Although Miles was renowned for his sexism, Wilson featured female musicians such as Regina Carter and Quartette Indigo as well as her regular male band.

Her album *Traveling Miles* grew out of that commission and allowed her to combine a devotion to the jazz tradition with the desire to open out into different musical arenas.

The inside cover of the album portrays Wilson sitting, apparently in a recording studio. Surrounded by music stands, she sits casually, dressed in a sweater, khakis, and loafers. The portrait echoes a photograph of Davis during the recording of *Kind of Blue*. She even wears an ascot as he did in the earlier photographs. Advertisements for the album show Wilson, dressed in a white petticoat and brown leather jacket, walking along the railroad like legendary blues men. Within the lyrics and the music Wilson conjures Miles the ancestor, who is not unlike those legendary blues men. He travels from country roads to Seventh Avenue, from Manhattan to the mythical land of the Yoruba Deities—Ile Ife, from this world to the world beyond. His horn, like the voice of the old black woman, floats from the landscape and through the heavens. Though the music, lyrics, and stories they tell evoke Davis, Wilson is the teller of this tale, the conjurer of this set. Davis paved the road she travels to this space—a space she creates by producing, writing lyrics, composing music, and singing. She is in full control of the narrative.

The very first song on the album is Miles's "Run the VooDoo Down," for which she provides lyrics: the musician, conjurer of these lyrics, is a female, "she'll run the voodoo down." It closes with a reprise of the song, and this time she is accompanied by West African vocalist Angelique Kidjo. The duet between the two women dominates: sung in English and in Yoruba, the song returns the sound to the source: the black woman's voice. The duet is among the most complicated music on the album. Wilson recalled, "It was tough, singing that section, but I love that weird intervalic stuff." The song, like the spiritual tradition it invokes, makes connections between Africa and the Americas. Kidjo calls in Yoruba; Wilson responds in Yoruba. Eventually the women's voices overlap and it becomes impossible to distinguish the call from the response. Finally, Wilson answers in the first person blues narrative that opens the album.

On at least three other songs, "Seven Steps," "Someday My Prince Will Come," and "Never Broken (ESP)," Wilson features another female artist, the violinist Regina Carter. On "Seven Steps to Heaven", where we have come to expect a dialogue of horns, two "feminine" instruments, the woman's voice and the violin, are featured. At first, Lonnie Plaxico's bass lays the ground, and Stefon Harris's vibraphone and Eric Lewis's piano create a sphere where a humming Wilson and Carter begin to talk to each other. Wilson pulls from her lowest register, her voice becoming androgynous and only reaching into its upper limits to plead, "Help me climb that road." Regina Carter does just that with a quick-paced, ebullient climb.

Wilson feels a particular affinity for Davis: "Miles was the man who introduced me to the depth and breadth of jazz: he allowed me to understand how far it could be stretched. Like Jimi Hendrix, he could open windows, break the rules and get away with it."[7] This is the path that Davis forged for Wilson. She uses the Miles album as an opportunity to combine the interests and emphases that she has found compelling her throughout her career. In addition to writing the lyrics to five Davis classics, she also composes four of her own and she produced the album as well. For fans of easy listening, she offers one of Miles's more controversial choices, Cindy Lauper's "Time After Time." On *Traveling Miles*, Wilson is composer, lyricist, producer, and leader. While Horn focused on an earlier Miles, Wilson is most interested in the post–*Bitches Brew* works. These fit within her own emerging musical philosophy, which entailed refusal to be contained by categories and tradition.

Miles Davis's legacy is not one that binds but one that allows Shirley Horn and Cassandra Wilson to explore their own individuality. In June of 1999 the two women played on a double bill at Carnegie Hall. Both performed from their Miles tributes. The presentations and styles could not have been more different. Horn, with Charles Ables on bass and Steve Williams on drums, sang to an almost silent house, the audience hanging on her every word, sitting on edge, anticipating each note. Wilson had them dancing in their seats with her funk-inflected set. Drummer Marcus Baylor, percussionist Jeffrey Haynes, and bassist Lonnie Plaxico were joined by Carter and Harris, creating a mix of genres where the spirit of Miles playfully hovered above. One gets the sense that he would have felt at home in either set. Miles Davis's music gives Cassandra Wilson and Shirley Horn space to explore their own creative visions. Their voices render the exquisite feminine quality at the core of his own distinct sound.

1   Miles Davis with Quincy Troupe, *Miles: The Autobiography* (New York: Simon and Schuster, 1989), 29.

2   Quincy Troupe, *Miles and Me* (Berkeley: University of California Press, 2000), 3.

3   Pearl Cleage, "Mad at Miles," in *Deals with the Devil and Other Reasons to Riot* (New York: Ballantine, 1993), 40–41.

4   Salim Washington, conversation with author, July 8, 2000.

5   Hazel Carby, *Race Men* (Cambridge, Mass.: Harvard University Press), 144, 155–56.

6   *Miles: The Autobiography*, 55.

7   Cassandra Wilson in Bob Spitz, "The Hottest Voice in Music," *Sky Magazine* (September 1998); 50.

Kind of Blue sessions,
New York, 1959.
Photograph by
Don Hunstein.

Miles Davis was from St. Louis. The "from" is important: as in the cases of T. S. Eliot, Tennessee Williams, Charles Eames and other prominent twentieth-century artists, St. Louis did not become the base from which he produced his mature art. Easy as it is to view Miles Davis as just another expatriate from the artistically benighted hinterland, his relationship to his home region provides important clues for understanding his directions in music. His musical background in East St. Louis and St. Louis, including training in a variety of musical styles and participation in a music scene with high standards, provided crucial contexts for his development as an artist.

In addition, his relationship to St. Louis reveals as-yet-unresolved issues of identity and community contained in American culture in general and St. Louis in particular. St. Louis at large suffers from a kind of cultural amnesia; Miles Davis never has been a major cultural icon beyond East St. Louis itself. Many St. Louisans, even those who may have heard of Davis, are unaware of his origins in this region. For the St. Louis region to embrace Miles Davis as one of its own, it must confront the racism so deeply ingrained in its history and acknowledge a legacy full of division and compromised hopes. It also must acknowledge and seek to understand East St. Louis, the region's "pariah of poverty."[1] Finally, it has to contend with Davis's own controversial persona and attitudes toward home.

The most egregious example of St. Louis's cultural amnesia with regard to Davis occurred when he died in 1991. Indeed, his passing in California made the front pages in much of the world on Sunday, September 29. The *New York Times*, for example, ran a full story with a photo on the front page. The *St. Louis Post-Dispatch*, the region's only major daily, put an Associated Press–penned obituary on page 11 of section D, along with the other notices.[2] The *Post* did run a lengthy appreciation of Miles the next day, but Harper Barnes's lively piece followed the sub-headline: "Jazz Genius Leaves Legacy of 'Brass.'" In this way, Miles's taciturn reputation remained an important part of the story for St. Louisans. New York and East St. Louis held memorial services; St. Louis itself remained silent.[3]

A week later, Larry Fiquette, in a reader's-advocate column, acknowledged that the *Post* had erred, and that a couple of dozen readers had complained. The editor of the Sunday edition had decided that Miles Davis was not "that big a

Remembering Miles in St. Louis:

A Conclusion

by Benjamin Cawthra

person in his field." The editor had considered a Page One promotion of the obituary, but Cardinal relief pitcher Lee Smith had tied the National League save record Saturday, and that story received the promotion. Davis partisans might have pointed out that by the time baseball had created the save statistic in the 1960s, Miles Davis had changed improvised music three times and was bidding for a fourth.[4]

It is easy to make too much of one assistant editor's misjudgment, but it is hard to avoid finding symbolism in the coverage. The treatment of his death seemed to reinforce the city's fundamental realities: economic stratification and racial segregation. The seams in the urban landscape are obvious: private places dating from the late nineteenth century that retain their gates and faux guardhouses, bastions against encroaching poverty, crime, color, or whatever else is undesirable; long stretches of cleared real estate in the middle of the city, punctuated here and there by crumbling brick residences like some mockery of the picturesque ruins praised by romantic poets. And

East St. Louis is to be avoided by whites at all costs.

This is the context for remembering Miles Davis. Doing so provides a means of uncovering part of the region's cultural history. The education he received back in the 1930s and 1940s, detailed by Eugene Redmond elsewhere in this volume, served him very well, as did the after-hours gigs and sit-ins on both sides of the river. Rock writer Stephen Davis, asking in 1973 whether Miles listened to rhythm and blues, elicited as pure a statement as Miles ever made about the influence of St. Louis on his work, electric or otherwise:

I'm from *St. Louis*, man. The only reason my records sound the way they do is because I studied music. It's my background. We always played the blues in St. Louis. Bands came up on the boats from New Orleans, guys came from Kansas City and Oklahoma City, all playing the blues. I mean, there's some funky shit in St. Louis even today. . . . They can't all go to New York or San Francisco because there ain't enough there for all of them.[5]

Davis always acknowledged his St. Louis teachers Elwood Buchanan and Joseph Gustat. It also should be noted that Miles Davis was not necessarily the most obvious trumpet talent in Buchanan's extraordinary Lincoln High music program. If he actually played better than his good friends Red Bonner

and Frank Gulley, it wasn't by that much. For social, economic, and family reasons, those men remained based in the region after graduating. Dr. Miles Dewey Davis II had deeper pockets and passed on a sense of ambition to his son. As biographer Quincy Troupe notes, "Miles Davis always had backup."[6]

What was the foundation for that "backup"? The fate of Miles Davis, III, had been influenced inexorably by historical forces. The Great Migration of African Americans to East St. Louis and other northern cities had created a large segregated black population in need of a professional class: teachers, ministers, doctors, nurses, and, yes, dentists. Dr. Davis relocated his practice from Alton to East St. Louis in 1927 to serve this new population, and it meant that young Miles would be able to grasp the opportunity Dr. Davis's patients hoped to enable for their own children. Of course, it is one thing to have ambition and opportunity, and something else again to become Miles Davis, revolutionary.

Miles also credited older players such as Clark Terry and the trumpeter and bandleader Eddie Randle as important factors in his development as a person and as an artist. The twenty-something Terry's hip clothes and burnished tone provided a model for the teenaged Miles (and for Gulley and other young friends). The rest of his life Davis would be known for his fashion sense and his pure tone on trumpet. Randle's recognition of Davis's musical grasp led him to shift responsibility for getting music together and rehearsing the band to the young Miles. "I became the musical director of the band," Miles writes in his autobiography, "because most of the other guys in the band were working regular gigs in the daytime, so they didn't have time to get the music together. I was in charge of setting up rehearsals and rehearsing the band. They had other acts at the Rhumboogie, like dancers and comedians, singers. . . . So sometimes the band accompanied another act and I had to get the band ready."[7] As critic Bob Blumenthal asserts, perhaps Davis's greatest achievement was as the best small group leader in jazz history.[8] His ability to recognize and nurture talent made him the virtual trunk on the family

tree of postwar jazz. That early responsibility with the Randle band surely increased his confidence in these areas. He played the same role in the Charlie Parker Quintet because of Bird's indispositions, and he reached an early peak as musical organizer with the Miles Davis Nonet in the late 1940s before he had reached the age of twenty-five.

There is something more than mere musical experience in East St. Louis that informed Davis's development. The river city's landscape provides a sense of expansiveness. A great black railroad bridge and trestle crosses the Mississippi and bisects East St. Louis from thirty feet in the air above the flood plain. Trains and their tracks used to dominate the city; twenty rail lines once converged here. Eugene Redmond, poet laureate of East St. Louis, once showed me a railroad grade near the Rush City neighborhood where fourteen tracks used to run parallel. The trick as children, Redmond said, was to try to cross the tracks in a more or less straight line while the trains were moving, jumping on one train headed south, then another moving north, and finally end up on the other side of the grade. A few of the less nimble didn't make it.

Many of the tracks led to the National Stockyards, today a mostly abandoned edifice whose decaying bulk looms just outside the city limits, between downtown and the river. Irene Cawthon, Miles's first girlfriend and mother of his first child, lived in the Goose Hill neighborhood near the stockyards. In

Miles, Davis remembers the "real bad smell in the air, of burnt meat and hair . . . the smell of death."[9] Miles's prominent family ensured that Davis would never work on the killing floors, but he did understand where his early audiences spent their days.

Writer John Gennari mentioned to me that East St. Louis impressed him with "the overwhelming power of the horizontal."[10] Certainly there is a sense of space within East St. Louis and in the larger city across the river. Gennari opined that Miles's musical approach encompassed that physical sense of open space. The great tension-building rests, the long horizontal melody lines, and the drummers who kept insistent time all gave a sense of this. I cannot look at the great railroad bridge of East St. Louis without hearing Tony Williams's steady pulse on *In a Silent Way*. It seems the very embodiment of movement across that landscape. In fact, "Shhh/Peaceful" originally was titled, "Mornin' Fast Train from Memphis to Harlem."[11] The train tracks that led to St. Louis represented lines of hope for thousands during the Great Migration. Whether attempting to escape from the pinions of poverty, to dodge the blows of violent racism, or to pursue happiness in the form of better opportunities for their children, the people who rode those tracks into the river cities found plenty of disappointment when they disembarked. The 1917 East St. Louis riot set the tone, but even in the midst of that lingering memory, and of day-to-day incidents that kept Miles Davis's antenna tuned to racism for the rest of his life, African Americans partially remade the drab brick river cities. St. Louis was, in Davis's word, "country," not only in physical space, but in attitudes and in the best of African American culture.[12]

And perhaps the crossroads nature of St. Louis bore fruit in surprising ways later in Miles's career. As Gary Giddins notes in *Visions of Jazz*, "West Coast jazz (cool) and East Coast jazz (hard bop), had the same Midwestern parent: one Miles Dewey Davis. . . ."[13] The blues always had been an important element in his music, especially with the Coltrane-Garland-Chambers-Jones band of the 1950s, and his film soundtrack for Louis Malle's *Ascenseur pour l'échafaud* contains stark and beautiful blues playing, particularly on "Gérénique." Certainly sixties rhythm and blues had a major impact on the electric period. And as late as the 1980s he returned to more or less overt examinations of the blues, finally collaborating with John Lee Hooker on a spare blues project for the Dennis Hopper film *The Hot Spot*. As guitarist Carlos Santana has said, Miles brings to

the blues "that elegance thing that Duke Ellington has. It's gutbucket, but it has Tiffany's, man. It ain't cheap like Woolworth's; it's got that real one-of-a-kind phrasing."[14] St. Louis's place in the development of jazz history may be ambiguous, but that lack of clear definition, of a sound as definable as that of New Orleans or Chicago, is perhaps embodied in an artist whose greatest legacy is near-constant stylistic change.[15]

As we have seen, even in death Miles Davis continued to generate controversy. And even in death, his relationship to home remained problematic. Was this because Miles had lived across the river in East St. Louis? East St. Louis in 1991 had changed dramatically from the small, multiethnic city where Davis had been raised, and its status as an unmentionable member of the regional family is another barrier St. Louis has erected that prevents it from embracing Miles Davis. By 1990 East St. Louis perhaps had reached the low point of a decades-long economic crisis. The fate of his hometown saddened Davis, and he admitted that even though he still felt close to his East St. Louis "homeboys," he almost never saw them.

East St. Louis remains invisible to its own region and the nation at large unless the news is tragically parodic or spectacularly bad. The city's status as the home of twenty-two Superfund sites makes it a kind of environmental grotesque. To begin his 1990 book *Savage Inequalities*, Jonathan Kozol chose the impoverished East St. Louis

school system to contrast with plush New Trier High School in suburban Chicago. Kozol's equal funding argument for public schools seems almost quaint in the wake of today's proposals for educational reform, but the chapter reiterated the image of East St. Louis as a toxic, crime-ridden, and mismanaged city in crisis.[16] Despite the problems, that school system had produced high achievers, especially in the arts and athletics, and one of its most famous pupils was none other than Miles Davis. His alma mater's high school jazz band in 1990 was one of the very best in the nation. As East St. Louis began to take steps toward a more stable economy, President Bill Clinton made East St. Louis a stop on his 1999 "Poverty Tour."

Pleased to be noticed, the city nevertheless hoped that one day it could remove itself from the itinerary.

East St. Louis today slowly is recovering from decades of crisis, partially due to the presence of legalized gambling and mostly because of a strength of resolve in so many of its tenacious residents. Abandoned by the middle class, both white and black, and by industry and business, the city's population plummeted nearly 50 percent between 1960 and 1990. According to urban planner Kenneth Reardon, citizen-driven neighborhood stabilization initiatives have contributed to a safer and cleaner environment over the past few years and also have spurred a degree of economic development.[17] While East St. Louis may never become a place where middle-class whites feel comfortable, the fact is that it doesn't need bourgeois approval to feel, understand, and test its own cultural strength. And, in any case, the white middle class and its tax dollars left decades ago and is careful to remain in its automobiles, literally speeding above the city on the tangled federal freeway system.

Still, the sense of loss in East St. Louis is palpable. The Spivey Building, a Louis Sullivan–inspired design and the city's tallest structure, is slated for demolition. The city's remaining architecture finds its way into salvage lots across the river. East St. Louis always has contained open spaces (even today agricultural areas exist within city limits) but in 1990, for example, only 422 of the Emerson Park neighborhood's 1,407 residential lots contained buildings, and the few structures built since then rarely aspire to the classically aesthetic.[18] This image of East St. Louis, one of poverty, crime, and despair, impairs St. Louis's ability to embrace Miles Davis. To do so, it would have to shine a spotlight on the world below the freeways and attempt to understand that place's history and culture. For East St. Louisans, Miles Davis remains a very important cultural and historical symbol of excellence. In that place, he represents not only the best of jazz, African American culture, and St. Louis, but the very best of East St. Louis, a shining star among many others who came from that city and accomplished worthwhile things. The river provides a

barrier of one kind and the state line it represents another, but East St. Louis is situated in the heart of an eleven-county metropolitan area. And if the story sounds familiar, there indeed are similar urban examples throughout the country. Miles Davis and American culture, indeed.

The act of cultural remembrance is, almost by definition and certainly in terms of historical practice, a middle-class gesture.[19] And Miles Davis, though he was born into a black, middle-class family, seemingly did everything he could to puzzle, infuriate, shock, and flout middle-class sensibilities. Why he did this is perhaps best left to others, but it surely had impacted how he is viewed at home. The autobiography's themes and language certainly are eye-openers in the conservative Midwest. Even before its publication, however, Davis had a reputation as a disdainful and angry black man, a performer who did not chat with his audience or smile and who seemed most unguarded when discussing race in interviews.

Perhaps St. Louis has felt insulted. Miles was to have visited St. Louis on a book tour to promote *Miles: The Autobiography* in 1990, but a dispute with his publisher, Simon and Schuster, meant that coauthor Quincy Troupe made the appearance alone. Some St. Louisans interpreted the move as typical of an ungrateful prodigal, and the tone Davis took toward his hometown in the book itself could not have helped.

Davis typically is unsparing in evaluating his home region. In *Miles*, one finds the following: "East St. Louis and St. Louis were country towns full of country people," writes Davis. "Both towns are real square, especially the white people from around there—*really* country, and racist to the bone."[20] Among the many citations in *Miles* is Billy Eckstine's engagement at the Club Plantation in 1944. The band, featuring Dizzy Gillespie, Charlie Parker, and many other future greats, failed to complete its engagement there because it was dismissed from the gig for flouting the club's policy of segregation. As Clark Terry recalls in this volume, only whites were allowed in the audience. Jordan Chambers's Club Riviera on Delmar, a black-owned club that catered to black audiences, booked the Eckstine band instead. At the Club Riviera, Miles Davis filled in as a trumpet replacement, and afterward, he knew that he would leave for New York to play with Bird and Diz. St. Louis's racism changed music history.[21]

African Americans, notes Davis, were also "country," but "kind of hip in their countryness. It was a hip place." Both blunt and enigmatic, the statement is typically Milesian. The roots of "countryness" among African Americans in St. Louis during Miles's childhood are easily accounted for: the already discussed Great Migration brought thousands to the region from the rural South during the First World War and after.

Davis claims that musical culture, and specifically African American musical culture, determined the "hipness in the black people then." He describes this milieu:

After St. Louis closed down at night, everybody over there came to Brooklyn [Illinois] to listen to the music and party all night long. People in East St. Louis and St. Louis worked their asses off in them packing and slaughterhouses. So you know they was mad when they took off work. They didn't want to hear no dumb shit off nobody, and would kill a motherfucker quick who brought them some stupid shit. That's why they were serious about their partying and listening to music.[22]

Another element of "countryness" is in the wariness of East St. Louisans, writes Davis, who "don't get into people right away." Surface conviviality is "just a mask so they can check you out . . . Country people are skeptical. . . ."[23]

There is a sense in *Miles* that despite Davis's continuing preference for East St. Louis–style barbecue, his personal connection with the place has receded. Clearly, he identifies with some aspects of "country"; the wariness he ascribes to East St. Louisans certainly finds an analogue in his own self-presentation. And how Davis presents himself elsewhere in the book is probably a reason why St. Louisans and others remain reticent to embrace him.

In particular, Davis's unfeeling recounting of domestic violence is cause for the proverbial shudder and led to several withering critiques of Davis's concept of masculinity.[24] Indeed, much of jazz history has relied on the biographies of great men, and only recently have the contours of a broader jazz life been sketched in. In particular, the role of spouses or domestic partners in creating the conditions for jazz cultural production are becoming clearer; and the costs of linking one's fate to "genius" continue to be counted and perhaps serve as a caution when erecting cultural memorials. In the case of Miles, two examples will suffice.

Irene Cawthon shared Miles Davis's dream of making it in New York. She aspired to be a dancer and share a life in the arts with him and even ordered an application form from the Juilliard School of Music for him. Davis's drug addiction and related acts effectively derailed not only his career for a time, but his relationship with Irene and his children with varying degrees of permanence. By 1960, Irene had picked up the pieces and forged a new life. She moved back to St. Louis where she worked in the St. Louis Public School system for twenty-nine years, supporting herself and her children.[25]

Frances Taylor fulfilled her own dreams of becoming a professional dancer. She already had succeeded in classical ballet, and with the innovative Katherine Dunham troupe, and on Broadway in *West Side Story* and other productions when she married Davis. Her career ended at Miles Davis's insistence, and his abusive and drug-fueled behavior eventually inspired her to leave him in an act of self-preservation. She made a new life for herself in California, having loved the man, not the great musician.[26]

When considering how Miles Davis should be remembered, it is difficult to navigate the many contradictions: of beauty and violence, generosity and selfishness, art and commerce, that seem to maintain a dual presence at nearly every turn. Just putting on the music and enjoying it doesn't seem to be enough, as Pearl Cleage reminds us, but it is also true that the music will stand as a monument of sorts, portable bits of

recorded culture that will continue to influence and astonish.

Physical reminders of Miles Davis's presence in St. Louis are few. Today the Rhumboogie Club in St. Louis is long gone. Eddie Randle's Blue Devils, with a sixteen-year old Miles Davis in the trumpet section, played there as the Rhumboogie Orchestra. Most of the other "Miles Davis" sites around St. Louis are no longer extant, victims of the instability of clubs, the marginal popularity of jazz, economic decay, or urban renewal. Peacock Alley, where the first Davis Quintet played in July 1956, in their second engagement with John Coltrane on tenor, is gone, a victim of the largest urban clearance project in America in 1959. Davis's Lincoln High in East St. Louis is now a junior high, the high school having been merged into East St. Louis High, and the original Lincoln building is no more. The building containing the Davis dental office and residence on Broadway was demolished long ago.

Even so, efforts to understand and even embrace Miles Davis are underway. Miles D. Davis Elementary

School opened in 1983 in East St. Louis with the trumpeter in attendance. University City, Missouri's Delmar Loop Walk of Fame contains a star for Davis. Washington University's series of conferences on Miles Davis in the 1990s increased the trumpeter's visibility in the region. The Missouri History Museum's 2001 exhibition on Miles Davis was the first major historical exhibit on the subject. The *Miles 2001* celebration in St. Louis and East St. Louis began as an effort to bridge the issues of race and the river, with the seventy-fifth anniversary of Miles Davis's birth as the catalyst.

Exhibitions, concerts, and other special programs have been designed to cure the amnesia and form new collaborative relationships. The most significant tribute to Davis may be that the jazz scene is St. Louis is stronger than it has been for several decades. You may even hear "So What" in a local restaurant.

Historians have long left behind the notion of great men, and even of heroes. And certainly in the case of Miles Davis's personal life, it would be difficult to position him as, in our culture's tired phrase, a role model. But surely the remembrance of one's own is an important cultural function, not only for families but for cities, regions, and countries, even if that function is mostly symbolic. As we know, even symbolism can be painful. For the St. Louis region to remember Miles Davis, it must do more than simply acknowledge one of the twentieth century's great musicians. It must also re-examine a rich heritage of African American musical culture in this region and confront the legacy of racism that traces back to slavery. In addition, it must also acknowledge one of the country's most distressed urban areas where that musician lived so many years ago. And it must try to weigh and understand what heroes are, and why music matters. Only as this slow, incremental process continues can Miles Davis, contradictions and all, truly be claimed as one of St. Louis's own. And that goes for the rest of America, as well.

Miles Davis was a New Yorker who kept a second home in Malibu at the end of his life. He loved Paris. He didn't need a passport in Warsaw, and the city of Grenada honored him. In a burst of international devotion, the December, 1999 cover of *GQ Japan* emphatically declared that "Miles is God!" His daughter Cheryl Davis, reflecting on the continuing international interest in her father, says simply that "he belongs to the world."

He belongs to St. Louis, too.

1   Eugene B. Redmond, interviewed by Benjamin Cawthra, September 8, 2000.

2   "Miles Davis, 65; Jazz Trumpeter." *St. Louis Post-Dispatch*, September 29, 1991.

3   Harper Barnes, "Miles Davis: Jazz Genius Leaves Legacy of 'Brass,'" *St. Louis Post-Dispatch*, September 30, 1991.

4   Larry Fiquette, "Davis Obituary Placement Hit A Sore Spot," *St. Louis Post-Dispatch*, October 6, 1991.

5   Stephen Davis, "My Ego Only Needs a Good Rhythm Section," 158. Collected in Gary Carner, ed., *The Miles Davis Companion: Four Decades of Commentary* (New York: Schirmer Books, 1996).

6   Quincy Troupe, *The Miles Davis Radio Project*, Program 1, 1990.

7   Miles Davis with Quincy Troupe, *Miles: The Autobiography* (New York: Simon & Schuster, 1990), 42–43.

8   Bob Blumenthal, *The Complete Live at the Plugged Nickel 1965*, liner notes. Columbia/Legacy, 1995.

9   *Miles: The Autobiography*, 39.

10 John Gennari to Benjamin Cawthra, June 21, 1999.

11 Artist Session Sheet, *In a Silent Way* folder, Macero Collection Box 2, American Music Collection, New York Public Library for the Performing Arts.

12 A full-length study of the Great Migration to St. Louis has yet to emerge, in part because scholars often have not been able to decide whether St. Louis is a southern place from which migration occurs or whether it is a destination. Often it was the place where the money ran out on the way to Chicago. An important study of the Great Migration to Chicago is James R. Grossman's *Land of Hope: Chicago, Black Southerners, and the Great Migration* (Chicago: University of Chicago Press, 1989), but the motivations for movement were often similar no matter the destination. For a look at the way the Great Migration found expression in literature and the arts, see Farah Jasmine Griffin, *Who Set You Flowin': The African American Migration Narrative* (New York: Oxford University Press, 1996).

13 Gary Giddins, "Miles Davis (Kinds of Blues)" in *Visions of Jazz: The First Hundred Years* (New York: Oxford University Press, 1998), 341.

14 Carlos Santana, *The Miles Davis Radio Project*, Program 5, 1990.

15 In jazz history as well as that of the Great Migration, St. Louis's role remains unclarified. Burton W. Peretti's excellent *The Creation of Jazz: Music, Race, and Culture in Urban America* (Urbana: University of Illinois Press, 1992) treats St. Louis as a place from which musicians migrated to Chicago. John Szwed, in his forthcoming biography of Miles Davis, points out that in the great mythology of jazz,

the music flowed northward along the river from New Orleans to Chicago; of course, the Mississippi River never comes close to Chicago.

16 Jonothan Kozol, *Savage Inequalities: Children in America's Schools* (New York: Crown, 1991), 7–39.

17 Kenneth Reardon, "Back from the Brink: The East St. Louis Story," *Gateway Heritage* 18, no. 3 (winter 1997–98): 5–15.

18 Ibid., 7.

19 Michael Kammen's *Mystic Chords of Memory: The Transformation of Tradition in American Culture* (New York: Knopf, 1991) contains extensive discussions of the imperatives toward commemorative activity.

20 *Miles: The Autobiography,* 38

21 The incident plays a central role in the "Prologue" to *Miles,* 7–10.

22 *Miles: The Autobiography,* 38.

23 *Miles: The Autobiography,* 356–57.

24 See Hazel V. Carby, "Playin' the Changes," in *Race Men* (Cambridge, Mass.: Harvard University Press, 1998), 135–68; and Pearl Cleage, "Mad at Miles," collected in Carner, 210–16. Cleage's critique of Davis found expression at the first Miles Davis in American Culture conference, held at Washington University in St. Louis in 1995. Coming as they did at the beginning of the conference, her remarks sparked an intensity of debate that perhaps best symbolizes the continuing controversy surrounding Miles Davis.

25 Irene Cawthon, interviewed by Benjamin Cawthra, November 18, 2000.

26 Frances Davis, interviewed by Benjamin Cawthra, November 19, 2000.

The technical and emotional brilliance of the trumpet played by Miles Davis has made him one of the most provocative influences in modern jazz. We spent two days with Miles not long ago in his rather unusual five-story home, a converted Russian Orthodox Church on West 77th Street near the Hudson River in New York City. Miles was between gigs at the time and we accompanied him on his restless daily home routine, asking questions at propitious moments while he worked out in his basement gymnasium, made veal chops Italian style for his family, took telephone calls from fellow musicians, his lawyer and stockbroker, gave boxing lessons to his three sons, watched TV, plucked out beginner's chords on a guitar and, of course, blew one of his two Martin trumpets, running up and down the chromatic scale with searing speed. Spending time with Miles in the refuge of his own home, and seeing him surrounded by the activities and people he loves, it was hard to reconcile this reality with his sometimes flinty and truculent public posture. It was on this facet of his personality that we first queried him.

AH: Linked with your musical renown is your reputation for bad temper and rudeness to your audiences. Would you comment?

MD: Why is it that people just have to have so much to say about me? It bugs me because I'm not that important. Some critic that didn't have nothing else to do started this crap about I don't announce numbers, I don't look at the audience, I don't bow or talk to people, I walk off the stage, and all that.

Look, man, all I am is a trumpet player. I only can do one thing—play my horn—and that's what's at the bottom of the whole mess. I ain't no entertainer, and ain't trying to be one. I am one thing, a musician. Most of what's said about me is lies in the first place. Everything I do, I got a reason.

The reason I don't announce numbers is because it's not until the last instant I decide what's maybe the best thing to play next. Besides, if people don't recognize a number when we play it, what difference does it make?

Why I sometimes walk off the stand is because when it's somebody else's turn to solo, I ain't going to just stand up there and be detracting from him. What am I going to stand up there for? I ain't no model, and I don't sing or dance, and I damn sure ain't no Uncle Tom just to be up there

Appendix 1

The *Playboy* Interview with Alex Haley

grinning. Sometimes I go over by the piano or the drums and listen to what they're doing. But if I don't want to do that, I go in the wings and listen to the whole band until it's the next turn for my horn.

Then they claim I ignore the audience while I'm playing. Man, when I'm working, I know the people are out there. But when I'm playing, I'm worrying about making my horn sound right.

And they bitch that I won't talk to people when we go off after a set. That's a damn lie. I talk plenty of times if everything's going like it ought to and I feel right. But if I got my mind on something about my band or something else, well, hell, no. I don't want to talk. When I'm working I'm concentrating. I bet you if I was a doctor sewing on some son of a bitch's heart, they wouldn't want me to talk.

Anybody wants to believe all this crap they hear about me, it's their problem, not mine. Because, look, man, I like people. I love people! I'm not going around telling everybody that. I try to say that my way—with my horn. Look, when I was a boy, 10 years old, I got a paper route and it got bigger than I could handle because my customers liked me so much. I just delivered papers the best I could and minded my business, the same way I play my horn now. But a lot of the people I meet now make me sick.

AH: What types of people do you find especially irritating?

MD: Well, these people that's always coming up bugging me until they get me to act like this crap they heard. They ask you things, you say what you think, and if it ain't what they want to hear, then something's wrong with you and they go away mad and think you don't like them. I bet I have had that happen 500 times. In this last club I played, this newspaper reporter kept after me when I told him I didn't have no more to say. He wasn't satisfied with that. After the next set, he come up again, either drunk or playing drunk, and shoved into me. I told him to get the hell out of my way, and then he was fine—he went right out and wrote that. But he didn't tell how it happened.

And I'm mad every time I run into the Jim Crow scene. I don't care what form it takes. You can't hardly play anywhere you don't run into some of these cats full of prejudice. I don't know how many I've told, "Look, you want me to talk to you and you're prejudiced against me and all that.

Why'n't you go on back where you're sitting and be prejudiced by yourself and leave me alone?" I have enough problems without trying to make them feel better. Then they go off and join the rest saying I'm such a big bastard.

I've got no plans of changing what I think. I don't dig people in clubs who don't pay the musicians respect. The average jazz musician today, if he's making it, is just as trained as classical musicians. You ever see anybody go up bugging the classical musicians when they are on the job and trying to work?

Even in jazz—you look at the white bandleaders—if they don't want anybody messing with them when they are working, you don't hear anybody squawking. It's just if a Negro is involved that there's something wrong with him. My troubles started when I learned to play the trumpet and hadn't learned to dance.

AH: You feel that the complaints about you are because of your race?

MD: I know damn well a lot of it is race. White people have certain things they expect from Negro musicians— just like they've got labels for the whole Negro race. It goes clear back to the slavery days. That was when Uncle Tomming got started because white people demanded it. Every little black child grew up seeing that getting along with white people meant grinning and acting clowns. It helped white people to feel easy about what they had done, and were doing, to Negroes, and that's carried right on over to now. You bring it down to musicians, they want you to not only play your instrument, but to entertain them, too, with grinning and dancing.

AH: Generally speaking, what are your feelings with regard to race?

MD: I hate to talk about what I think of the mess because my friends are all colors. When I say that some of my best friends are white, I sure ain't lying. The only white people I don't like are the prejudiced white people. Those the shoe don't fit, well, they don't wear it. I don't like the white people that show me they can't understand that not just the Negroes, but the Chinese and Puerto Ricans and any other races that ain't white, should be given dignity and respect like everybody else.

But let me straighten you—I ain't saying I think all Negroes are the salt of the earth. It's plenty of Negroes I

can't stand, too. Especially those that act like they think white people want them to. They bug me worse than Uncle Toms.

But prejudiced white people can't see any of the other races as just individual people. If a white man robs a bank, it's just a man robbed a bank. But if a Negro or a Puerto Rican does it, it's them awful Negroes or Puerto Ricans. Hardly anybody not white hasn't suffered from some of white people's labels. It used to be said that all Negroes were shiftless and happy-go-lucky and lazy. But that's been proved a lie so much that now the label is that what Negroes want integration for is so they can sleep in the bed with white people. It's another damn lie. All Negroes want is to be free to do in this country just like anybody else. Prejudiced white people ask one another, "Would you want your sister to marry a Negro?" It's a jive question to ask in the first place—as if white women stand around helpless if some Negro wants to drag one off to a preacher. It makes me sick to

hear that. A Negro just might not want your sister. The Negro is always to blame if some white woman decides she wants him. But it's all right that ever since slavery, white men been having Negro women. Every Negro you see that ain't black, that's what's happened somewhere in his background. The slaves they brought here were all black.

What makes me mad about these labels for Negroes is that very few white people really know what Negroes really feel like. A lot of white people have never even been in the company of an intelligent Negro. But you can hardly meet a white person, especially a white man, that don't think he's qualified to tell you all about Negroes.

You know the story the minute you meet some white cat and he comes off with a big show that he's with you. It's 10,000 things you can talk about, but the only thing he can think of is some other Negro he's such close friends with. Intelligent Negroes are sick of hearing this. I don't know how many times different whites have started talking, telling me they was raised up with a Negro boy. But I ain't found one yet that knows whatever happened to that boy after they grew up.

AH: Did you grow up with any white boys?

MD: I didn't grow up with any, not as friends, to speak of. But I went to school with some. In high school, I was the best in the music class on the trumpet. I knew it and all the rest knew it—but all the contest first prizes went to the boys with blue eyes. It made me so mad I made up my mind to outdo anybody white on my horn. If I hadn't met that prejudice, I probably wouldn't have had as much drive in my work. I have thought about that a lot. I have thought that prejudice and curiosity have been responsible for what I have done in music.

AH: What was the role of the curiosity?

MD: I mean I always had a curiosity about trying new things in music. A new sound, another way to do something—things like that. But man, look, you know one of the biggest things that needs straightening up? The whole communication system of this country! Take the movies and TV. How many times do you see anybody in the films but white people? You don't dig? Look, the next movie or TV you see, you count how many Negroes or any other race but white that you see. But you walk around in any city, you see the other races—I mean, in life they are part of the scene. But in the films supposed to represent this country, they ain't there. You won't hardly even see any in the street crowd scenes—because the studios didn't bother to hire any as extras.

Negroes used to be servants and Uncle Toms in the movies. But so much stink was raised until they quit that. Now you do have some Negroes playing feature parts—maybe four or five a year. Most of the time, they have a role that's special so it won't offend nobody—then it's a big production made like that picture is going to prove our democracy. Look, I ain't saying that people making films are prejudiced. I can't say what I don't know. But I see the films they make, and I know they don't think about the trouble a lot of colored people find with the movies and TV.

A big TV network wanted to do a show featuring me. I said no, and they asked me to just look at a show featuring a big-name Negro singer. No, I ain't calling no names. Well, just like I knew, they had 18 girls dancing for the background—and every one of them was white. Later on, when I pointed this out to the TV people, they were shocked. They said they just hadn't thought about that. I said I knew they hadn't. Nobody seems to think much about the

colored people and the Chinese and Puerto Ricans and Japanese that watch TV and buy the things they advertise. All these races want to see some of their own people represented in the shows—I mean, besides the big stars. I know I'd feel better to see some kids of all races dancing and acting on shows than I would feel about myself up there playing a horn. The only thing that makes me any different from them is I was lucky.

This black-white business is ticklish to try to explain. You don't want to see Negroes every time you click on your set. That would be just as bad as now when you don't see nobody but white people. But if movies and TV are supposed to reflect this country, and this country's supposed to be democratic, then why don't they do it? Let's see all kinds of people dancing and acting. I see all kinds of kids downtown at the schools of dancing and acting, but from what I see in the movies and TV, it's just the white ones that are getting any work.

Look, man, right in music you got the same thing happening. I got this album, *Someday My Prince Will Come*, and you know who's on the jacket cover? My wife—Frances. I just got to thinking that as many record albums as Negroes buy, I hadn't ever seen a Negro girl on a major album cover unless she was the artist. There wasn't any harm meant—they just automatically thought about a white model and ordered one. It was my album and I'm Frances' prince, so I suggested they use her for a model, and they did it.

But it ain't all cases where white people just didn't think about the other races. It's a lot of intended discrimination, right in music. You got plenty of places that either won't hire Negroes, or they hire just one that they point out. The network studios, the Broadway pit bands, the classical orchestras, the film studios, they all have color discrimination in hiring.

I tell you why I feel so strong about the communication system. I never have forgotten one time in Europe this nice old man told me how in World War II, the Europeans didn't know what to make of Negro troops. They had their picture of this country from our magazines and movies, and with a very few exceptions like Pops Armstrong and Joe Louis and Jesse Owens, they didn't know about any Negroes except servants and laborers.

AH: Do you feel that your views are shared by most Negroes? And Puerto Ricans? And Orientals?

MD: I can't speak for them last two. I'm in no position.

I just know what I personally feel for them. But I know that pretty nearly all Negroes hardly have any other choice about how they feel. They ain't blind. They got to see what's happening. It's a thousand big and little ways that you run into the prejudices of white people. Just one thing—how long have Negroes been looking at immigrants coming into this country and can't even speak the language, and in the second generations, they are in places the Negroes haven't got to yet.

Look, not long ago this big magazine had this Southern truck driver saying he'd carry sandwiches if they let Negroes eat in them Maryland highway restaurants. But where he wants to eat ain't my point—I'm talking about what he said. He said, "You give them a finger, they take an arm" and a lot more. You dig? When it comes to human rights, these prejudiced white people keep on acting like they own the damn franchise! And, man, with the world in the mess it's in now, we trying to influence on our side all them Africans and Arabs and Indians and Chinese. . . . You know two thirds of the people in the world ain't white? They see all this crap with Negroes and supposed to feel white people really think any different about them? Man, somebody better get straight!

Another thing—there was no upset about them restaurants not serving Negroes, until it was an African they turned away. You think every Negro in the country don't see what it says? It says that we been here 400 years, but it wasn't no mess until they put out an African that just flew over here on a jet.

AH: Do you, in your position as a famous Negro, meet prejudice?

MD: I told you, someway or other, every Negro meets it, I don't care who he is! Look, man, I sent for an electrician to fix something in the house. When he rang the bell, I answered and he looked at me like I was dirt, and said, "I want to see the owner, Mr. Davis." When I said, "You looking at him," the cat turned beet red. He had me figured as the porter. Now he's mad and embarrassed. What had I done to him but called to give him work?

That same week, I had seen a lot of them West Point cadets, and in a bar I asked why there was so many of them in town. Man, I just asked the cat a question and he moved up the bar and didn't speak! But then somebody recognized me and he got red as that electrician. He came trying to apologize and saying he had my records. I told him I had just paid enough taxes to cover his free ride at West Point, and I walked out. I guess he's somewhere now with the others saying I'm such a bastard. It bugged me so, man, I wasn't worth a damn for two or three days. It wasn't just him ignoring me I was thinking about, but in two or three years, Gregory, my oldest boy, may be doing some Army time. How am I supposed to feel about him maybe serving under this cat?

Then take this tour I made—Frances and I had train reservations to California. But this clerk I showed my identification to, he took it and looked at me just like the West Point cat. When he said he had to check with somebody else, I asked him what was the trouble. You know he had the nerve to tell me I might have forged it! Ain't no need of me telling you what I told him, nobody would

print it. But we went to the airport and took a plane. I'm spending my money, the railroads are broke, even this son of a bitch's job's in trouble, but all he can see is I'm black, so it's all right to insult me. Bad as I hate to fly, I ain't been on a train since, because I haven't met Jim Crow on the airlines.

AH: In your field, music, don't some Negro jazzmen discriminate against white musicians?
MD: Crow Jim is what they call that. Yeah. It's a lot of the Negro musicians mad because most of the best-paying jobs go to the white musicians playing what the Negroes created. But I don't go for this, because I think prejudice one way is just as bad as the other way. I wouldn't have no other arranger but Gil Evans—we couldn't be much closer if he was my brother. And I remember one time when I hired Lee Konitz, some colored cats bitched a lot about me hiring an ofay in my band when Negroes didn't have work. I said if a cat could play like

Lee, I would hire him. I didn't give a damn if he was green and had red breath.

AH: Do you find that being the head of your band adds to your problems?
MD: Fronting a band ain't no fun. A lot of people don't understand that music is business, it's hard work and a big responsibility. I hate to even think what all I've been through to play my horn, and still go through. I put everything I've got into it. Even after a good rehearsal, I feel empty. And you add to playing your instrument the running of a band and you got plenty of problems. I got my own family, and the guys that work for me and their families to think about. On one tour, I had this white woman in Kansas City meet me when I came off the stand and wanted me to come to her table with her and her husband for a drink. I told her I didn't like to do that, and she hollered, "They said you're like that!" I felt like throwing down my horn and kicking it. But I said to myself I was going to try and educate at least that one couple. So I went over and talked to them.

I told them an artist's first responsibility was to himself. I said if he kept getting upset with what other people think he ought to do, he never would get too far, or he sure wouldn't last. I tried to make them see how I had worked all my life to play myself and then to get a band worth people paying to hear. I said that a lot of times when people in a club wanted to talk to me, I needed to be worrying about something about my band. They said they understood. I hope they did.

AH: You have been quoted as not being in favor of jazz concerts. Why?

MD: Nobody can relax at concerts, the musicians or the people, either. You can't do nothing but sit down, you can't move around, you can't have a drink. A musician has to be able to let loose everything in him to reach the people. If the musician can't relax, how's he going to make the people feel what he feels? The whole scene of jazz is feeling.

AH: Do you now ever indulge in jam sessions?

MD: I wish there was some jam sessions to sit in. But there ain't none left—at least not in the big cities. I used to sit in some great ones around St. Louis and in Brooklyn, Illinois. We would blow sometimes clear up until the next afternoon. When I go back there now, I sit in with a little blues band. They have the feeling.

AH: You've won all the trumpet polls. After yourself, how would you rank others?

MD: After me! Hell, it's plenty great trumpet players don't come after me, or after nobody else! That's what I hate so about critics—how they are always comparing artists . . . always writing that one's better than another one. Ten men can have spent all their lives learning technical expertness on their instruments, but just like in any art, one will play one style and the rest nine other ways. And if some critics just don't happen to like a man's style, they will knock the artist. That bugs the hell out of musicians. It's made some damn near mad enough to want to hang up their horns.

Trumpet players, like anybody else, are individualized by their different ideas and styles. The thing to judge in any jazz artist is does the man project, and does he have ideas. You take Dizzy—he does, all the time, every time he picks up his horn. Some more cats—Clark Terry, Ray Nance, Kenny Dorham, Roy Eldridge, Harold Baker, Freddie Hubbard, Lee Morgan, Bobby Hackett—a lot of them. Hell, that cat down in New Orleans, Al Hirt, he blows his ass off, too!

AH: Is there any special reason you didn't mention Louis Armstrong?

MD: Oh, Pops? No, why I didn't mention him is because I was talking just about modern-jazz players. I love Pops, I love the way he sings, the way he plays—everything he does, except when he says something against modern-jazz music. He ought to realize that he was a pioneer, too. No, he wasn't an influence of mine, and I've had very little direct contact with Pops. A long time ago, I was at Bop City, and he came in and told me he liked my playing. I don't know if he would even remember it, but I remember how good I felt to have him say it. People really dig Pops like I do myself. He does a good job overseas with his personality. But they ought to send him down South for goodwill. They need goodwill worse in Georgia and Alabama and Mississippi than they do in Europe.

AH: To go back a moment, you expressed a sharp. dislike of critics. Are there other reasons besides their comparing musicians?

MD: Well, aside from that, I get sick of how a lot of them write whole columns and pages of big words and still ain't saying nothing. If you have spent your life getting to know your business and the other cats in it, and what they are doing, then you know if a critic knows what he's talking about. Most of the time they don't.

I don't pay no attention to what critics say about me, the good or the bad. The toughest critic I got, and the only one I worry about, is myself. My music has got to get past me and I'm too vain to play anything I think is bad.

No, I ain't going to name critics I don't like. But I will tell you some that I respect what they write—Nat Hentoff, Ralph Gleason and Leonard Feather. And some others, I can't right off think of their names. But it ain't a long list.

AH: Are there any particular places or clubs that you don't like to play?

MD: There are plenty I won't play! I won't take a booking nowhere in the South. I told you I just can't stand Jim Crow, so I ain't going down there in it. There's enough of it here in the North, but at least you have the support of some laws.

I won't play nowhere I know has the kind of audiences that you waste your breath to play for. I'm talking about them expense-account ofays that use music as a background for getting high and trying to show off to the women they brought. They ain't come to hear good music. They don't even know how to enjoy themselves. They drink too much, they get loud, they got to be seen and heard. They'll jump up and dance jigs and sing. They ain't got no manners—don't pay their women no respect. What they really want is some Uncle Tom entertainment if it's a Negro group on the stand. These are the

kind will holler, "Hey, boy, play Sweet Georgia Brown!" You supposed to grin and play that. I hate to play in a place full of those kind of squares so bad that if there wasn't nobody else to play to, I'd invest in some more property and just stay home and collect rents. I can't stand dumb-ass people not respecting the other customers that have come to hear the music. Sometimes one table like that has bugged me so that when I get home or to my hotel, I walk the floor because I can't sleep.

I told you I ain't going to play nowhere in the South that Negroes can't come. But I ain't going to play nowhere in the North that Negroes don't come. It's one of two reasons they won't, either because they know they ain't wanted, or because they don't like the joint's regular run of music. Negroes ain't got as much money to throw away in night clubs as white people. So a club that Negroes patronize, you can figure that everybody that goes there comes expecting to hear good music.

AH: What is your opinion of the jazz audiences in Europe?

MD: European audiences are generally more hip about the background of jazz than most of the fans here. Some cats hardly heard of here are big record sellers in Europe. In this country, it's more following of personalities. You want to hear something funny? One club-owner friend of mine said a lot of people pay their money to come where I'm playing just because they want to see me—they heard I'm so bad. Ain't that a bitch?

But this country has a lot of great fans. You know, they appreciate what you're trying to do, and that inspires a musician to give his best. I know some Americans that don't stop with just knowing jazz, but that even think just like musicians.

AH: Do you plan another European tour soon?

MD: Maybe. I like to play in Europe every now and then, but I don't like to spend no more time out of this house than I can help. Jack Whittemore, my booking agent at Shaw Artists, schedules me so I don't stay long on the road. I like to have time at home to be with my kids and Frances, and to just think about things—like worrying about the people running this government maybe slipping and getting us into another war. But I like them Kennedy brothers—they're swinging people.

AH: Would it please you if the image of you changed, that people quit regarding you as a tough guy?

MD: Well, nobody wants to be always accused of something he ain't done. But people that want to think that, it's their worry, it ain't mine. I'm like I am, and I ain't planning to change. I ain't scared of nothing or nobody. I already been through too much. I ought to be dead from just what I went through when I was on dope. I ain't going around anywhere trying to be tough and a racist. I just say what I think, and that bugs people, especially a lot of white people. When they look in my eyes and don't see no fear, they know it's a draw.

AH: Have you always been so sensitive about being a Negro?

MD: About the first thing I can remember as a little boy was a white man running me down a street hollering "Nigger! Nigger!" My father went hunting him with a shotgun. Being sensitive and having race pride has been in my family since slave days. The slave Davises played classical string music on the plantations. My father, Miles the first, was born six years after the Emancipation. He wanted to play music, but my grandfather wanted him to be more than an entertainer for white folks. He made him go to Northwestern to be a dental surgeon. My father is worth more than I am. He's a high-priced dental surgeon with more practice than he can handle—because he's good at his business—and he raises hogs with pedigrees. It's a special breed of hogs with some funny name I would tell you, but I never can remember it.

AH: You're said to be one of the financially best-off popular musicians. Is this correct?

MD: Well, I don't have any access to other musicians' bankbooks. But I never have been what you would call poor. I grew up with an allowance, and I had a big newspaper route. I saved most of what I made except for buying records. But when I first left home as a musician, I used to spend all I made, and when I went on dope, I got in debt. But after I got enough sense to kick the habit, I started to make more than I needed to spend unless I was crazy or something.

Now I got a pretty good portfolio of stock investments, and I got this house—it's worth into six figures, including everything in it. My four kids are coming up fine. When the boys get in from school, I want you to see them working out on the bags in our gym downstairs. I keep myself in shape and teach the kids how to box. They can handle themselves. Ain't nothing better that a father can pass along.

Then I got my music, I got Frances, and my Ferrari—and our friends. I got everything a man could want—if it just wasn't for this prejudice crap. It ain't that I'm mad at white people, I just see what I see and I know what's happening. I am going to speak my mind about anything that drags me about this Jim Crow scene. This whole prejudice mess is something you would feel so good if it could just be got rid of, like a big sore eating inside of your belly.

1926 Born at home in Alton, Illinois, on May 26. Father Miles Dewey Davis, II, of Arkansas was a dental surgeon and prosperous landowner. Mother Cleota (Henry) Davis, is also of Arkansas. Older sister Dorothy born in Alton in 1924 shortly after the Davis family moved there.

IN JAZZ HISTORY: Louis Armstrong is in the midst of recording his *Hot Fives* records that would become the most highly regarded small-jazz band sessions in the history of American music.

IN AFRICAN AMERICAN CULTURAL HISTORY: The Young Turks of the Harlem Renaissance, led by Langston Hughes, Zora Neale Hurston, Richard Bruce Nugent, and Wallace Thurman, publish *Fire!!,* an experimental literary magazine meant to challenge the taste and control of the older black literary establishment. The publication lasts for only one issue.

Historian Carter G. Woodson establishes the annual celebration of Negro History Week in February.

1927 Davis family moves to East St. Louis, Illinois. They live behind the dental office at Fifteenth and Broadway on the second floor of a commercial building in an all-white neighborhood.

IN JAZZ HISTORY: Duke Ellington and the Washingtonians open at the Cotton Club (December 4), the engagement that makes Ellington famous.

Bix Beiderbecke records, among other tunes, "I'm Coming Virginia," "Singin' the Blues," "Trumbology," "Krazy Kat," and his famous "In a Mist."

IN AFRICAN AMERICAN CULTURAL HISTORY: Black nationalist leader Marcus Garvey, convicted of mail fraud, is deported to Jamaica after having served three years in federal prison.

1929 Brother Vernon born (November 3). Depression begins but Davis family weathers its effects.

IN AFRICAN AMERICAN CULTURAL HISTORY: King Vidor's touching black folk film *Hallelujah!,* starring Nina Mae McKinney, is released.

1932–34 Davis begins attending John Robinson Elementary School, an all-black school.

IN AFRICAN AMERICAN CULTURAL HISTORY: The country is in the midst of the Scottsboro case. Nine black boys had been tried and convicted in 1931 of raping two white girls in a boxcar, producing worldwide protests and demonstrations against the convictions. Langston

Chronology
Miles Dewey Davis III

by Benjamin Cawthra and Gerald Early

Hughes writes his famous play, *Scottsboro Limited*. The case makes the Communist Party, which had defended the boys, well-regarded among African Americans.

1935 Davis receives his first trumpet, a gift from Dr. John Eubanks, a friend of his father. He has been exposed to music at home as his mother plays the violin and his sister, Dorothy, the piano.

IN AFRICAN AMERICAN CULTURAL HISTORY: Joe Louis defeats Italian Primo Carnera in a highly politicized heavyweight bout shortly after fascist Italy invaded Ethiopia. There is great concern expressed and considerable coverage about the invasion in black newspapers.

W. E. B. Du Bois publishes *Black Reconstruction*, a Marxist interpretation of the Reconstruction era.

IN JAZZ HISTORY: Duke Ellington writes and records his first concerto-like piece, "Reminiscing in Tempo," in honor of his late mother.

Benny Goodman and his orchestra are a hit at the Palomar in Los Angeles (August 21, 1935), which officially ushers in the swing era for mainstream America.

1938 At Crispus Attucks Grade School, Elwood Buchanan becomes Davis's first music teacher. Buchanan gives lessons once a week.

IN AFRICAN AMERICAN CULTURAL HISTORY: Joe Louis, after becoming heavyweight champion of the world a year earlier, defeats German Max Schmeling on June 22 in one round in one of the most highly publicized and politicized sporting events in American history. Louis becomes the first black to hold the title since Jack Johnson (1908–1915).

IN JAZZ HISTORY: Swing music enters the citadel of high culture when Benny Goodman and his racially integrated orchestra perform a concert at Carnegie Hall.

Mayor and boss Tom Pendergast is arrested and convicted on charges of tax evasion, ending the era of a wide-open Kansas City that produced great black swing music. The most famous outfit to come from Kansas City in the 1930s is Count Basie's orchestra.

Dorothy Baker publishes *Young Man With a Horn*, loosely based on the life of Bix Beiderbecke and inspired by articles by jazz critic Otis Ferguson. It becomes the most famous American novel about jazz ever written.

1939 Father gives Davis a new trumpet for his thirteenth birthday. Family moves to house at 1701 Kansas in East St. Louis. Davis begins taking additional lessons in St. Louis with Joseph Gustat, first chair of the St. Louis Symphony. Outbreak of Second World War in Europe.

IN AFRICAN AMERICAN CULTURAL HISTORY: Denied permission by the Daughters of the American Revolution to use Constitution Hall, Marian Anderson gives her famous Easter Sunday concert on the steps of the Lincoln Memorial to an audience of 75,000.

Hattie McDaniel is awarded an Academy Award for her performance in *Gone With the Wind*, the first African American actor so honored.

IN JAZZ HISTORY: Tenor saxophonist Coleman Hawkins records his famous version of "Body and Soul."

Billie Holiday records a protest song against lynching called "Strange Fruit" for Commodore Records. It is jazz's first overtly political tune.

1940 Forms small band with friends that performs at Huff's Beer Garden, playing hits such as "In the Mood." Befriended by Clark Terry, who plays with Davis at various clubs over the next couple of years.

IN AFRICAN AMERICAN CULTURAL HISTORY: Novelist Richard Wright publishes *Native Son*, one of the most influential works of fiction by a black writer in the twentieth century.

1941–42 Davis's parents divorce. Davis enters Lincoln High School, East St. Louis. Joins Lincoln High Marching Band directed by Elwood Buchanan. Meets Irene Cathorn, his first girlfriend. Begins earning money performing at night; some of his earnings will support sister Dorothy's studies at Fisk University in Nashville.

IN AFRICAN AMERICAN CULTURAL HISTORY: In the summer of 1941, A. Philip Randolph announces the March on Washington movement, which forces President Roosevelt to issue executive order 8802, banning racist hiring practices in the defense industry and establishing the Fair Employment Practices Commission. United States enters World War II in December 1941. Black leaders and the black press announce a Double-V campaign: victory in the war and victory over racism at home.

IN JAZZ HISTORY: A gathering of younger musicians including Dizzy Gillespie, Thelonious Monk, Kenny Clarke, Jimmy Blanton, and Charlie Christian had begun meeting after-hours at Minton's and Monroe's Uptown in New York as early as 1939, experimenting with a new sound that would become bebop. They were joined in the early 1940s by Kansas City saxophonist Charlie Parker.

Stan Kenton's Artistry in Rhythm band becomes a huge success.

Innovative guitarist Charlie Christian dies on March 2, 1942, at the age of 25.

Ellington *wunderkind* bassist Jimmy Blanton dies on July 30, 1942, at the age of 24.

1943 Joins Eddie Randle's Blue Devils. Becomes musical director of the band, preparing music and leading rehearsals. Plays with visiting musicians, including Howard McGhee, Sonny Stitt, and Lester Young.

IN JAZZ HISTORY: Ellington premieres a new long work, *Black, Brown, and Beige*, a "tone parallel."

IN AFRICAN AMERICAN CULTURAL HISTORY: What is considered the first "modern" urban race riot occurs in Detroit on June 20, with blacks not simply defending themselves from white mob violence but attacking white persons and property. Nine whites and 25 blacks die as military police have to restore order.

A similar riot occurs in Harlem on August 1, resulting in six African Americans dead and 185 injured.

Lena Horne, Ethel Waters, and Eddie Anderson star in Vincente Minnelli's black musical, *Cabin in the Sky*. In the same year, Horne also would be featured in *Stormy Weather*, the black musical biopic of bandleader James Resse Europe.

Rex Ingram is widely acclaimed for his portrayal of a courageous African soldier in *Sahara*, a film about World War II starring Humphrey Bogart.

1944 Completes high school studies in January; graduates in absentia in June. Daughter Cheryl born in June. Later that month he substitutes in Billy Eckstine's touring big band at Club Riviera in St. Louis, playing with Charlie Parker, Dizzy Gillespie, Sarah Vaughan, Art Blakey, and Lucky Thompson for the first time. Leaves for New York in September; once there, he passes Juilliard audition. Spends some time in classes, but devotes more energy to uptown club scene. Begins building relationships with Parker, Gillespie, Freddie Webster, and others in the bebop movement. Irene and Cheryl join him in New York in December; they live in same building as Parker.

IN JAZZ HISTORY: Both Charlie Parker and Dizzy Gillespie lead bands in engagements on Fifty-second Street, the new mecca of jazz, and succeed in pushing bebop into the mainstream.

1945 First recording session in New York with singer Rubberlegs Williams, April. Following summer session at Juilliard, Davis decides not to register for autumn term; he now has become devoted to jazz. Following the breakup of the Parker/Gillespie quintet, he joins Parker for engagement at Three Deuces and other clubs on Fifty-second Street in October. Plays with Coleman Hawkins at Minton's engagement in Harlem. Participates in November 26 Savoy sessions with Charlie Parker's Reboppers including Gillespie, Sadik Hakim, Curley Russell, and Max Roach performing such bebop classics "Now's the Time" and "Billie's Bounce." During police shutdown of Fifty-second Street clubs, Davis returns to East St. Louis for holidays.

World War II officially ends on August 14 after the dropping of atomic bombs on Japan.

IN AFRICAN AMERICAN CULTURAL HISTORY: Jackie Robinson signs Major League baseball contract with Brooklyn Dodgers in December.

Richard Wright publishes controversial autobiography *Black Boy*.

John H. Johnson starts *Ebony* magazine.

1946 Davis joins Benny Carter's big band in St. Louis and accompanies it to California. Plays with Carter's small band and with Parker, who had gone west with Gillespie. In March, records with Parker for Dial Records; tunes include "Moose the Mooche," "Yardbird Suite," "Ornithology," and "A Night in Tunisia." In summer, begins working sporadically with bassist/composer Charles Mingus. Son Gregory born in East St. Louis. When Eckstine's band arrives in Los Angeles, Davis fills trumpet chair vacated by Fats Navarro. Accompanies band back to New York late in the year; visits East St. Louis during Eckstine's stopover in Chicago.

IN AFRICAN AMERICAN CULTURAL HISTORY: Sugar Ray Robinson defeats Tommy Bell on December 20 to win world welterweight title.

Chester Himes publishes *If He Hollers, Let Me Go*, his first novel.

1947 January/February: Eckstine Orchestra breaks up; Davis performs with Illinois Jacquet and Gillespie's big band. Irene, Cheryl, and Gregory live with him in New York. Parker forms new band with Davis and Roach in April; they perform with Duke Jordan and Tommy Potter for much of the year and record "Donna Lee," "Cheryl," (named for Davis's daughter) and other singles in May. Davis's first Savoy session as a leader features Parker on tenor saxophone in August; the date also features pianist John Lewis and bassist Nelson Boyd and includes "Milestones," "Half Nelson," and "Sippin' at Bells." Davis records under Parker's leadership for Dial later that year before touring Detroit and Chicago.

IN AFRICAN AMERICAN CULTURAL HISTORY: Jackie Robinson becomes the first black to play Major League baseball in the twentieth century when he joins the Brooklyn Dodgers, is voted Rookie of the Year.

Chester Himes publishes *Lonely Crusade*, his second novel.

1948 Parker quintet returns to New York, March, then joins a Jazz at the Philharmonic tour, including a stop in St. Louis on April 30. In August, Davis turns down offer to join Duke Ellington's orchestra; he is rehearsing a new nine-piece band with Gil Evans and Gerry Mulligan. The Miles Davis Nonet opens for Count Basie at Royal Roost for two weeks in September; it is the band's only engagement. Rejoins Parker but quits in December, frustrated by Parker's erratic behavior.

IN AFRICAN AMERICAN CULTURAL HISTORY: President Truman issues an executive order desegregating the armed services.

The Supreme Court declares racially restrictive housing covenants unconstitutional in *Shelly v. Kramer*.

1949 Recording sessions with nonet for Capitol, January and April; recordings such as "Move" and "Boplicity" sell poorly but will have large influence on "cool" or "west coast" jazz. Performs with Tadd Dameron Quintet at Paris International Jazz Festival, May, his first journey abroad. Meets writer Jean-Paul Sartre and singer Juliette Greco, with whom he has a love affair that endures for many years. Returns to United States, finds little work, and slides deeper into heroin addiction. Joins pianist Bud Powell for engagement in October.

IN AFRICAN AMERICAN CULTURAL HISTORY: Rioting occurs in Peekskill, New York, when Paul Robeson tries to perform at a concert there. Robeson had said earlier in the year that he considered it "unthinkable" that African Americans would go to war against the Soviet Union.

IN JAZZ HISTORY: Dave Brubeck leads both a trio and octet in recording sessions that come to define many aspects of west coast jazz.

1950 In March, Davis leads another nonet recording session for Capitol with Mulligan, Roach, Lewis, and J. J. Johnson among others. Performs on Sarah Vaughan sessions for Columbia. Leads sextet featuring Johnson, Dameron, and Art Blakey. Miles IV born, his third child. Joins Eckstine for stands in Chicago in August and Los Angeles in September. Davis arrested in Los Angeles for possession of heroin; he is acquitted of charges but publicity makes it more difficult to find work. Performs opposite Billie Holiday in successful Chicago engagement, December.

North Korea invades South Korea leading to intervention by United Nations Troops headed by U.S. armed forces. First war to be fought with racially integrated American troops.

IN AFRICAN AMERICAN CULTURAL HISTORY: Young black actor Sidney Poitier stars in his first film, Joseph Mankiewicz's *No Way Out*, a breakthrough dramatic role. Gwendolyn Brooks wins the Pulitzer Prize for poetry for *Annie Allen*, published in 1949.

Ralph Bunche is awarded the Nobel Peace Prize.

1951 Davis returns to New York at the bidding of Prestige Records, January. Sessions for Prestige mark first recordings with tenor saxophonist Sonny Rollins, bassist Percy Heath, and drummer Roy Haynes. Leads "Miles Davis All-Stars" sporadically, featuring at various times Johnson, Blakey, Rollins, Mingus, and altoist Jackie McLean. Records again for Prestige In October, but Davis's drug habit is out of control. He becomes a pimp. His father comes to New York to retrieve him.

IN AFRICAN AMERICAN CULTURAL HISTORY: Davis's idol, Sugar Ray Robinson, wins the middleweight title in February and

is featured on the cover of *Time* magazine on June 25.

1952 While in East St. Louis, Davis sits in with St. Louis tenor man Jimmy Forrest at the Barrelhouse. Davis returns to New York, living with McLean. Briefly leads a group featuring Mclean and pianist Gil Coggins; they record Davis's first sessions for Blue Note in May. Joins Symphony Sid's package tour for several weeks in summer. He is virtually inactive through the end of the year.

IN AFRICAN AMERICAN CULTURAL HISTORY: Idol Sugar Ray Robinson retires from the ring after his June fight against Joey Maxim.

Ralph Ellison publishes *Invisible Man*, one of the most important African American novels in American literary history, and is awarded the National Book Award the following year.

Chester Himes publishes *Cast the First Stone*, a novel about prison.

IN JAZZ HISTORY: Basie reorganizes his big band after several years of working with a smaller unit. It becomes known as the "Second Testament" band.

The Modern Jazz Quartet is formed with pianist John Lewis, Vibist Milt Jackson, bassist Percy Heath, and drummer Connie Kay.

1953 Davis gathers Rollins, Parker, Heath, pianist Walter Bishop, and drummer Philly Joe Jones for Prestige session in January, which results in his first recording of Thelonious Monk's

"Round Midnight." Eventually, he rides the bus home to East St. Louis. In August he joins Roach and Mingus's cross country drive to Los Angeles. Davis occasionally sits in with Lighthouse All-Stars. Meets dancer Frances Davis. Erratic behavior in Los Angeles leads to his departure; he goes to San Francisco in September, then Chicago in late fall, picking up engagements as he goes. Returns to East St. Louis. At father's farm in Millstadt, Illinois, Davis attempts to break heroin addiction, but backslides when he goes to Detroit to feel his way back into music.

Korean War ends with an officially divided Korea.

IN AFRICAN AMERICAN CULTURAL HISTORY: James Baldwin publishes *Go Tell It On the Mountain,* his first novel.

Richard Wright publishes *The Outsider,* his first novel since the publication of *Native Son* in 1940.

1954 Inspired by Sugar Ray Robinson, Davis returns to New York in February determined to stay clean. He schedules recording dates with both Prestige and Blue Note. In April, records "Walkin'" and "Blue 'N' Boogie" for Prestige. The *Walkin'* album, featuring pianist Horace Silver, Percy Heath, and Blakey, signals start of "hard bop." Begins perfecting ballad style with tunes such as "It Never Entered My Mind," recorded for Blue Note. In May, Capitol releases *The Birth of the Cool* sessions in album format. In December records for Prestige with vibraphonist Milt Jackson and pianist Thelonious Monk. Tunes include "Bags' Groove" and "The Man I Love." Irene and the children eventually will live with Davis's sister Dorothy Wilburn and mother Cleota in Chicago.

IN AFRICAN AMERICAN CULTURAL HISTORY: U.S. Supreme Court issues the *Brown* decision that declares "separate but equal" doctrine of racial segregation unconstitutional.

IN JAZZ HISTORY: Dave Brubeck makes the cover of *Time* magazine.

George Wein starts the Newport Jazz Festival.

1955 Charlie Parker dies in March. Davis forms new working band and is determined to keep it together: Rollins, pianist Red Garland, bassist Paul Chambers, and Jones. He performs at jam session at second Newport Jazz Festival, July; his performance of "Round Midnight" makes him the star of the festival. Signs recording contract with Columbia Records, but the company is unable to release Davis material until 1957. Tenor saxophonist John Coltrane replaces Rollins in September; the group's popularity ensures full bookings.

IN AFRICAN AMERICAN CULTURAL HISTORY: Sugar Ray Robinson returns to boxing after a nearly three-year retirement, during which he worked as a dancer.

Montgomery bus boycott starts in December.

Dorothy Dandridge is nominated for an Academy Award for her performance in *Carmen Jones,* released in 1954.

Marian Anderson becomes the first African American to appear at the Met.

Arthur Mitchell becomes the first African American to dance with the New York City Ballet.

Emmet Till, a black teenager from Chicago, is murdered in Mississippi for allegedly whistling at a white woman.

IN JAZZ HISTORY: Jazz avant-gardist Sun Ra begins recording *Angels and Demons at Play* for his own Saturn label.

1956 Davis Quintet tours major cities. Begins relationship with Frances Taylor. Stress placed on larynx after node operation results in permanent damage to his voice. In May (sixteen tunes) and October (twelve), Davis makes two famous long recording sessions over two days for Prestige to fulfill contract; the resulting material is released on the albums *Cookin'*, *Workin'*, *Steamin'*, and *Relaxin'* to be released over the next four years. Recordings made for Columbia later will be released on *Round About Midnight*. Davis is principal soloist for Gunther Schuller's Brass Ensemble of the Jazz and Classical Music Society on Columbia recording sessions. Returns to Europe with Birdland All-Stars, November.

IN JAZZ HISTORY: Duke Ellington and his orchestra perform an historic concert at Newport that revives public interest in the band.

Nat "King" Cole hosts a weekly television show. The show lasts only one year because it is unable to attract sponsors.

Avant-garde pianist Cecil Taylor records *Jazz Advance*.

Sonny Rollins records *Blue 7* and *St. Thomas*, both landmark tunes.

IN AFRICAN AMERICAN CULTURAL HISTORY: Jackie Robinson retires from baseball.

James Baldwin publishes *Giovanni's Room*, a novel about white homosexuals.

1957 Another national quintet tour precedes long engagement at Café Bohemia (it will become home base for the band), New York. In May, Davis fires Jones and Coltrane because of drug addiction. Art Taylor and Rollins replace them. Sessions with a nineteen-piece orchestra conducted by arranger Gil Evans begin, with Davis playing flugelhorn on *Miles Ahead*. Alto saxophonist Cannonball Adderley joins quintet in October. Davis goes to Europe to join Barney Wilen Quartet (featuring Kenny Clarke on drums). While in Paris, he records the soundtrack for the Louis Malle film *Ascenseur pour l'échafaud*. On Davis's return, Coltrane rejoins the band, making it a sextet.

IN AFRICAN AMERICAN CULTURAL HISTORY: A crisis caused by the racial integration of Central High School in Little Rock leads President Eisenhower reluctantly to send in federal troops to protect black students. Louis Armstrong bitterly denounces the federal government's foot-dragging.

Dr. Martin Luther King, Jr., a major leader as a result of the Montgomery bus boycott, leads a prayer vigil in Washington, D.C.

The 1957 Civil Rights Act is passed.

The Southern Christian Leadership Conference is formed and Martin Luther King, Jr., is elected president.

IN JAZZ HISTORY: Count Basie records his historic *Atomic Basie* album, featuring arrangements by Neal Hefti.

1958 Sextet records "Milestones" for album of the same name in February. The tune is one of Davis's earliest experiments in modal playing. Garland and Jones leave the band and are replaced by Bill Evans and Jimmy Cobb. Davis performs on Adderley's *Somethin' Else* album on Blue Note later that month. Columbia records appearance at Newport Jazz Festival in July; Davis then begins sessions with Gil Evans for album based on Gershwin opera *Porgy and Bess*.

IN JAZZ HISTORY: Although he had been on the scene for a few years, Jimmy Smith's recording of "The Sermon" makes the Hammond B-3 a popular jazz instrument and makes him a star.

Saxophonist Sonny Rollins records "The Freedom Suite," which suggested a political sensibility and identification that was to become more explicit for other black jazz musicians in the 1960s.

1959 Wynton Kelley replaces Bill Evans on piano, though Evans's influential harmonic conception leads Davis to bring him back for sessions in March and April comprised in the classic *Kind of Blue*, featuring signature tunes such as "So What" and "All Blues." Between the sessions in April, Davis performs "So What" with the band and a medley of *Miles Ahead* material with Gil Evans on the *Robert Herridge Theatre*, a syndicated CBS television arts program (broadcast 1960). In August, Davis is beaten by New York police officers between sets outside of Birdland for refusing to give way after escorting a white female friend to a cab. Davis is booked for disorderly conduct and assault; the charges are dismissed in October. Adderley leaves the band to perform with his brother Nat. Davis begins recording *Sketches of Spain* with Gil Evans and orchestra in November.

IN AFRICAN AMERICAN CULTURAL HISTORY: Lorraine Hansberry's *A Raisin in the Sun* is awarded the New York Drama Critics Circle Award.

Otto Preminger's *Porgy and Bess*, starring Sidney Poitier and Dorothy Dandridge, is released and generates a spate of *Porgy and Bess* albums.

Malcolm X and the Nation of Islam, popularly known as the Black Muslims, become known to a broad American audience as a result of the CBS broadcast, "The Hate that Hate Produced."

IN JAZZ HISTORY: Saxophonist Ornette Coleman releases the controversial *Tomorrow is the Question* and *The Shape of Jazz to Come* to a startled jazz audience.

The Dave Brubeck quartet records Paul Desmond's *Take Five* which becomes one of the most popular instrumental records ever made.

Lester Young dies in New York on March 15.

Billie Holiday dies in New York on July 17.

Charles Mingus records his influential Columbia album, *Mingus Dynasty*.

John Coltrane records his seminal Atlantic album, *Giant Steps*.

1960 With *Sketches of Spain* completed in March, the quintet tours Europe as part of a Jazz at the Philharmonic tour organized by Norman Granz. The group performs in Norway, Sweden, Denmark, West Germany, Italy, Austria, Switzerland, the Netherlands, Italy, and France. Coltrane leaves the band and is replaced by Sonny Stitt. The quintet tours England and Sweden in the early fall. Davis marries Frances Taylor on December 21. Hank Mobley replaces Stitt on saxophone for a Chicago engagement at the end of the year.

IN AFRICAN AMERICAN CULTURAL HISTORY: African American college students start the sit-in movement and the civil rights movement moves into high gear as a form of political protest.

Cassius Clay wins the gold medal in boxing at the Olympic Games in Rome.

Richard Wright dies in France.

Sidney Poitier stars with Paul Newman in *Paris Blues*, a film about jazz musicians.

Civil Rights Act of 1960 is passed.

IN JAZZ HISTORY: Max Roach records *We Insist: The Freedom Now Suite*, featuring tunes co-written by Oscar Brown, Jr., and performances by Abby Lincoln and Coleman Hawkins. It is the first jazz album to reflect explicitly the sensibilities and protest of the civil rights movement.

Ornette Coleman records *Free Jazz*.

1961 In March, Davis quintet, with Coltrane substituting for Mobley on two tunes, records album *Someday My Prince Will Come*. The album cover features Frances on the cover. Columbia records Davis's April engagement at the Blackhawk, San Francisco, for later release as two albums. In May, the Davis Quintet and Gil Evans Orchestra appear in benefit concert at Carnegie Hall for the African Research Foundation, at which drummer Max Roach led an on-stage protest. Columbia later releases material as an album. For the next year, Davis is largely inactive, struggling with calcium deposits and performing less at his engagements.

IN AFRICAN AMERICAN CULTURAL HISTORY: CORE (Congress of Racial Equality) begins its freedom rides on public transportation into the deep south to challenge segregation laws.

IN JAZZ HISTORY: Saxophonist Stan Getz records the come-back album, *Focus*.

1962 Davis returns to the studio in July for another Gil Evans collaboration. The resulting bossa nova album, *Quiet Nights*, is only half-finished but is released anyway. Davis's father dies two years after car accident leaves him in poor health. Davis rarely records in the studio over the next few years, and the band becomes unsettled with frequent personnel changes. The Kelley-Chambers-Cobb rhythm section quit at the end of the year as they get more work as a trio.

IN AFRICAN AMERICAN CULTURAL HISTORY: James Baldwin publishes his controversial novel, *Another Country*.

James Meredith, with the help of federal troops, registers as the first black student at the University of Mississippi.

Jackie Robinson inducted into Baseball's Hall of Fame, the Hall's first African American player.

IN JAZZ HISTORY: Stan Getz records "Desafinado," which becomes a pop hit, launching the bossa nova craze.

Herbie Hancock has a pop hit with "Watermelon Man," one of the most recognized jazz tunes of the 1960s.

Pianist Vince Guaraldi's "Cast Your Fate to the Wind" becomes a major pop hit.

1963 Davis begins building a new band, eventually settling on bassist Ron Carter, seventeen-year-old drummer Tony Williams, saxophonist George Coleman, and pianist Herbie Hancock. Sessions in Los Angeles and New York featuring these and other players are released as *Seven Steps to Heaven*. Angered at the release of *Quiet Nights*, Davis does not enter the studio again for twenty-two months and begins increased touring with his new group. They are recorded live at Antibes by Columbia.

President John F. Kennedy is assassinated in November.

IN AFRICAN AMERICAN CULTURAL HISTORY: Alabama governor George Wallace, an ardent segregationist, stands in front of the University of Alabama to prevent black students from enrolling.

Martin Luther King leads his campaign against segregation in Birmingham, Alabama, one of the most dramatic of the entire civil rights movement.

Four black girls are murdered in a church bombing in Birmingham in September.

The March on Washington for Jobs and Freedom, organized by various civil rights, religious, and labor groups, attracts 250,000 marchers and features Martin Luther King's "I Have a Dream" speech.

W. E. B. Du Bois dies in Ghana.

LeRoi Jones (Amiri Baraka) publishes the highly influential study of black music *Blues People*.

NAACP field secretary Medgar Evers is murdered in Mississippi.

1964 With the young new rhythm section jelling, Davis performs on Lincoln's Birthday at Philharmonic Hall for a benefit concert raising funds for voter registration drives in the South. The concert results in two albums, *My Funny Valentine* and *"Four" and More*. His mother dies in February. Sam Rivers replaces Coleman in June and the saxophonist is heard on material recorded live in Tokyo in July. Unhappy with Rivers's avant-garde tendencies, Davis and the band recruit tenor saxophonist Wayne Shorter for west coast engagement.

IN AFRICAN AMERICAN CULTURAL HISTORY: Freedom summer of 1964 sees hundreds of black and white college-age students go south in a massive voter registration drive.

The murder of three civil rights workers— James Chaney, Michael Schwerner, and Andrew Goodman—in Philadelphia, Mississippi, startles and provokes the nation.

Cassius Clay wins the heavyweight title by defeating champion Sonny Liston. After the fight, he announces that he is a member of the Nation of Islam and changes his name to Muhammad Ali.

LeRoi Jones (Amiri Baraka) writes *Dutchman*, his most famous play, which is performed off-Broadway.

James Baldwin's play *Blues for Mister Charlie*, based on the Emmet Till case, is performed on Broadway.

The 1964 Civil Rights Act is passed.

Sidney Poitier becomes the second black actor to win an Academy Award when he is recognized for his performance in *Lilies of the Field*, released in 1963.

Martin Luther King is awarded the Nobel Peace Prize.

IN JAZZ HISTORY: John Coltrane records the highly influential album, *A Love Supreme.*

Saxophonist Archie Shepp records *Four For Trane*, in tribute to Coltrane.

1965 Satisfied with his current band, Davis returns to studio to record *E.S.P.* in January. The album features compositions by all five band members. His health continues to decline and in April he has hip replacement surgery. His continued cocaine and alcohol abuse leads to Frances's departure and eventual divorce. He does not perform again until November. In December Columbia records the band live at the Plugged Nickel in Chicago.

IN AFRICAN AMERICAN CULTURAL HISTORY: Malcolm X is murdered in New York in February.

Sugar Ray Robinson retires from the ring.

The Voting Rights Act is passed.

Martin Luther King leads a dramatic march on Selma.

A race riot in Watts that begins on August 11 becomes one of the worst urban disturbances in American history, leaving thirty-one blacks dead.

IN JAZZ HISTORY: The Association for the Advancement of Creative Musicians is founded in Chicago, a nonprofit organization devoted to the black jazz avant-garde. Its most important members were pianist Muhal Richard Abrams and the Art Ensemble of Chicago. John Coltrane records *Ascension*.

1966 Hospitalized with oxygen deficiency in January, Davis nevertheless continues heavy concert schedule. In October, the quintet records material for *Miles Smiles*, including the Shorter classic "Footprints." Davis no longer composes; in addition to their own work, the group records Jimmy Heath's "Gingerbread Boy" and Eddie Harris's "Freedom Jazz Dance." Live, the band continues to feature the standards and Davis originals such as "So What," and the sets begin to resemble long suites of music with no breaks between tunes.

IN AFRICAN AMERICAN CULTURAL HISTORY: Huey Newton and Bobby Seale found the Black Panther Party in Oakland, California.

Sammy Davis, Jr., stars in *A Man Called Adam*, a jazz film whose lead character is loosely based on Miles Davis. The film also stars Cicely Tyson, who will become Davis's third wife, as well as Louis Armstrong.

1967 Session for the album *Sorcerer* in May; it features compositions by Shorter, Hancock, and Williams and a cover photo of Davis's new love interest, actress Cicely Tyson. In June the quartet records *Nefertiti*, with Shorter's haunting title tune. Late in the year, Davis begins experimenting with longer forms, and with employing a guitarist.

In African American Cultural History: Boxer Muhammad Ali is convicted of violating the Selective Services Act in refusing to be drafted into the Army. His defiance of federal law leads to comparison with the first black heavyweight champion, Jack Johnson, who was prosecuted for violation of the Mann Act. This comparison leads to a revival of interest in Johnson.

Martin Luther King becomes a critic of the Vietnam War.

Race riots continue to afflict many major cities; one of the worst occurs in Detroit between July 23 and 25, which results in the deaths of forty-three blacks.

John A. Williams publishes the apocalyptic novel, *The Man Who Cried I Am.*

President Lyndon Johnson appoints Thurgood Marshall to the Supreme Court.

In Jazz History: Saxophonist Charles Lloyd releases two jazz albums, *Love-In* and *Journey Within*, both recorded at the Fillmore, a rock venue, in effect making jazz a crossover music. Lloyd's sidemen includes pianist Keith Jarrett and drummer Jack DeJohnette, both of whom would join Davis's electric band in the early 1970s.

John Coltrane dies.

1968 Davis's increasing interest in rhythm and blues and soul music inspires him to begin writing again. The results on *Miles in the Sky* (January and May) show a greater interest in funk-based rhythms than in traditional bop chord clusters, and the album cover reveals a new affinity for the psychedelic style popular in rock. Hancock and Carter play electric instruments, providing new textures. Between sessions for *Filles de Kilimanjaro*, in June, Hancock and Carter leave the band, replaced by Chick Corea (piano) and Dave Holland

(bass). Gil Evans assists on album. In September, Davis marries Betty Mabry, an aspiring rhythm-and-blues singer who influences his musical and fashion choices and who appears on the *Kilimanjaro* cover.

In African American Cultural History: Martin Luther King is assassinated in Memphis.

LeRoi Jones (Amiri Baraka) publishes *Black Music*, a popular collection of essays promoting the black jazz avant-garde. Baraka is one of the leading black literary figures, black jazz authorities, and political revolutionaries in the United States.

Eldridge Cleaver publishes *Soul On Ice*.

The Last Poets are formed, one of the groups that served as a forerunner to rap.

Track stars Tommie Smith and John Carlos give a clenched-fist salute during the medals ceremony at the Mexico City Olympic Games. They are expelled.

1969 February: records material that will become *In a Silent Way*, featuring guitarist John McLaughlin and pianist-composer Josef Zawinul, as well as the developing cut and paste editing methods of producer Teo Macero. Williams leaves band and is replaced by Jack DeJohnette. Begins relationship with Marguerite Eskridge, who will be companion for four years and who will bear son Erin. Quintet tours through summer, making appearances at Newport Jazz Festival and Jaun le Pins

Festival. Records double album *Bitches Brew* August 19-21, his quintet augmented by bass clarinet, additional drums, percussion, and keyboards. The album will go on to sell 300,000 copies in 1970, popularizing the concept of jazz-rock fusion. Many older fans and critics are unsympathetic to the new music. Davis is featured in a cover story in *Rolling Stone*, December.

IN JAZZ HISTORY: John Coltrane sideman Pharoah Sanders records *Karma*, a highly influential album combining lyricism, eastern mysticism, and the avant-garde. It features the vocals of East St. Louisan Leon Thomas.

Tony Williams forms the jazz-rock group Lifetime, featuring John McLaughlin on guitar and Larry Young on organ.

Quincy Jones scores commercial success with *Walking in Space*.

1970 The Davis band, with Steve Grossman having replaced Shorter, debuts at rock promoter Bill Graham's Fillmore West in April, the material released in Japan as the double-album *Black Beauty*. With pianist Keith Jarrett and percussionist Airto Moreira added to the band, Davis plays four nights at the Fillmore East in New York in June, live recordings of which would be released as the double album *At Fillmore*. The Davis band plays a forty-minute set at the Isle of Wight Festival in England as a late addition to the bill. Corea and Holland leave to form a band. Soul bassist Michael Henderson replaces Holland. Davis records *A*

Tribute to Jack Johnson, the soundtrack for the documentary on the boxer's life, a film that results from the revived interest in Johnson also embodied in Howard Sackler's popular play of the period, *The Great White Hope*. Gary Bartz replaces Grossman, and the band records live in December at the Cellar Door in Washington, D.C., with McLaughlin sitting in. The material will be used for the 1971 double album *Live-Evil*.

IN AFRICAN AMERICAN CULTURAL HISTORY: Muhammad Ali returns to boxing after being denied a license to fight for three and one-half years as he appealed his draft conviction.

Chester Himes's *Cotton Comes to Harlem* is made into a film and leads a wave of "blaxploitation" films to come in the 1970s.

Toni Morrison publishes her first novel, *The Bluest Eye*.

Maya Angelou publishes the first volume of her autobiography, *I Know Why the Caged Bird Sings*.

Alice Walker publishes her first novel, *The Third Life of Grange Copeland*.

Novelist Gil Scott-Heron releases his first album, *Small Talk at 125th and Lenox*. He is a forefather of rap.

IN JAZZ HISTORY: Saxophonist Albert Ayler dies.

The jazz-rock group Weather Report is founded with Joe Zawinul, Wayne Shorter, Miroslav Vitous, Alphonse Mouzon, and Airto Moreira. Jazz critics consider it the most innovative of all the jazz-rock groups.

1971 Davis is inactive for some months; his divorce of Betty Mabry becomes final. He begins performing again in late spring, making the summer festivals and touring Europe in the fall, but does not record.

IN AFRICAN AMERICAN CULTURAL HISTORY: Melvin Van Peebles directs and stars in the X-rated controversial film, *Sweet, Sweetback's Badass Song*, the making of which inspired later black filmmakers like Spike Lee.

Gordon Parks directs *Shaft*, arguably the most famous of all blaxploitation films. Isaac Hayes wins an Academy Award for best song, "The Theme from *Shaft*."

Ralph Bunche dies.

IN JAZZ HISTORY: Louis Armstrong dies.

Chick Corea records *Piano Improvisations* for ECM.

John McLaughlin, after his religious conversion, forms the jazz-rock group, The Mahavishnu Orchestra.

Carla Bley records her "jazz opera," *Escalator Over the Hill*.

1972 Facing deteriorating health once again, Davis does not record until June. Using a wah-wah pedal to distort his sound, *On the Corner*, with its cartoon cover and music clearly based on funk and Stockhausen, fail to meet Davis's expectations. As Davis's working band begins to disintegrate, he calls on a pool of musicians with divergent backgrounds. Records double album *In Concert: Live at Philharmonic Hall* in September, with electric guitars, sitar, talba, electric bass, drums and percussion, and saxophones on stage with Davis playing organ and trumpet. On October 21, Davis is involved in serious accident in his Lamborghini, breaking both ankles.

IN AFRICAN AMERICAN CULTURAL HISTORY: Diana Ross stars as Billie Holiday in the film *Lady Sings the Blues*, directed by Berry Gordy, founder of Motown Records. Ross nominated for an Academy Award for her work.

Jackie Robinson dies.

IN JAZZ HISTORY: Keith Jarrett records the solo piano record *Facing You* for ECM.

Chick Corea records his first *Return to Forever* album, featuring Airto Moreira, Stanley Clarke, Flora Purim, and Joe Farrell.

Former Coltrane pianist McCoy Tyner records *Sahara* in 1972.

Tyner, Corea, and Jarrett become the major jazz keyboard players of the 1970s.

1973 Arrested in February for possession of cocaine and an automatic pistol; the drug charge is later dropped. Suffers from ulcer and new hip problems caused by the walking casts on ankles. Occasional sessions will be collected on albums *Big Fun* and *Get Up With It*. Begins touring again with band featuring saxophonist David Liebman in July and tours Europe in the fall.

IN JAZZ HISTORY: Keith Jarrett releases his first set of solo piano concerts, *Bremen Lausanne*, to much commercial and critical acclaim. Nearly single-handed, he generates a solo-piano-recording craze and, along with McCoy Tyner and some others, revives interest in acoustic jazz.

Herbie Hancock records the remarkably successful jazz-funk album, *Headhunters*.

1974 Performs in March at Carnegie Hall; material later released in Japan as double album *Dark Magus*. *Get Up With It*, a double album of material recorded between 1970 and 1974, released. Includes dirge "He Loved Him Madly," dedicated to the late Duke Ellington. Tours South America in November and December.

IN JAZZ HISTORY: Duke Ellington dies.

1975 Davis band, featuring alto saxophonist Sonny Fortune, tours Japan and records live double albums *Agharta* and the Japan-only release *Pangaea* at Osaka in February.

Following a March concert at Kiel Opera House in St. Louis, Davis collapses with bleeding ulcer and is hospitalized. Has throat surgery to remove more nodes in April. Davis performs at Schaefer Festival in Central Park in September, then cancels a date in Miami. Davis has second hip operation in fall and does not record or perform again for six years.

IN AFRICAN AMERICAN CULTURAL HISTORY: Elijah Muhammad, Messenger of the Nation of Islam, dies.

1976 Certifies his first gold record, *Bitches Brew* (500,000 units sold in U.S.). Davis, still recovering from hip surgery, makes no plans to perform or record.

IN JAZZ HISTORY: To much acclaim, saxophonist Dexter Gordon returns to the United States after a fifteen-year absence and further revitalizes interest in acoustic jazz.

1978 Visits Columbia Studios and observes, but does not participate in, aborted recording session featuring guitarist Larry Coryell in February. Columbia releases vault material as *Water Babies*.

1979 Columbia releases vault material as *Circle in the Round*. Rumors swirl around Davis, some predicting his imminent death due to health problems and substance abuse and others a return to music, but he neither touches his trumpet nor enters a studio during

the year. Cicely Tyson reenters Davis's life and he begins to revive.
IN JAZZ HISTORY: Stan Kenton dies. Charles Mingus dies.

1980 Encouraged by nephew Vince Wilburn, Jr., and his young Chicago friends Robert Irving, III, Randy Hall, and Felton Crews, Davis enters the studio in May and July and makes tentative efforts at recording. Most of the material remains unissued.

1981 Davis's comeback begins in earnest. He completes new material for the album *The Man With the Horn* in March, then in June performs live for the first time since 1975 at Kix in Boston with a band comprised of saxophonist Bill Evans, guitarist Mike Stern, bassist Marcus Miller, drummer Al Foster, and percussionist Mino Cinelu. A July performance at Avery Fisher Hall in New York receives mixed reviews. Material recorded at these shows and Tokyo in October will be released as *We Want Miles*, which wins Grammy in 1982. Marries Cicely Tyson on Thanksgiving Day, but health

is in decline again.
IN AFRICAN AMERICAN CULTURAL HISTORY: Joe Louis dies.
IN JAZZ HISTORY: Trumpeter Wynton Marsalis signs with Columbia Records to do both jazz and classical records.

1982 Suffers stroke in January and temporarily loses use of right hand. Begins to take care of health for the first time. In August, December, and January 1983 Gil Evans contributes arranging skills to *Star People,* which also features Davis's artwork on the cover for the first time. Davis begins to take up art at this time. Guitarist John Scofield joins band in November.
IN AFRICAN AMERICAN CULTURAL HISTORY: Michael Jackson releases *Thriller,* which becomes the biggest-selling album of all time.
IN JAZZ HISTORY: Thelonious Monk dies.

1983 Tours Japan and Europe. Begins working on *Decoy* in early fall. Miles D. Davis Elementary School dedicated in East St. Louis with Davis present. Tours Europe, and makes first appearance in Warsaw. Feted at Radio City Music Hall in November. Has third hip operation and suffers from pneumonia.
IN AFRICAN AMERICAN CULTURAL HISTORY: Harold Washington becomes the first black mayor of Chicago.
Congress establishes the Martin Luther King, Jr., holiday.
Alice Walker wins the Pulitzer Prize for her novel *The Color Purple.*

1984 Begins work on *You're Under Arrest,* to be released the next year. Davis awarded Denmark's Sonning Award, the first nonclassical winner. Davis travels to Denmark to perform and then record composer Palle Mikkelborg's orchestral suite "Aura," written in honor of the trumpeter.
IN AFRICAN AMERICAN CULTURAL HISTORY: Jesse Jackson competes for the presidential nomination of the Democratic Party.
IN JAZZ HISTORY: Count Basie dies.

1985 *You're Under Arrest,* featuring versions of Cyndi Lauper's "Time After Time" and Michael Jackson's "Human Nature" released. It will be his last album on Columbia due to Davis's frustration at the label's refusal to release *Aura.* Signs with Warner Bros. Performs on protest album *Sun City: Artists United Against Apartheid.*
IN AFRICAN AMERICAN CULTURAL HISTORY: *The Color Purple* becomes a successful Hollywood film, directed by Steven Speilberg and produced by Quincy Jones.
IN JAZZ HISTORY: Wynton Marsalis releases *Black Codes from the Underground.*

1986 On first album for Warner Bros., takes a new approach to recording, soloing over producer Marcus Miller's prerecorded synthesizer tracks. Wins Grammy for Best Jazz Instrumental Performance for the resulting album, *Tutu.* Davis appears on television show *Miami Vice* as a pimp and former drug dealer in the episode "Junk Love," and in award-winning commercials for Honda scooters. Tours Europe and America.

In AFRICAN AMERICAN CULTURAL HISTORY: Spike Lee releases *She's Gotta Have It.*

In JAZZ HISTORY: Duke Ellington is honored with a postage stamp bearing his likeness.

1987 Davis and Miller create soundtrack for Mary Lambert's feature film set in Spain, *Siesta.* Again tours Europe and America. Performs with Prince for New Year's Eve benefit concert.

In AFRICAN AMERICAN CULTURAL HISTORY: Toni Morrison publishes *Beloved,* wins the Pulitzer Prize.

In JAZZ HISTORY: Woody Herman dies. Wynton Marsalis becomes cofounder and artistic director of Jazz at the Lincoln Center.

1988 Gil Evans, described by Davis as his best friend, dies in March. Exhibitions of his paintings in Spain, Germany, and Japan result in strong sales of his work. Maintains heavy concert schedule. Tours Europe and also performs in Turkey and Japan. On November 13, he is dubbed a Knight of Malta in Grenada, Spain.

In AFRICAN AMERICAN CULTURAL HISTORY: Jesse Jackson, again, competes for the presidential nomination of the Democratic Party.

1989 Records music to be released as *Amandla* in January; album produced by Miller and features alto saxophonist Kenny Garrett as second soloist. The album later reaches the top of the jazz charts. Divorce from Cicely Tyson complete. Columbia issues *Aura* four years after its recording, and the album receives strong reviews. *Miles: The Autobiography,* co-written with Quincy Troupe, released by Simon and Schuster. Despite the controversy it generates, the book wins the American Book Award.

In AFRICAN AMERICAN CULTURAL HISTORY: David Dinkins becomes the first black mayor of New York.

Sugar Ray Robinson dies.

Spike Lee releases *Do the Right Thing.*

1990 The eight-hour *Miles Davis Radio Project,* produced by Steve Rowland, airs across the country on American Public Radio. Davis, John Lee Hooker, and Taj Mahal perform the blues score to Dennis Hopper film *The Hot Spot.* Davis plays an aging trumpeter in Rolf de Heer's film *Dingo,* released in 1991, and collaborates with composer Michel Legrand on the soundtrack.

1991 Begins work on jazz/rap album with Easy Mo Bee, to be released late in the year as *doo-bop.* Performs with Gil Evans Orchestra and Montreux Festival Band conducted by Quincy Jones on July 8 in Montreux, his first performance of classic Evans material in more than thirty years. Performs retrospective concert in Paris July 10; joined onstage by members of his working bands from the 1960s on. Plays final concert with current working band at Hollywood Bowl, August 25. Hospitalized in early September, suffering from bronchial pneumonia. While there, suffers stroke and goes into coma. Dies September 28 at St. John's Hospital and Health Care Center, Santa Monica.

In AFRICAN AMERICAN CULTURAL HISTORY: Los Angeles Police use excessive force in arresting drunken motorist Rodney King on March 3. This eventually leads to two trials for the police officers involved and a bloody race riot in Los Angeles in 1992 when, at one trial, the officers are acquitted.

This book received nourishment from many sources, but the two main streams that made it possible were the intellectual crosscurrents created by Gerald Early's three *Miles Davis and American Culture* conferences (held at Washington University, 1995–1997) and the Missouri Historical Society's major exhibition on Davis called *Miles: A Miles Davis Retrospective*, curated by Benjamin Cawthra beginning in 1998. In these respective projects, we quickly became immersed in the contentious world of Miles Davis—a kind of subset of controversy in the larger jazz world—that nevertheless united on the overriding belief in Davis's continuing importance and the strong desire to help in remembering his life and legacy.

The book is not an exhibition catalog in the traditional sense, although each of the images used are among those selected for the exhibition. It is a complementary piece that delves more deeply into some of the themes addressed in necessarily brief fashion in the exhibition, but it aims as well to preserve some of the gallery's ambience within its covers. As we have learned, Miles never took a bad picture. Several of the contributors also served as panelists and presenters for the Washington University series of conferences.

Josh Stevens, Matt Heidenry, Robyn Morgan, and Director Lee Ann Sandweiss of the Missouri Historical Society Press all lent their varied and considerable talents to the production of this book, and they never let their own exacting standards eclipse their remarkable patience. Thanks to all.

Miles: A Miles Davis Retrospective was the product of many more heads and hands at MHS, but these meant the most to the project: the exhibition team of Shannon Berry, John Dalzell, Linda Hendricks, Caitlin McQuade, and Thomas Sleet, led by the exhibition designer, Becki Hartke, who also consulted on the book design. Missouri Historical Society President Robert Archibald, Susan Alan, Ken Anderson, Donna Bruner, Steve Call, Erika Chawla, Amanda Claunch, Angie Dietz, Myron Freedman, Jenny Heim, Marsha Jordan, Douglas Kemp, Nicola Longford, Kathy Petersen, Diane Ryberg, Eric Sandweiss, Noel Schiber, David Shultz, Duane Sneddeker, and Tamaki Harvey Stratman also made crucial contributions to the Miles Davis project.

We would like to especially thank the following for their help in creating *Miles: A Miles Davis Retrospective* as well as *Miles Davis and American Culture*. Irene Cawthon, Cheryl Davis, the late Vernon Davis, Vince Wilburn, Sr., Vince Wilburn, Jr., and the family of Miles Davis were gracious and helpful throughout. Cheryl joined Peter Shukat, Ronald Carter, Gerald Early, John Gennari, Ingrid Monson, Eugene B. Redmond, Quincy Troupe, and Lee Tanner on the exhibition advisory committee, a useful and warm-spirited group. Tom Alexios of *Down Beat* assisted in tracking artifacts with indefatigable zest. Gene Dobbs Bradford, executive director of Jazz at the Bistro in St. Louis, served the entire region well as chair of *Miles 2001*, a commemoration of Miles Davis's seventy-fifth birthday, and helped arrange some of the interviews found in this book.

The following individuals and institutions assisted the Missouri Historical Society in a variety of ways. They shared ideas and phone numbers, provided valuable research assistance, and in some cases actually contributed artifacts and photographs to the exhibition. Thanks to Anthony Barboza; George Boziwick of the New York Public Library's American Music Collection; William Cayton; Lynne Clifford of Bag One Arts; Todd Coolman; Frances Davis; Jack and Lydia DeJohnette; Mike Dibb; Anita Evans; Greg Dickinson; Robert Frost; Ken Burns and Vicky Gohl of Florentine Films; Debra Granger; JoAnne Jimenez; Ashley Kahn; William Kenney; Marc Kirkeby of Sony Music Studios; Murray Lerner; Jerry Mandell; Gordon Meltzer; Dan Morgenstern, Tad Hershorn and the Institute of Jazz Studies; Gerry Mulligan; the Museum of Television and Radio; Joanne Nerlino; Claude Nobs; Robert O'Meally and Jazz Studies Group, Columbia University; Gary Paris; David Peck of Reelin' In The Years; Matt Pierson of Warner Bros. Jazz; Loanne Rios-Kong of Sony Photographic Archives; Michael Roberson and Seth Rothstein of Sony; Steve Rowland; Darlene Roy; William Sacks; John and Susan Scofield; Joe Schwab of Euclid Records; the Schomburg Center for Research in Black Culture; Jeff Sedlik; Janet Sommer of Archive Photo; John Szwed; Ken Vail; Mel Watkin of the Forum for Contemporary Art, St. Louis; Dorothy Weber; George Wein.

Special thanks to George Avakian, Ron Carter, Joey DeFrancesco, Ahmad Jamal, Quincy Jones, and Clark Terry.

For their kind hospitality and warm friendship on visits to New York, Benjamin Cawthra also thanks Jaime Rodriguez and Linda Abdel-Malek.

For assistance with the chronology, thanks to Ian Carr, Jack Chambers, Eugene B. Redmond, John Szwed, Quincly Troupe, and Ken Vail.

Gerald Early would like to thank particularly Quincy Jones for his friendship and his caring, Ken Burns for his tenacious intelligence and generosity, and Rafia Zafar, Bill Paul, Wayne Fields, Ingrid Monson, and Jeff Smith, colleagues at Washington University, for all their help and support.

Acknowledgments

Martha Bayles is the author of *Hole in Our Soul: The Loss of Beauty and Meaning in American Popular Music*. She has taught at Harvard University, served as television and arts critic for the *Wall Street Journal*, and has contributed to the *Atlantic Monthly, Harper's* and the *Wilson Quarterly*, among numerous other publications.

Benjamin Cawthra is Special Projects Historian at the Missouri Historical Society in St. Louis. He served as lead historian for *Reflections, 1904–2000*, a permanent exhibition on the history of twentieth-century St. Louis, and for the temporary exhibition *Miles: A Miles Davis Retrospective*. His interests include American culture and public memory, and he has written on African American St. Louis.

Gerald Early is Merle Kling Professor of Modern Letters at Washington University and one of America's most respected essayists. His interests in American and African American culture are reflected in books such as *Tuxedo Junction, The Culture of Bruising* (National Book Critics Circle Award), and *One Nation Under a Groove*, a book on Motown. He has edited collections on African American speeches, black consciousness, sports, Muhammad Ali, and African American writing about St. Louis.

John Gennari is Assistant Professor of American Studies at Pennsylvania State University–Harrisburg. He has written extensively on music and American culture with an emphasis on jazz, including the forthcoming *Canonizing Jazz: An American Art From and Its Critics*. He was a National Endowment for the Humanities fellow in 1996 and later a visiting fellow at the Carter G. Woodson Institute, University of Virginia.

Farah Jasmine Griffin is Visiting Professor of English at Columbia University. Her major fields of interest include African American literature, music, history, and politics. She is the author of *Who Set You Flowin'?: The African American Migration Narrative* and co-editor of *Stranger in the Village: Two Centuries of African American Travel Writing*. Her forthcoming work is *If You Can't Be Free Be A Mystery: In Search of Billie Holiday*.

William Howland Kenney is Emeritus Professor of History at Kent State University and an expert in early jazz history. His books include *Chicago Jazz: A Cultural History, 1904–1930* and *Recorded Music in American Life: The Phonograph and Popular Memory, 1890–1945*. He is currently researching musical culture in the Mississippi River valley.

Waldo E. Martin is Professor of History at the University of California–Berkeley. His interests include the development of African American identity, U.S. and African American intellectual history and culture, and the history of social movements. He is the author of *The Mind of Frederick Douglass* and numerous other essays and articles.

Ingrid Monson is Assistant Professor of Music at Washington University and is a leading ethnomusicologist with an emphasis on jazz. Her book *Saying Something* won the 1996 Lowens Prize for best monograph on American music. Her forthcoming works include an edited volume featuring musical perspectives on the African Diaspora and *Freedom Sounds*, her work on the impact of the civil rights and African independence movements on the history of jazz.

Eric Porter is Assistant Professor of American Studies at the University of New Mexico. His interests include African American history and culture, jazz studies, popular music, and film. His current work is an intellectual history of African American jazz musicians titled "Out of the Blue: Creative Musicians and the Challenge of Jazz."

Eugene B. Redmond is Professor of English and Creative Writing at Southern Illinois University–Edwardsville. An East St. Louis native, Redmond is the poet laureate of that city. He is the author of *Drumvoices: The Mission of Afro-American Poetry* and six volumes of his own poems. He is founder and editor of *Drumvoices Revue* and associate editor of *Literati Internazionali* and the *Original Chicago Blues Annual*.

Quincy Troupe is Professor of Creative Writing and African and Caribbean literature at the University of California–San Diego. He has authored nine books, including six volumes of poetry and *Miles: The Autobiography*, a collaboration for which he received his second American Book Award, and *Miles and Me*, a memoir. A St. Louis native, Troupe was co-producer of the *Miles Davis Radio Project* for American Public Radio.

Contributors